THE COMPLETE BOOK OF
CONTAINER GARDENING

THE COMPLETE BOOK OF
CONTAINER GARDENING

CONSULTANT EDITOR:
ALAN TOOGOOD

AUTHORS:
PETER McHOY
TIM MILES
ROY CHEEK

Trafalgar Square Publishing

NORTH POMFRET, VERMONT

A QUARTO BOOK

Copyright © 1991 Quarto Publishing plc

First published in the United States of America
in 1993 by Trafalgar Square Publishing
North Pomfret, Vermont 05053

ISBN 0 943955 66 1
Library of Congress Catalog Card Number: 92-85301

This book was designed and produced by
Quarto Publishing plc
The Old Brewery
6 Blundell Street
London N7 9BH

Senior Editor Kate Kirby
Designer Anne Fisher
Illustrators Valerie Price, Christine Wilson,
Gordon Hurden
Symbols and zone maps David Kemp
Picture research Liz Eddison
Assistant art director Chlöe Alexander
Art director Moira Clinch
Publishing director Janet Slingsby
Special thanks to Stefanie Foster

Manufactured in Singapore by Chroma Graphics Pte Ltd
Typeset by Bookworm Typesetting, Manchester
Printed in Hong Kong by Leefung Asco Printers Ltd

CONTENTS

FOREWORD

Balconies and windowboxes overflowing with continental cascade pelargoniums, well-planted tubs, hanging baskets and other vessels creating complete little gardens on patios and in tiny paved plots – this is container gardening, or rather part of it, for today there is no limit to what can be achieved in these restrictive habitats.

Indeed, container gardening has probably never been more popular, possibly because it provides additional growing space in a given area.

It is a versatile form of gardening, too. It enables colour to be put where it is needed and displays are easily changed to maintain interest throughout the year.

Skilfully used and planted, containers can create atmosphere in a garden or on a patio. For instance, a Mediterranean atmosphere, very popular today, is easily achieved with tubs of *Agave*, *Aeonium*, *Trachycarpus fortunei* (the hardy Chusan palm), *Cordyline* and even *Oleander* and trained *Bougainvillea*.

Tubs, baskets and windowboxes overflowing with glorious mixtures of old-fashioned flowers will create a cottagey atmosphere in a town or country garden, and it is even possible to have a wildflower garden in containers. I once admired some hanging baskets planted with *Viola tricolor* (heartsease or wild pansy) – a most attractive display in purple and yellow.

Formality can be created with Versailles tubs, now back in fashion, planted with topiary specimens (also highly fashionable) and other trained plants such as *Citrus* and *Laurus nobilis* (bay).

The surging interest in container gardening has resulted in a wealth of fresh and inspired ideas for container use, plants and planting schemes, many from *Container Gardening's* team of authors. So you can be sure of a totally fresh approach to the subject in these pages.

No longer do traditional bedding plants form the only means of providing summer colour. Hanging baskets can be ablaze with the bright scarlet *Alonsoa warscewiczii* (mask flower), grown as an annual, or overflowing with the "cool" blue perennial *Convolvulus mauritanicus*. There is even a tomato specially bred for hanging baskets or other containers called 'Tumbler' which makes a colourful display with trailing blue *Lobelia* growing through it.

Other unusual ideas I have seen for hanging baskets include *Fragaria* 'Pink Panda' (the pink-flowered strawberry) grown with the multicoloured foliage perennial *Houttuynia cordata* 'Chameleon'; and I can vouch that the new *Heuchera micrantha* 'Palace Purple', an evergreen perennial with purple foliage, looks great in baskets.

The range of permanent plants that has proved suitable for tub culture is expanding all the time. It includes topiary, which is enjoying renewed popularity, and it is even possible to have a mini orchard by planting the new non-branching columnar Ballerina apple trees.

Plants with grassy and sword-like foliage are in vogue and specially popular with container gardeners. In 1990 a new bamboo was launched (a rare occurrence) called *Arundinaria murielae* 'Simba', with a graceful arching habit and specially recommended for tubs, together with a new *Cordyline* named 'Purple Tower' whose broad sword-like leaves are deep purple.

Dramatic schemes can be created with permanent plants in containers. While on the subject of grassy foliage, try golden *Hakonechloa macra* 'Alboaurea', a true grass, with the new dwarf *Hebe* 'Margaret' which produces flushes of sky-blue flowers from late spring till autumn. Other inspired schemes I have admired include the dwarf blue *Agapanthus* 'Lilliput' (African lily), alongside the comparatively new evergreen shrub, *Choisya ternata* 'Sundance', with bright gold foliage. Or the recently introduced birch, *Betula* 'Golden Cloud', with golden yellow leaves, would make a good partner for *Agapanthus*, especially if grown as a bush.

Containers also provide the opportunity of growing some good but rampant plants as they are kept in check. This applies to such kinds as the beautiful green and white striped grass, *Phalaris arundinacea* var. *picta* (gardener's garters), and *Aegopodium podagraria* 'Variegatum' (variegated ground elder), both delightful foils for strongly coloured plants.

Sadly few of today's small gardens have space for a vegetable plot, but vegetables can be grown in containers on a patio. I have already mentioned 'Tumbler' tomato, but try other colourful subjects, too, like yellow courgettes (*Cucurbita*) and red-stemmed rhubarb chard (*Beta*). Growing bags, suitably disguised with pots of summer bedding plants, are ideal for vegetables but herbs, which are currently enjoying great popularity, are very attractive when planted in "warm" terracotta containers, particularly if the more colourful varieties are chosen.

I hope these few observations will start you rethinking this exciting and challenging method of growing plants. Certainly the wealth of fresh and inspired ideas that follow will turn you into an adventurous and artistic container gardener.

Alan Toogood

SECTION ONE

BASICS

A huge wine jar has been selected as a container for this splendid example of Clematis macropetata 'Maidwell Hall'.

BASICS:
INTRODUCTION

Container gardening is a hobby in its own right – with no more than a balcony or a tiny backyard it may be the only kind of gardening possible, but anyone fortunate enough to have a large garden will know the special, more intimate type of gardening that containers afford. It is an intensive as well as interesting form of cultivation, often compressing into a single container the same number of plants that might normally cover a sizeable area of bed or border. Plants of many different habits, sizes, and even growing requirements are often forced to cohabit in the same confined environment, yet the results are often breathtakingly beautiful and often more eyecatching than ordinary garden displays. Despite all the handicaps, the results can be stunning. And although plants in containers require a level of care that few plants receive in a bed or border, the rewards are well worth the effort.

Because container gardening is intensive, the difference between success and failure can depend on attention to detail, and, above all, a willingness to give the plants the best chance by considering the type of container, the compost, or simply the way both plants and containers are arranged.

The second section of this book provides all the ideas and inspiration for planting combinations that anyone is likely to need, and the designs can be adapted and modified to suit individual tastes or the plants available. But choosing the right container to complement the plants, giving them the best compost, and making sure they are fed and watered adequately, are the things that bring success. Container gardening is about containers and compost, design concepts and deadheading as much as about the choice of plants: it is when all these elements are right that container gardening is at its best.

The first section of this book provides the practical advice that will help to get the best from the inspirational plantings in the second section, but the information and illustrations that it contains show that things like containers and compost, focal points and fertilizers are far from dull topics. Getting to grips with the basics will bring out the best from the plants.

Choosing containers
The container itself can sometimes be visually unimportant; if the planting is profuse and designed to cover the container completely, it is purely practical considerations like capacity and durability that are important.

Conversely an ornate vase or antique trough may require very restrained planting so that the beauty of the container remains an important visual element. For the well-being of the plants, aspects like depth and compost capacity, or the insulation provided on very hot or very cold days can be important. Financially, the choice may be between materials that are cheap but with a relatively limited life, and more expensive but more durable (and often more attractive) containers.

Pots and Planters, starting on page 12, provides the kind of practical advice on materials, sizes and shapes, that will help in choosing the right kind of container for the purpose and the plants. And there are tips for improving the appearance of the cheaper materials like plastic and concrete, as well as sound advice on making sure windowboxes and hanging baskets are safe as well as super to look at.

Containers can be fun as well as practical, however, and there are plenty of suggestions for different and delightful ways of displaying plants – from boots and baskets to old paint tins and tyres.

Containers in garden design
With only a balcony or space for a hanging basket and a couple of windowboxes, the principles of good garden design may seem irrelevant, but wherever there is enough space for a proper garden – no matter how small – looking at garden design as a whole rather than pots and planters in isolation will make the most of containers of all kinds.

Garden Design, which starts on page 24, provides ideas and suggestions for using containers creatively, whether

simply by grouping containers imaginatively or using them as focal points and design devices.

Containers can be more than mere receptacles for plants; a suitable container can serve as a punctuation point in garden design, form a focal point at the end of a walk, the centrepiece of a formal garden, or simply draw the eye away from an unattractive view. It can break up a long expanse of dark hedge or bring an unexpected touch of style within a shrub or herbaceous border. A wall pot may be all that an uninteresting wall requires to transform it into an attractive and integrated part of the garden.

This part of the book also suggests how container gardening can be an integral part of the patio garden.

Making containers

There is nothing wrong with bought containers – few people could possibly achieve the fine detail and quality of many terracotta and reconstituted stone containers even with the right equipment and materials. Even plastics are not to be dismissed, as they often make useful liner containers for home-made windowboxes and troughs as well as being perfectly acceptable in their own right where it is the floral display rather than the container itself that forms the focus of attention.

However, there is something extremely satisfying about making a container to fit a particular position or to design one to fulfil a particular need, and decorating them individually.

The DIY projects starting on page 36 show you how to make a windowbox, a planter, a hanging basket, a hypertufa sink, miniature water gardens, and even raised beds.

None of the containers or raised beds described requires more than basic DIY skills, and by making at least some containers the hobby can become even more absorbing, and at the same time make a garden that little bit more distinctive.

Composts and care

Composts deserve careful consideration. Unlike a container, a compost cannot be judged by its appearance or even the name on the bag (unless tried and tested before – but even then formulations can be changed).

Certainly the texture of the compost may be obvious, but the nutrients it contains, and how quickly these will be depleted, is largely taken on trust. With so many different brands of peat-based composts and the increasing range of composts now based on peat alternatives (because of concern about depleting the peat bogs) the choice can be bewildering.

Container Care, starting on page 46 is a guide to some of the options and choices, with advice about the all-important feeding that follows, whichever compost is chosen. Help is also on hand in this section when it comes to keeping both plants and containers looking good at all times.

CHOOSING CONTAINERS is a decision as important as the plants you put in them. Think carefully about materials, size and shape.

PRIORITIES AND PRACTICALITIES

No matter how desirable the plants, or how inspired their arrangement, if they are in unattractive or unsuitable containers the effect will be disappointing. It is not necessary to spend a fortune on buying containers – you can make your own from junk or scrap and still have a superb display (as the illustrations on pages 22–23 demonstrate) – but the containers do help to set the tone of the garden. They indicate whether it is a fun garden, or a serious one, a garden where plants are paramount or one where design and taste are the hallmark. Choosing the right containers to go with the right plants, in a suitable setting, is what makes a garden distinctive. Whether your taste is for subdued bamboos in oriental-style containers or bright and brash annuals in simple plastic windowboxes, choosing suitable containers is as important as selecting the plants.

The container will also affect how well plants grow. They will almost certainly do less well in one of very limited capacity, which will hold less compost and thus a smaller reservoir of nutrients, and will dry out more quickly than one with more generous proportions.

Information on how to make or convert your own containers is given on pages 36–47, but a garden with *only* improvised containers generally lacks good taste unless it is clearly done with a sense of fun or outrage. Different kinds of containers are required to indicate different moods and styles within the garden. The section on *Garden Design* (page 24) has ideas for all tastes and styles of gardening.

Size and shape
Size has to be a compromise between what the plants would like and what you can lift and move easily, and what supports or sills will hold safely.

Windowboxes should be large enough to hold an adequate reservoir of compost and to support a reasonable selection of plants. The minimum practical depth (except for a few special cases such as alpines like sempervivums, which require very little soil) is 15cm (6in). As it is necessary to deduct space for a drainage layer and to leave about 2.5cm (1in) of watering space between the top of the container and the compost, 20cm (8in) is only just adequate. Length is less important, as several boxes can be butted together if one is not long enough; lifting and handling them is the major restraint. A 1.8m (6ft) space is best filled with two 0.9m (3ft) boxes; as even a 1.2m (4ft) box is very difficult to lift when filled; two 0.6m (2ft) boxes might make life easier.

The width from front to back has a significant effect on the type of display that can be achieved. Some are so narrow that there is space only for a single row of plants; at most a row of bushy plants and trailers along the front. An extra few centimetres may allow an additional row of plants to be squeezed in, or bushier plants (perhaps dwarf shrubs or conifers) to be used. The extra width also makes it more practical to plunge plants while still in their pots, an invaluable technique for maintaining continuity of display by changing plants around as some die or pass their best. A width of 20cm (8in) is the minimum for a bold display of mixed plants.

Hanging baskets should be as large as possible, bearing in mind the support available; a large half-basket well secured to the wall may be better than a small full basket

Long-lasting glass-reinforced plastic Also known as glassfibre, this long-lasting material can be coloured and moulded to interesting shapes, sometimes not easily achieved with other materials, and can be made to look like lead. The shallow dish shape is ideal for low, compact plants like *Hyacinthus* (hyacinths).

on an insubstantial bracket. The bigger the basket the bolder and better the display, but this has to be weighed (in both senses) against the drawbacks associated with supporting and handling a very heavy basket. A 30cm (12in) basket is a practical size, but larger is preferable if particularly strong supports are available.

Tubs, pots, troughs and urns generally hold a generous amount of compost, and the skill comes in choosing a container and plant that are well balanced and look right together (see page 48). Beware of containers that slope inwards at the top if planting trees or shrubs that will require moving to a larger pot in time as it may be difficult to remove them without damaging the roots or breaking the container.

Material merits

The majority of containers are made from various plastics or from terracotta, but other materials are used and they all have their merits and their drawbacks. Occasionally, different and very striking containers can be found, such as windowboxes with steel frames into which can be slid ceramic tiles of your choice and, if you can afford to consider antique or replicas of antique containers, you may even find metals like lead used.

Glass-reinforced cement looks rather like reconstituted

Short-term but cheap and practical Recycled cellulose-fibre containers will only last one or two seasons, but they are a practical choice where a lot of containers are required and the flower display is more important than the container itself. To buy more permanent containers for this vibrant display of pansies would have been very expensive, but here the cost has

been kept down without any loss of impact.

If these containers do not become too waterlogged, they can often be used for a second season.

Although not an attractive material, it can be almost hidden if plenty of trailers are used around the edge. It is even possible to cut holes (V-shaped cuts are best) in the sides for plants.

stone, but it can be cast in thin sections, so they are generally more elegant. Cement is used to bind glass-fibres, producing strength even in a thin profile. Containers made from glass-reinforced cement are usually too heavy for windowsills, but they make impressive troughs.

Glass-reinforced plastic (GRP or glassfibre) offers real scope for anyone with imagination. If you are prepared to pay, you can even have very elegant containers made in colours of your choice. One of the most effective off-the-shelf finishes is imitation lead. Although expensive there are some excellent and elegant windowboxes ideal for a period setting, and they are usually large enough to give even small shrubs plenty of room.

Glazed ceramic containers greatly expand the options where terracotta pots leave off. They are particularly useful for invoking oriental or exotic images. Generally they are generous in proportions and usually suitable for one shrub or large plant, possibly with a little under-planting around the base. Use ceramic containers to bring a touch of colour and decoration to the garden, but avoid garish plants that will detract from the pot itself. Always check that they are suitable for outdoors.

Plastic is widely used because it is cheap and easily moulded. Most plastic containers will become brittle after a few years, and may then split or break, but the initial low cost is an obvious attraction. The main problem is colour. Whites look too bright when new and grubby when dirty; green never looks really happy, despite being a "garden" colour. Browns are generally the least obtrusive. Plastic decorative urns and planters can be carefully painted to improve their appearance and make them look more "antiqued" (see page 29).

Plastic is an ideal material for cheap liner boxes (see page 19).

Recycled cellulose fibre containers will last a few seasons, but are cheap enough to be regarded as disposable. Although the usually brown peat-like colour is unappealing it can be hidden if trailing plants are allowed to cascade over the sides. These are containers strictly for seasonal plants.

Reconstituted stone is heavy and quite expensive. It is invaluable, however, for those large, elegant urns and *jardinières* that would be prohibitively expensive in real stone.

Terracotta has a timeless appeal that looks right in a garden of almost any period, as suitable for a modern

housing estate as a classic garden on the grand scale. Ornate and large hand-thrown pieces are expensive, but plain large pots are not much more expensive than their plastic equivalents given that they will last for much longer with a little care. Terracotta, being porous, ensures that roots do not become waterlogged, and the evaporation of water from the outside of the pot in hot weather helps to keep the roots inside relatively cool. In winter it offers more insulation than, say, plastic.

Timber is the obvious choice if making your own containers. Timber planters and windowboxes can be bought, and although expensive they will last for many years if looked after. Stained or painted, they can be integrated and co-ordinated with the house in a way that is difficult with other materials.

IS IT FROSTPROOF?

It is essential that terracotta containers used outdoors should be frostproof, except in areas where the temperature seldom falls to freezing. Unless the clay has been well prepared and baked to a high temperature, the pot will crumble or split as the moisture absorbed by the terracotta freezes and expands. Pottery made in warm climates or intended for indoor use may not have been fired to this high temperature – always receive an assurance from the seller that the pottery is frostproof.

Beware of "ali baba" pots, and others that curve inwards at the top. Even if the terracotta is frostproof, it may not be able to take the pressure from the expanding frozen compost that it contains. Either protect these pots from freezing conditions or use them for seasonal plants and empty the compost out at the end of autumn.

Strong and classy (left) Glass-reinforced cement can be cast in a much thinner profile than concrete and reconstituted stone, and it is possible to produce a finely-textured and detailed finish. Although very heavy to move, troughs like this have a generous compost capacity, ideal for dwarf shrubs. This one contains a mixture of dwarf conifers, *Hebe* and *Hedera* (ivy).

Elegant and permanent (right) Reconstituted stone is often used for large vases and urns, or any large and decorative container where a high quality finish with fine detailing is required. These vases are tastefully planted with pink *Petunia* and *Pelargonium*.

Warm and "sympathetic" (below) Terracotta is an ideal material for the garden. It has a timeless appeal that makes it look right whatever the style or period of the garden. Although some pots can be very ornate, and are focal points in their own right, here a fairly plain design has been chosen to let *Impatiens* (busy Lizzie) and *Pelargonium* take the stage.

Tubs and Troughs, Pots and Planters

Even the best garden centre or shop can only stock a limited range of containers; it is always worth shopping around before buying, and it may be necessary to send away for some of the more specialist types. It is worth looking at the advertisements in gardening magazines; the more expensive reconstituted stone or reproduction glassfibre containers are likely to be advertised in magazines for the experienced gardener, or in "lifestyle" home-and-garden magazines.

The containers illustrated here are a cross-section of those available. Not all of them will be obtainable everywhere, but it is usually possible to obtain something similar.

3 French urn This is a facsimile of a Renaissance bell-shaped urn. The plants should be colourful without detracting from the beauty of the classic urn shape.

4 Italian style *jardinière* Reconstituted stone enables the fine detail to be achieved in classic designs like this Corredo *jardinière*.

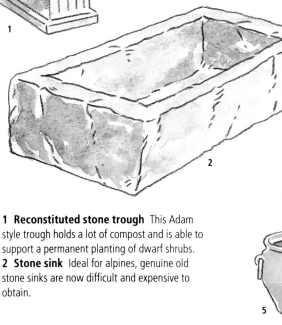

5 Terracotta ring handle terrace pot The drawback of this type of terrace pot is that the narrow neck makes repotting difficult and if the compost freezes it could crack the container.

6 Terracotta terrace pot A practical shape for many patio trees and shrubs. These pots come in a range of sizes.

7 Round terracotta pot Round pots like these are very useful for bringing variety to the patio.

8 Internally glazed Ali Baba pot This type of container gives a Mediterranean feel to a garden.

9 Herb or strawberry pot These terracotta or glazed pots are available in a range of sizes. If used for perennial herbs the roots will become entangled and compacted within the pot and removing them from the pockets can be very difficult. They are great for small bulbs in spring and for bedding plants in summer, as well as herbs and strawberries.

10 Pedestal and bowl Available in terracotta or glazed, this is a good choice for tender plants as you can take it indoors for the winter (it comes in two sections so it is easy to move) where it will still look elegant.

1 Reconstituted stone trough This Adam style trough holds a lot of compost and is able to support a permanent planting of dwarf shrubs.

2 Stone sink Ideal for alpines, genuine old stone sinks are now difficult and expensive to obtain.

11 Textured plastic container Plastic containers are very much lighter to move around than real stone or concrete. The range illustrated has holes fitted with drainage plugs so that they can be used indoors – just remove the plug to use them outside.

11

12 Tower pot Plastic tower pots are a good way to grow strawberries, as it keeps them off the ground, but they can be used for bedding plants too.

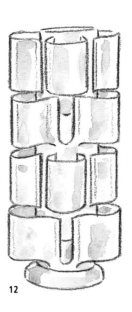

12

13 Versailles tub Elegant and classic outline, Versailles tubs also hold plenty of compost. They are one of the best containers for trees and fairly large shrubs. Although traditional timber ones are still available less expensive plastic versions are easier to obtain.

14 Imitation lead tank and cistern Reproduction antique lead containers like this are worth their high cost to help recreate a period-style garden. They are very convincing and hold plenty of compost.

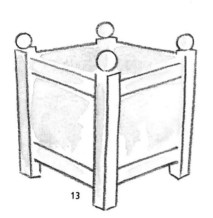

13

14

15 Oriental glazed pot If fired to a high enough temperature these pots will be frost-proof, but in the winter raise them slightly off the ground.

17 Recycled cellulose fibre planter Useful for a seasonal display, choose plants that bush out well, and plant some trailers, then the flowers will dominate.

15

16

16 Barrel Because of the proportions and depth of compost, barrels (or more usually half-barrels) are ideal for trees and shrubs. Wooden barrels are particularly attractive (leave them natural or paint them white, perhaps with black hoops), but plastic simulated wood barrels are also available.

18 Plastic shrub tub Plain plastic shrub tubs are inexpensive yet very practical for a wide range of plants that need a generous amount of compost.

19 Concrete container Generally lacking in refinement, they are useful for trees and shrubs that require firm anchorage.

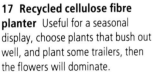

17

18

19

WINDOWBOXES

The distinction between windowboxes and troughs is not always clearcut. Many troughs can be used as windowboxes if the sill is broad and deep and provided there is absolutely no risk of the additional weight of some of the heavy ones, such as those made from glass-reinforced cement, being unstable or dangerous. Windowboxes are generally more modest in size, especially depth and width, but in a suitable setting most windowboxes can also be set on the ground as small troughs. Plastic and lightweight materials such as glass-reinforced plastic are particularly suitable where excessive weight is a problem, for instance where sills are narrow or the windowbox is mounted on brackets.

Permanent yet seasonal
Permanent dwarf shrubs, *Hebe* and *Hedera* (ivies), can be livened up with a few flowering pot-plants like *Campanula carpatica*.

FINISHING TOUCHES

Plastic boxes are often plain and unattractive. A false front can give them more character. This technique is also a good way to disguise the fact that two small boxes have been used instead of one long one.

A simple front can be made from 6mm (¼in) marine grade plywood cut to the height of the boxes and the width of the window. This can be fixed to the frame with hooks or to the front of the actual boxes. Seal the ends of the wood, and varnish or paint it to make it look more attractive, perhaps matching the colour to that of the paintwork of the house. Alternatively the false front could be painted artistically with an attractive design (see page 37). For a more rustic finish, fix pieces of cork bark to the front of the boxes (often available from a florist).

FIRM FIXING

Securing a windowbox safely is important at any time, but especially so if used above ground-level. Old houses sometimes have large, flat sills which make them relatively safe, but it is still worth taking additional precautions if there is any chance they could fall and cause injury.

A simple but effective way to provide additional security is to fix eye hooks into the windowframe and thread a 1mm galvanized wire through these and small holes drilled through each end of the box (right). With plastic or metal windowframes it may not be possible to screw in eye hooks, but it should be possible to drill and plug the wall to take them.

Sills usually slope slightly so that they shed water more easily. If the slope is steep, cut small wedges from scrap wood to level the box (right). It is in any case desirable to raise the box off the sill so that air can circulate: there is a risk of the sill rotting if water is allowed to stagnate beneath the box.

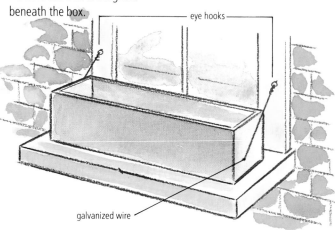

wooden wedges

eye hooks

galvanized wire

Brackets
It may not be possible to use the sill as in many modern homes it is too narrow, and with casement windows a box would cause an obstruction. However, boxes can sometimes be fitted *below* the window, on special brackets. This is unlikely to be an option for heavy terracotta or large

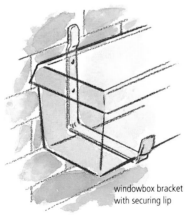

1

2

3

4

1 Plastic Polypropylene will last for years, but look for a thick, solid rim to reduce the risk of splitting.
2 Wood Timber boxes can look superb but they are expensive to buy. Ensure that the box is supported so that there is a free circulation of air beneath.
3 Terracotta These tend to be heavy, and some of them hold relatively little compost.
4 Glass-reinforced plastic These are light, generally capacious, and often extremely attractively designed.

A sense of unity Windowboxes can be integrated with both the home and the surrounding plants by choosing a sympathetic colour that blends (sometimes a strong contrasting colour is used to make a bold statement), and using plants that harmonize. Trailing *Glechoma hederacea* (ground ivy) ties in with the vertical habit climbing *Ipomoea* (morning glory).

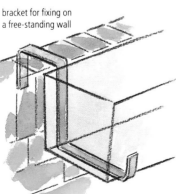

windowbox bracket with securing lip

bracket for fixing on a free-standing wall

glass-reinforced plastic windowboxes, but brackets can be bought suitable for many plastic types (left). Ordinary shelf brackets are unsuitable as they lack the lip on windowbox brackets that prevents the box slipping or being knocked off. They are screwed to the wall using wall plugs.

Some brackets can be used to hang a box on a low wall (left). Most garden centres sell brackets suitable for mounting plastic windowboxes.

When fixing a bracket below a window, allow for the height of the plants when calculating the clearance needed for opening the window.

CHEAP AND CHEERFUL

Consider using some short-term cheap "boxes" if you are using a false front, or you can place the containers on a balcony where they will not be very obvious from below. The kind of trays sold for moistening ready-pasted wallpaper are very cheap and hold just as much compost as many windowboxes.

Some plastic trays are reasonably robust to handle and will last for a couple of seasons. Those made of expanded polystyrene are much more fragile and should not be moved when full of compost; they are unlikely to be usable for a second season. Make a few holes for drainage in both types.

RINGING THE CHANGES

Cheap plastic windowboxes, or improvised liners, can be dropped into more impressive outer boxes, or hidden by a false front on the sill. A supply of liner boxes can be planted to follow on and replace earlier ones as they pass their best. Proprietary boxes are available designed to take a

series of "segments" that can be bought ready-planted or empty for planting up. With spare segments planted up and waiting in the wings, it is possible to keep a windowbox looking good almost throughout the year.

CONTAINERS IN THE AIR

Hanging baskets, hanging pots, and wall baskets and wall pots all make use of space that would otherwise be wasted. Although these containers often require much more attention than windowboxes and tubs – being more exposed and generally holding less compost, they dry out more quickly – they are invaluable where space is very limited, and even in a backyard garden can bring an otherwise uninteresting wall to life.

If you do not want to fix a lot of containers directly on to the wall (which involves a lot of masonry drilling and plugging), fit a stout wooden trellis to the wall, and hang wall pots to this.

Single-subject planting Planting just one type of plant, perhaps in mixed colours as with this lobelia, can often work better than a mixed basket containing many different plants. Here a little *Glechoma hederacea* 'Variegata' (variegated ground ivy) has been used to add a touch of contrast.

1 Traditional wire basket
Galvanized or plastic-covered wire baskets are the most versatile for all-round planting.

2 Open mesh wire basket
Planting through the sides is easier than with a small mesh, but if the mesh is too wide it is more difficult to use moss as a liner.

3 Recycled cellulose fibre
These come with a metal frame that holds the container which may last a couple of seasons.

4 Half basket Large half baskets can be as effective as full hanging baskets.

5 Wall pot Wall pots hold only a limited amount of compost, and are often best with a few small plants.

6 Plastic hanging containers
Planting is only possible in the top, and it is difficult to disguise this type of container.

7 and 8 Hanging pots Hanging pots are usually large enough to take one bushy plant, and if suitably planted can be very effective.

POT HOLDERS

These are a great way to display an attractive plant in an ordinary pot. Ring the changes and bring out plants when they are at their best. There are several pot holders that are simply screwed to a wall, and some will hold pots of various sizes.

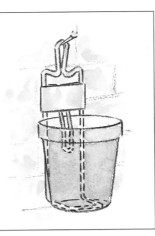

Improvise for interest (above) Here an old manger that once held hay for horses now has another use. Often improvised containers are useful because they hold plenty of compost. This display contains lobelia, trailing *Pelargonium*, cascading *Fuchsia*, and *Tropaeolum* (nasturtium).

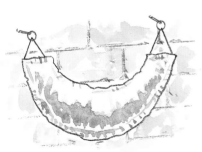

Swags (left) A novel way to grow plants. The bags, available in a range of shapes including garlands, tubes, and drops, come complete with compost. Suitably compact plants, such as *Impatiens* (busy Lizzie), are planted through small slits made in the covering and grown on a flat surface (such as a greenhouse bench or on the ground) for a month before hanging. They are suitable only for one season.

LINERS

Sphagnum moss is the traditional basket liner, and still one of the best – but it must be bought while still fresh and alive. Unless you keep it constantly damp it will soon die and turn an unattractive brown. The big advantage of moss is that it is so adaptable and plants can be inserted anywhere in a wire basket with ease.

Polythene is often used because it is cheap and readily available (you can even cut up an old plastic bag). Black polythene is usually chosen, but only on visual grounds. It is difficult to line a basket neatly with polythene and wrinkles are almost inevitable, so slit the sheet and overlap it as necessary. To plant through the sides, simply slit the polythene as required. Once well covered with plants, polythene is acceptable, but it is very unattractive during the early stages of growth.

Coir fibre liners are made from jute and coconut fibre. They look rather like a coconut on one side and sacking on the other. The coconut fibre side faces outwards. They will last more than a season, but planting through the side is not easy.

Polyurethane foam liners are widely available and easy to use, and are made in various sizes. They last for several seasons, and planting between the slits is easy.

Recycled cellulose fibre liners must be used in wire baskets designed to take them, otherwise they will not fit properly. Moss is a better choice for a wire basket, and if you don't want to plant in the sides a normal plastic basket may be a better choice.

Whalehide (bitumenized cardboard) liners are made in a range of sizes to fit particular baskets. Plants can be inserted through the sides where the slits occur and some have a capillary matting disc at the base to help retain water.

Basket liners (right to left) cellulose fibres; polyurethane foam; whalehide liner with capillary mat; moss.

DELIGHTFULLY DIFFERENT

For some people gardening is a way of expressing their personality and creativity. Making and adapting containers that are unique or unusual can be part of that expression. A plantsman will probably be more concerned with the plants than with the containers; for other gardeners it is the good taste of a well-made oriental glazed earthenware pot or an elegant piece of hand-thrown terracotta that is part of the charm of container gardening. For those with a sense of fun, or perhaps an inability to throw away something that could be put to good use, and for those who simply want to save on the sometimes considerable cost of bought containers, improvisation has much to offer.

The ideas on these pages are suggestions to whet the appetite; more can be found in the pictures within the rest of the book. Part of the pleasure of improvisation, however, is coming up with an original idea, putting something unwanted to unexpected good use, or modifying and improving upon an idea already seen.

A word of caution is necessary. Except in those few rare cases where a sense of fun or mischief has influenced the whole garden, unusual containers are easily overdone. A single surprising container discovered as you walk round an otherwise conventional garden will bring a smile or a touch of admiration; if there are too many or they are too vulgar, the effect can be off-putting.

Barrels or purpose-made wooden tubs that resemble barrels are widely available, but they lack the natural look and better proportions of a real old barrel. They are usually sold already sawn in half (occasionally lengthwise, but usually across the middle). If they are in good condition they will be waterproof enough to use as miniature pools (see page 42), but they are really at their best as shrub tubs. Make at least three holes about 18-20mm (¾in) diameter in the bottom with a brace and bit and char the inside with a blowlamp to help preserve it, if this has not been done already. If a wood preservative is used, choose one safe to plants, and avoid creosote.

Baskets of many kinds can be pressed into service. Large baskets such as old litter baskets of the size used in public places can look fantastic planted as a column of, say, fibrous-rooted begonias or impatiens. Line it with black polythene then fill with compost. Slit the polythene to plant the seedlings. Smaller baskets can be treated in a similar way but will require less compost.

Boots and shoes will give a season or two of use in the garden after they have served their owner. But retain a bit of dignity – fashion shoes will look silly but old gardening boots, wellingtons, or perhaps even clogs, have the right image. Choose small plants that are not going to grow so large that they hide the container. Try a single boot, or a pair, near the front door (perhaps by a boot scraper), or make a shelf somewhere and have a whole row of them!

Buckets and bowls do not look elegant, but they can serve a season in the garden after they have been evicted from the kitchen. Drill some drainage holes in the bottom and plant very bold and bushy bedding plants, with plenty of trailers too. Then the plants and not the container will catch the eye.

Chimney pots are always popular as "alternative" containers. Many of them are quite ornate, and being made from clay they always seem to blend naturally in a garden setting. Some are quite tall, so as it is only the top that is planted pack the lower part with gravel or some other coarse material, topped with something like capillary matting to retain the compost and prevent its being washed away.

Growing bags may not appear to be particularly attractive, but once covered with bushy and spreading annuals like *Petunia* the bag itself is scarcely visible. Use

Beauty in a barrow (below) A simple planting of *Impatiens* (busy Lizzie) and *Glechoma hederacea* 'Variegata'(variegated ground ivy), made special by being planted in this old barrow.

New life for old boots (right) Most of us would have thrown these old shoes and boots away, but someone has used their imagination to create this delightful and colourful scene.

new bags for vegetables, such as tomatoes, which require a high nutrient level, then use them the second year for flowers. After that spread the contents around the garden.

Paintpots provide a real opportunity to use colour. Make some drainage holes in the bottom, then paint the outside white to hide any printing on the tin. Once that is dry, paint brightly coloured drips and splashes down the side (perhaps in red or yellow). Use compact upright plants, maybe in a matching colour, like red tulips or yellow pansies.

Plastic kitchen containers should be used in moderation, but there is plenty of scope. Plastic bottles can have drainage holes drilled in the base and a "window" cut in the side about halfway up, into which you can plant, say, parsley or chives. Hang the bottle by its neck.

Tyres can be stacked several high. Paint the outsides white, and plant in the top. This arrangement would take an enormous amount of compost to fill, much of which would be washed away as there is no base, so place a suitably sized bucket (with drainage holes) in the top and fill this with compost. The bucket will not be noticed once the plants bush out.

If a tyre with wheel is available, it can be cut and reversed to make an attractive urn-like planter. Drill a hole in the tyre about three-quarters of the way up the tread to enable a hacksaw blade to be inserted. Cut right round the tyre with the saw blade, then fold back the largest (the three-quarter part), so that the tread is on the inside of the "vase" (help may be required). Finally, paint it with an emulsion paint.

Wheelbarrows are popular for conversion. Metal or plastic barrows can be used, but for real impact the old-fashioned high-sided wooden gardener's barrow is difficult to beat — especially brightly painted, perhaps in red or green.

GARDEN DESIGN – by looking at pots and planters as garden features as well as containers for plants, they can add to the sense of garden design.

CONTAINERS IN PERSPECTIVE

Container gardening is particularly popular in these days of small gardens, the interest in patios, and the insatiable quest for the "instant garden" (you can now go along to the garden centre and buy ready-planted containers in full bloom!). There is nothing new about container gardening, however, as the Ancient Egyptians used pots as a design feature in an ornamental setting.

There are wall paintings in Egyptian tombs depicting garden scenes, some of which show plants, including formal conical shrubs, being cultivated in pots. It is known that Rameses III (1198-1166BC) was a great gardener, and in his reign trees and shrubs were grown in decorated earthenware vases. These early Egyptian gardens were formal, divided in compartments by trees, arbours and walls. Plants in pots were used to punctuate the symmetry, on the corners of ponds or in straight lines along a path or wall. Woodcuts, tapestries and prints from late medieval times and during the Italian Renaissance show that a wide range of flower pots, many ornately decorated, with both informal and formal plants, including topiary, were popular.

Containers with plants can be found in most of the world's great gardens. Scrutiny of their function soon reveals that they are strong elements of design. They act as focal points and punctuation marks, or form an integral part of the design. Many containers are ornamental in their own right, and the plants they contain are merely supplementary decoration.

All this may seem irrelevant if your problem is how to brighten up a balcony, bring a touch of colour to a boring fence or provide a cheery floral welcome at the front door. Yet the principles and objectives of good design are valid, albeit modified, whatever the size of garden. If containers can be used with taste and imagination they will add to the garden as a whole.

Are containers necessary?

Perhaps an odd question in a book on containers, but it is worth asking. It may be preferable to grow plants in the ground if you have the option, and use fewer but more impressive containers. A garden where almost everything is grown in containers, no matter how pretty and tasteful individually, can look cluttered. In a backyard or on a balcony this may be acceptable: it provides a sense of dense vegetation, an area bustling with life, in a place that would otherwise be rather sterile. However, in a garden where space is not at quite such a premium, the effect can be a negative one.

The more containers you have, the more time you need for their maintenance, so if time is at a premium it

Exotic expressions (left) Anyone with a heated conservatory to over winter plants like these – the large-leaved plant is *Musa* (banana); the big pink trumpets belong to *Datura* – can create a "tropical oasis". Of course they must be carefully acclimatized, and taken in before the first frost.

New life for old chimneys (right) Old-fashioned chimney pots used to be thrown away when their useful lives were over. Nowadays their value as garden ornaments is appreciated, but group several together as an isolated chimney pot can look too tall in proportion to the plants.

Creating an image The plants used in this English garden (*Cordyline australis* 'Purpurea' in the centre and *Agave americana* 'Variegata' behind) generate a special impact because they look "foreign" in a place where traditional hardy shrubs and herbaceous plants abound. Although both of these plants sometimes survive without protection in a favourable winter in very mild areas, they clearly create the illusion of a warmer climate.

makes sense to grow as many plants as possible in the ground or in raised beds (these have many of the merits of containers but are less likely to need daily watering in warm weather).

From a design viewpoint, a garden ornament can serve a similar purpose to a plant in a container. If it is necessary to provide a focal point some distance from the nearest water supply, an ornament may be more successful than a neglected container plant.

On a patio it may be possible to grow some plants, especially wall shrubs and climbers, in a small area of ground where a paving stone has been lifted. These will probably thrive better with less attention, and more time can be spent ensuring that those plants in containers are well maintained.

Raised beds and borders

Although not strictly containers, raised beds and borders provide an opportunity to grow many more plants in an elevated position, like containers. And as with pots and tubs, it is possible to create the right soil conditions for particular groups of plants that would be difficult in the open garden; they can be filled with an acid soil or compost in which to grow lime-hating shrubs for instance. And, of course, they are particularly relevant for anyone who finds bending difficult. Ideas for raised beds and borders can be found on pages 44–45.

Getting the best from containers

Hanging containers make good use of vertical space. Walls and fences can be transformed, especially in small or enclosed gardens where they always seem more oppressive. Used in porches, on balconies, even roof gardens, troughs and tubs enable plants to be grown where otherwise it would be impossible.

Just a couple of clipped *Taxus* (yews) or topiary specimens in Versailles tubs or painted half barrels flanking the front door is enough to set the tone of a garden, no matter what its size. Choosing the right combination of containers and plants, and positioning them for maximum impact, is part of the art of container gardening. This section of the book provides plenty of ideas for using containers to best advantage, and the plant directory starting on page 114 gives information on a wide range of plants from which to choose.

FOCUS ON FOCAL POINTS

Focal points are an essential part of good garden design. They give a garden a sense of purpose, and by acting as punctuation marks within the overall design, draw the eye to a particular view or angle. Such a point of interest may lure a visitor to admire it more closely, and view the garden from a particularly good position. It can also give purpose to other garden features: a path that has an ornament or seat at the end has more purpose than one that simply leads nowhere; an ornate container brimming over with bright flowers will lead the eye down a trained arch or an avenue of clipped hedges and encourage the visitor to explore. It can help to link various parts of the garden, and even create a sense of distance in a relatively small garden by drawing attention to an attractive view beyond.

Ornaments are widely used as focal points, distinctive plants can serve a similar purpose, but planted containers are also effective in the same way if chosen with care. The containers generally need to be bold, decorative, and distinctive. Often they need height, which can be provided by a pedestal, or a striking plant, such as a *Datura* or a large *Fatsia japonica*. Many reconstituted stone ornaments that are replicas of classic designs are ideal, but they should always reflect the style of garden. A large *jardinière* or a stone urn on a large pedestal could look incongruous in a small modern garden; a very modern-looking container in plastic could spoil the effect in an informal or period setting. Terracotta is one

of those fortunate materials that looks good almost anywhere.

In a small garden large containers may not look right, but it is possible to achieve impact by grouping together a cluster of smaller containers.

Accent plants

The container may be less important as a focal point than the plant it contains. A plant with a strong visual presence can set the mood of an area. A single palm immediately suggests the exotic. Conifers, although more commonplace, are ideal accent plants by nature of their variety of shapes and colours. An unusual and distinctive plant, such as a *Nerium* or *Clianthus*, in a temperate garden, will arrest the eye because neither of these is commonplace.

Backgrounds

To work, focal point containers should be clearly visible against their backgrounds. A dark hedge, or wooden fence, requires a light-coloured container, such as reconstituted stone. Terracotta and lead (imitation or genuine) require a light background, such as a wall of yellow bricks or pale stone, but more often it has to be created from plants such as grey-leaved shrubs or perhaps tall ornamental grasses.

The sky can be an effective background. On a sloping site it may be possible to position a large container in a prominent position, with a plant that creates a distinctive silhouette, such as a *Phormium* or a palm.

Creating a focal point
Containers do not have to be planted. If they are decorative enough in their own right let them make their own statement. These terracotta containers do everything a focal point is supposed to do.

A suitable setting (above left)
The juxtaposition of the large oriental-style container with the circular frame provided by the wall make this focal point doubly interesting. When container, plant and background all complement each other, container gardening is seen at its very best.

The plant here is *Astelia chathamica* 'Silver Spear', but a *Phormium*, would work just as well. The large plant in the background on the other side of the wall is *Mahonia* 'Charity'.

Focal point plants (above)
Sometimes the container is much less important than the plant as a focal point. In this picture the pot is not decorative, but the plant immediately dominates the scene and catches the eye.

ACCENTS IN THE GARDEN

● Use a pale-coloured container on a pedestal, perhaps with cascading silvery-leaved foliage plants such as *Helichrysum petiolatum*, and perhaps a white daisy-like *Argyranthemum (Chrysanthemum) frutescens,* to break up a long, dark hedge. The hedge will make an ideal background and the planted container will bring to life what would be an otherwise dull feature.

● Flank a garden seat with two matching containers, and plant them with fragrant shrubs or scented annuals.

● Provide a welcome by flanking the door with a pair of attractive containers filled with colour and preferably fragrance. Use an outer container that is easy to replenish with fresh plants and be prepared to use plenty of short-term plants, such as reasonably tough houseplants like all-the-year-round *Chrysanthemums*, to keep these key containers bright all through the year.

● Use a very colourful or ornate container at the end of a long path, to give a sense of direction and purpose. In a light position use a large, dramatic plant, such as a *Datura*. If the background is dark choose something pale and feathery or spiky, perhaps a yellow-variegated *Arundinaria* (bamboo), or yellow-flowered annuals.

● Move in a container with a striking plant (perhaps a well-established clump of *Agapanthus* or a variegated *Phormium*) to enliven a border that has passed its best. If the container is very decorative you could stand it just in front of the border; if the pot is not a feature itself, place it within the border.

● Steps are an ideal setting for container plants. They draw the eye to the steps and therefore help to create a focal point, yet they can trail down to soften a long or wide flight and use space that would otherwise be wasted. If the steps are too narrow to stand containers, it may be possible to use urns on a suitable support either side at the top of the steps.

● Containers are invaluable in flat, formal areas of the garden, such as a herb garden or a parterre. Formal shrubs, such as clipped *Laurus nobilis* (bay) in wooden tubs or Versailles tubs, act as focal points.

ORNAMENTAL CONTAINERS

Containers can be simple plant holders or ornaments in their own right. Bright seasonal bedding displays do not normally benefit from a particularly decorative container (lots of trailers will largely obscure the pot anyway), but if perennial plants, or mainly tall, upright bedding plants in muted colours are used, an attractive container is more important. Those in prominent positions should be chosen like an ornament, which is what they are.

The real test for a decorative container is whether it is worth looking at when empty. The majority of containers are bare, or hold only dormant plants, for at least part of the year, so one that makes an attractive feature in its own right is clearly an advantage. Some are works of great beauty in their own right.

Reproductions of large traditional designs, in Greek, Roman, Chinese, Italian, French and Victorian styles, among others, are most imposing where there is adequate space. Some of the best are made from reconstituted stone, and there is a wide range of plinths in this material to give the necessary height to urns and vases.

Terracotta containers can take a rightful place in the grandest gardens, yet they have a warmth that makes them equally suitable for a small cottage garden. They can be ornately decorated without appearing pretentious – a shortcoming of imitation stone in an unsuitable position.

An urn on an appropriate pedestal can form the centrepiece of a formal garden, but would look equally attractive set in an alcove of clipped hedge. This type of focal point depends as much on the container as an ornament as on the plants it contains. It is a worthwhile garden feature on a cold day in mid winter, covered with frost, and the summer foliage and flowers are a welcome bonus.

Oriental glazed pots are ideal for small modern gardens where a tranquil style has been achieved with the emphasis on shape and form and a restrained use of plants, or for a very plain garden. Whether simple dragon pots are chosen, or those with more sophisticated and colourful decoration, their colour and shape play an important role and any plants should not detract from their beauty. For instance, a flowered pattern may be best with a foliage plant; a dragon pot with a blue design might be best with a variegated dwarf bamboo or ornamental grass.

And remember, containers don't *have* to be planted.

A sense of fun (above) These containers show how a sense of fun can be achieved without the garden looking too gimmicky. Although the containers are clearly intended to bring a smile to the face, the planting is nevertheless thoughtful and impressive in its own right.

Balancing pots and plants (far left) Containers that are pleasantly decorated in a subtle way require plants that will look attractive yet remain compact and not mask the container itself. Here regal pelargoniums have been used, with a silver-leaved *Senecio bicolor cineraria* (usually sold as *Cineraria maritima*) to bring a little contrast in colour and texture.

Balance and proportion (left) Never let overplanting or large plants spoil the impact of an attractive ornament.

INSTANT AGEING

New concrete containers can look rather stark initially. Instant ageing can be achieved with the aid of a little paint!

Mix a little white emulsion paint with a few squeezes of raw umber acrylic paint (from a shop supplying artists' materials) and mix thoroughly. Test on the inside of the container to judge the colour, and adjust as necessary.

1 When satisfactory paint the outside, a little at a time. It does not matter if you have to mix several batches as a little variation adds to the appearance.

2 When the container has received its base coat, mix in some black acrylic paint to produce a darker colour, and with a small brush paint the recesses in any mouldings with this.

3 Before it dries, go over the darker paint with the brush used for the original colour to blend the colours.

As a finishing touch the raised edges of any moulding can be very lightly sandpapered with a medium grade paper, to take the paint off the raised ridges.

Plastic containers can be treated in a similar way, but they are unlikely to look so convincing and you should not use the sandpaper.

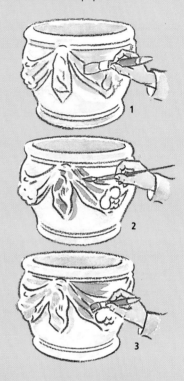

PATIOS, POOLS AND POTS

By their very nature patios are outdoor rooms in the truest sense of the word, and ornaments and containers provide ample opportunity to decorate them as one would the home. Being paved, they are ideal for grouping containers in an artistic and intimate way often difficult in other parts of the garden.

The intimate scale of a patio means that sink gardens and miniature water gardens are appropriate, and relatively small decorative glazed ceramic containers can be used more boldly without looking incongruous.

Troughs can be especially effective if they match the design and materials, or at least the planting scheme, of windowboxes. This helps to integrate the patio closely with the home. For instance, a herb or strawberry pot planted with a collection of herbs can be especially attractive on a patio. Herbs, which are often evergreen, are also attractive in a windowbox.

A small hedge or screen can be grown in a trough. If several are used, each mounted on castors, they can be moved around to form a living screen to suit the day and the mood.

Some containers that may seem out of place in a more rugged setting, such as highly decorated and colourful bowls on pedestals, can work well on a patio. These containers can be used indoors or in a conservatory and help to link home and garden. Plant them with some of the tougher houseplants, perhaps trailing *Tradescantia* or *Zebrina*, to strengthen the link.

Because patios are usually in a sheltered position, or have a shelter or screen wall, it is a good place to grow some of the more tender or exotic plants. A magnificent *Datura* in a big pot, a tender climber such as a *Bougainvillea* (grown in a trough with an integral trellis, so that it can be moved into a conservatory for the winter), and perhaps a few tropical-looking plants like palms or *Agaves*, will create an impression of warm climates and hot sunny days, and above all create an oasis for different plants to those grown elsewhere in the garden.

There is a natural temptation to fill patio beds with *Impatiens* (busy Lizzie), *Petunias*, and other dependable flowering plants but instead why not create an exotic look? A raised bed of cacti and succulents can be a real eye-catcher and they don't require much care or maintenance. If the pots are plunged to the rim in the soil, and the surface covered with stone chippings or fine gravel, the effect is really striking. This works well within a patio setting but would look too contrived in other parts of the garden.

If traditional summer bedding plants are used, try to introduce a few tropical-looking foliage plants. *Ricinus communis* (castor oil plant) is easily raised from seed along

with the other seasonal plants, and this will give height to a bed or container. The large, often colourful foliage will give the display more impact. If facilities for overwintering the plants are available, small *Abutilons* or perhaps a variegated × *Fatshedera lizei* are useful; *Cannas* are superb plants, combining striking flowers with bold foliage.

A water feature adds considerably to the appeal of a patio, and it does not have to be large to be effective. To achieve the sight and sound of water, a small wall-mounted gargoyle with a spout is sufficient. A small raised pool is even better, especially if combined with

Contrasting colours (left) Dark decking requires a light or bright plant as a contrast, here provided by an attractive golden grass, *Hakonechloa macra* 'Alboaurea'. In this setting a very decorative pot would detract from the beauty of the wooden decking and the surrounding planting.

Offsetting paving (below) Paved patios and courtyards can look bleak unless plenty of containers are used to add character and height. In this scene the use of pots at a higher level as well as on the ground helps to make the scene more cosy and "clothed".

Ingredients for a patio (above right) Three of the ingredients for an interesting patio are plants in pots, a water feature, and a few tasteful ornaments, all of which are present here. Raising some of the containers off the ground helps to provide much-needed height and also masks the background.

some form of running water, such as a tiny cascade or fountain, but failing that a miniature pool in a container has a charm of its own. A plastic shrub tub of suitable size and shape, provided it is waterproof, requires no preparation. A wooden half barrel makes a more appealing pool, but requires careful preparation (see page 42).

Keeping up appearances

A patio will generally benefit from a combination of permanent plantings (perennials, shrubs or small trees) in large containers, and a succession of seasonal plants in small pots, tubs and windowboxes. This is one area where it is well worth plunging fresh plants in pots into existing containers as other plants pass their best, to keep everything looking fresh and interesting, at least during the summer.

Going upwards

On the patio climbers help to create a sense of enclosure and, as there are almost inevitably walls to be covered, they are functional too. Annual climbers in containers such as *Lathyrus* (sweet peas) and annual *Ipomoea* (morning glories) can clamber up a simple wigwam of canes or a small trellis; annual climbers can be used in windowboxes if the windows are of the sash type, but are unsuitable for windows that open outwards.

Perennial climbers are better planted in the ground than in containers. Self-clingers such as the *Parthenocissus* will support themselves by clinging to a wall, but others like *Humulus lupulus* 'Aureus' (golden hop) are best given an arch to grow over, or wire mesh or wooden trellis fixed to a wall.

Table talk

Patio furniture can seem bleak and boring when it is not actually being used. Keep a selection of small-sized containers — perhaps containing herbs or alpines — to group on the patio table when it is not in use.

BALCONIES AND BACKYARDS

Containers can be at their most effective on balconies and in backyard gardens. Growing plants in containers is often the *only* way to enjoy them in a very small area. Walls can dominate a small balcony or backyard garden; basement apartments often have the additional handicap of concrete steps and a gloomy aspect. These conditions would deter many gardeners, yet some of the most dramatic container gardens have been created in response to this kind of challenge. By concentrating efforts in a small area the results can be particularly colourful and delightful. Watering and routine care is often easier when all the containers are close together and, without the demands on time from a larger garden they are often better cared for.

The key to successful container gardening in this situation is to use all available surfaces.

Decorating walls

A few hanging baskets may be possible, but with restricted space they are likely to be an inconvenience. Arrangements in wall baskets and wall pots can be just as effective, provided they are large enough, and they make better use of available space. The other advantage of wall baskets and pots is that you can have many more

Dense planting (left) In a small backyard it is perfectly acceptable to pack the plants in tightly. Plants in pots, like this *Acer* (maple), can be squeezed into a corner to avoid wasting space.

Roof gardens (above) In the warmest months lots of house- and greenhouse plants can be used to create an impression of luxuriant growth in the confined space of a roof garden.

of them. It is not practical to have more than a single row of hanging baskets, yet wall-mounted containers can be fixed in as many rows as you care to cram in; the only word of caution is to stagger them rather than have regimented rows.

A massed wall display with lots of containers needs to be planned with care. Too many of the same type, especially if wire half baskets are used, can look unattractive "off season". By choosing decorative terracotta containers it is possible to have dozens of them and all different. Choose interesting shapes and designs to create an arrangement of terracotta that looks good during the winter.

A large iron wall manger will add character to a bare wall and reproduction mangers are widely available. Because mangers have widely spaced bars, line them with black polythene or fix small-mesh wire-netting to the inside and line with sphagnum moss.

Troughs positioned at the foot of a wall will enable a range of climbers to be grown. Self-clingers such as

A dash of life (above) Basement steps and long flights of steps rising up between buildings can be depressing without a few plants.

Using space to the full (left) Porches and balconies provide a great opportunity for plants in containers. As the plants are convenient for watering and regular care, they usually do very well.

Parthenocissus may be too vigorous, but annual climbers or permanent wall shrubs, or perhaps large-flowered hybrid *Clematis*, (generally less vigorous than many of the species), can be trained up a decorative wooden trellis fixed to the wall.

Windowboxes can be used on walls as well as windowsills. If windows open outwards, boxes have to be secured to the wall below. Use them with caution on a plain wall as they are less attractive than wall pots, but they can be used to match boxes on adjoining windows. They are very useful for fixing to the top of a *low* wall.

Windows

In a limited space, windowboxes must work hard, and impact from a distance is less important than interest at close range. The container itself should be attractive, and a timber windowbox or a false timber front for a plastic box can be painted to match the woodwork of the house. Fixing ceramic tiles to the front of a timber box will also help to liven it up. Terracotta windowboxes are a good choice if terracotta wall pots have been used.

Steps

Planted containers will soften the harsh outline of steps. Freestanding pots can be stood on the treads if space allows. A climber or wall shrub planted in a large tub at the base of the flight will break up an expanse of a brick or concrete wall in a basement yard.

Balconies

Lightweight containers are a sensible precaution for balconies. It is unwise to use heavy containers, such as concrete tubs, unless you are sure that the structure is capable of supporting them.

Plastic containers and peat-based composts are suitable for most plants you are likely to want to grow, but larger trees and shrubs will need a heavier loam-based compost and a substantial tub (perhaps a wooden half barrel or a Versailles tub) to give stability in what can be an exposed and windy position.

A well-designed balcony garden should look good from the apartment and attractive from the ground. Making the most of windowboxes on balcony railings (hang them on the inside for safety), and using plenty of climbers and trailers, will ensure an attractive framework within which to use more intimate groupings of containers. Growing bags at the edge of the balcony are useful for trailers, which can do much to soften the outline of the building.

Try using large houseplants, such as *Yuccas* and *Monsteras*, which can be moved indoors again once the weather deteriorates.

33

An Element of Surprise

A garden that is predictable is usually boring. Even a small garden requires a few little surprises. In a plantsman's garden it could be an eccentric choice of plant – perhaps a container with insectivorous plants, or an interesting shrub such as *Corylus avellana* 'Contorta' (contorted willow). In other gardens the surprise might be the container itself.

In a patio garden packed with containers, a couple of large terracotta tubs or bowls with smiling faces, one perhaps winking knowingly at the other, will immediately take the eye and almost certainly raise a smile.

Paintpots (painted white, with drips and runs in bright colours) can have a similar impact and are more readily available. Many large paint pots are now made of plastic, and these are less likely to leave a rust mark on your patio than a conventional metal pot.

Conventional containers, or even earthenware jars from the kitchen, can be on their sides, perhaps partly submerged in the ground, with plants tumbling out as though spilling over the ground. In a gravel garden a

Fun with taste (left) Old-fashioned household items can be interesting, but they are not always attractive in their own right. Planting densely so that there is just a hint of the container, like this old bath tub, produces the right effect without being obtrusive.

Charm and elegance (above) This wall pot in the form of an elegant mask is planted quite simply with *Alyssum maritimum* (sweet alyssum). Such a combination can transform an uninteresting wall or fence for very little cost or effort. It is important not to overplant a charming container like this.

single trailing plant set in the container with the top growth allowed to run out over the ground may be effective. In a position where plants can be set in the soil as well as the container, a "river" of, say, small yellow or gold violas could be planted in the container and in a spreading pool of colour in the ground.

An upright container nestling among plants in a border, perhaps with trailers such as small-leaved *Hedera* (ivies) tumbling down the sides to mingle with the border plants, can also provide an element of surprise.

Painting a colourful picture
(above) Instead of throwing away those old paint tins, put them to use as plant containers. Drill some holes in the bottom for drainage, then paint the outsides white (to obliterate the lettering), using gloss or outdoor emulsion paint. When that is dry, use a brightly coloured paint to create the "drips". Traditional metal tins may produce stains if they start to rust, but many modern "cans", are plastic and cause no problem.

The right background (left)
Painting a wall can help to show off the plants in front. The effect of the contorted stem on this trained and clipped *Laurus nobilis* (bay) could be lost against a confused background of foliage; here shape and form are shown clearly.

It is worth having a few small plants in ordinary kitchen cups, soup bowls, or even an old teapot without its lid, which can be set on the patio table when you entertain. As these containers will have no drainage holes, the plants must be watered very carefully and kept out of the rain, otherwise they will become waterlogged and the plants will die.

Drainage holes can be made easily in plastic containers, but old washing-up bowls and the like need to be used with care if they are not to lower the tone of the garden (a bright red washing-up bowl put by the clothes line can work, because it is in context, elsewhere it could look cheap).

Small animal containers, such as those in the shape of frogs or hedgehogs, are worth trying to tuck into unexpected places, perhaps almost hidden by other plants, until suddenly "discovered".

An old gardening boot planted-up by the door can look both tasteful and amusing. Surprise containers should be set in context, positioned so that they are encountered unexpectedly, or be really bold.

DIY PROJECTS which are not too tricky to tackle; here we show you how to tailor-make containers to suit your own requirements.

WINDOWBOX

The advantages of making your own windowbox when there are so many good proprietary ones around are twofold: it can be made to fit a sill exactly (allow enough room at the ends to manoeuvre the box into place), and it will be unique.

Make the box to accommodate a proprietary plastic windowbox liner. This not only protects the wood and ensures that it lasts longer, but also enables a number of inner boxes to be grown on elsewhere and rotated to keep the decorative box filled and bright at all times.

The timber is more likely to warp and rot after a few years in direct contact with the compost so, if liner boxes are not used, make the windowbox out of a durable hardwood, such as elm. Softwoods are cheaper and can be used if thoroughly treated with a wood preservative safe near plants.

You will require
● Hardwood (for a long life) or good quality softwood:
● 2 pieces 210mm × 20mm (8¼ × ¾ in) × length of box, for sides
● 2 pieces 210mm × 20mm × 210mm (8¼in × ¾in × 8¼in), for ends
● 3 pieces 180mm × 55mm × 12mm (7¼in × 2¼in × ½in), for base braces
● 4 pieces 20mm × 20mm × 210mm (¾in × ¾in × 8¼in), for corner braces (omit if dovetailing)
● Screws and woodworking adhesive

To assemble
Dovetailing the sides (see inset, right) makes a strong and attractive box, but requires more patience and carpentry skills. A perfectly adequate windowbox can be made easily by using corner battens as shown.

Glue and screw the sides and ends together, using battens cut to the correct length. Carefully cut recesses for the three base braces, using a sharp chisel, and glue and screw these into position.

At this point you could insert a base if you don't want to use liner boxes. Cut a piece of 20mm (¾in) timber to size, and make plenty of large drainage holes with a brace and bit. Glue and screw it into position. Ensure that the box is raised off the sill to avoid the base standing in water.

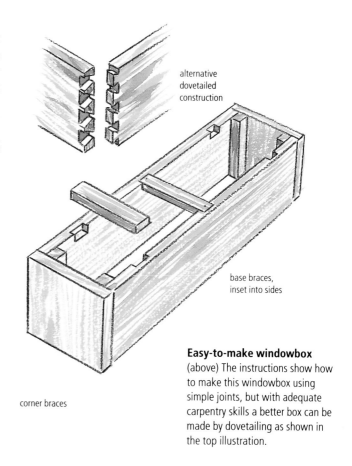

alternative dovetailed construction

base braces, inset into sides

corner braces

Easy-to-make windowbox (above) The instructions show how to make this windowbox using simple joints, but with adequate carpentry skills a better box can be made by dovetailing as shown in the top illustration.

Finishing off
Rub down all the surfaces with glasspaper to provide a smooth, unmarked finish – especially important if the front is to be varnished or painted, less so if it will be covered with tiles or other decoration.

To varnish, apply two coats of a good exterior grade varnish (yacht varnish is excellent).

To paint, apply two coats of primer, then two undercoats. Rub down lightly with glasspaper between each coat. The inside can be finished with a couple of coats of a dark gloss paint; if the outside is to be finished with paint apply a coat of enamel paint of a suitable colour.

This box is intended to take a plastic liner box. To fit

a particular make of box, adjust the dimensions accordingly and follow either metric *or* imperial measurements. Dimensions are approximate actual (prepared) sizes – always check as you work that pieces will fit before cutting and assembling as there may be variations in the timber which will require adjustment.

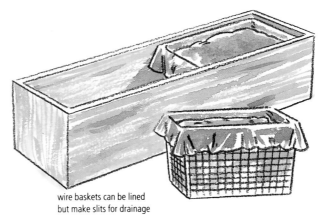

wire baskets can be lined but make slits for drainage

cheap plastic windowboxes can be used to change the display

Colour it bright One advantage of making a windowbox is that it can be painted to suit any taste and colour scheme. By making it large enough to take cheap plastic liner boxes or containers, the plants can be changed round to keep the windowbox looking bright and beautiful at all times.

DECORATIVE FINISHES

A bright and cheerful gloss finish like the one on the windowbox illustrated may be sufficient, especially if the plants are likely to obscure the box. But a more ornate box is invaluable for spring displays, which has to sit exposed through the winter with apparently little happening.

A decorative box can be a feature in its own right in which case upright pansies or *Begonia semperflorens* (fibrous-rooted begonias) are a better choice than sprawling plants.

Anyone with artistic skills can paint a freehand design, perhaps on a floral theme;

others may prefer a simple style, possibly using stencils.

Try painting the background with acrylic paint. Then use the same kind of paints to create a colourful or muted design to suit the mood. The windowbox below is decorated with acrylic paints, applied freehand.

Ceramic tiles provide an easy way for anyone to decorate a box with no more skill than the ability to apply a tile adhesive. (The box must be made to dimensions that will accommodate the tiles exactly.) Choose bold tiles or a floral theme; and try to avoid those designs that look as though they belong in the bathroom or kitchen.

TRELLIS PLANTER

Make this trellis planter Just follow the instructions given on this page.

This versatile planter can be made any length (90-120cm/3-4ft is a manageable size), with a trellis to suit the climbers being grown. Several can be coupled together to make a more substantial container where there is space.

You will require

- Good quality softwood, treated with a timber preservative (this can be applied after assembly, to give an attractive finish, as illustrated):
- 2 pieces 230mm × 25mm (9in × 1in) × length of planter, for sides
- 1 piece 280mm × 25mm (11in × 1in) × length of planter less 20cm (8in), for base
- 3 pieces 230mm × 25mm × 230mm (9in × 1in × 9in), for ends and central divider
- 2 posts 50mm × 25mm (2in × 1in) × height of trellis plus 230mm (9in), for trellis supports
- 4 pieces 25mm × 25mm (1in × 1in) × length of planter, for internal bracing
- 25mm × 25mm (1in × 1in) battens for trellis (the number and length required will depend on the dimensions of the trellis and the closeness of the mesh)
- 4 coach bolts
- Screws and woodworking adhesive
- Wood preservative safe to plants

Quantities are for a single unit (sizes are approximate actual sizes, but can be adjusted to suit the individual unit). Follow either metric *or* imperial measurements.

To assemble

Shape the corners of the sides carefully, using a saw and then a file or rasp to smooth them to an even curve. Mark the decorative holes in exactly the same position on each piece, and remove them by taking out an initial hole with a brace and bit and then cutting them out with a saw. Finish off with a file to produce a smooth surface.

Drill large drainage holes in the base of the planter using a brace and bit (take great care when carrying out this task so as not to splinter the wood).

Loosely assemble the pieces, positioning the central division in the middle of the planter, and cutting the 25mm × 25mm (1in × 1in) battens into lengths to run along both sides of the base between the ends and centre piece. You may adjust the width of the base by cutting or planing enough off to bring it to the correct width when the cross-sections and sides are in place.

When the pieces are ready for assembly paint them with a coloured wood preservative (green was used for the planter illustrated), paying special attention to end grain and cut surfaces.

Glue and screw the sections together, screwing both base and sides to the parallel battens at the base. Screw the ends and central piece directly from the outside, countersinking the screws. Fill the resulting depressions with a woodfiller.

Fix the trellis support posts with coach bolts (see illustration), having first painted them with wood preservative.

Nail the trellis to the posts. You can make your own or buy one ready made.

Finishing off

Paint the whole structure again with wood preservative.

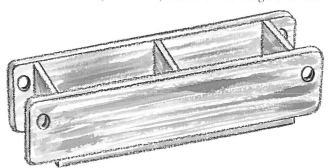

(Left) The planter could be used without a trellis. (Right) The trellis supports are easy to fix with coach bolts.

WOODEN HANGING BASKET

This is the kind of basket that would look good indoors or out, and it is an excellent choice for those plants that can go out in the summer but require overwintering indoors – perhaps a trailing *Asparagus sprengeri* (asparagus fern).

The basket will require lining and a square pond planting basket makes an ideal inner container that can be lined with moss (moss alone would fall through the gaps). If the mesh of the planting basket is too small to plant through, cut out a few sections with a sharp craft knife.

You will require
- Approx. 7.3m (24ft) of 20mm × 20mm (¾in × ¾in), actual size, softwood
- Approx. 3m (10ft) of small-link chain (from a hardware shop)
- Wood preservative

Follow either metric *or* imperial measurements.

To assemble
If using a pond planting basket, make the wooden basket just a little larger than this, so that it fits in snugly. The basket should be deep enough to bring the highest rung just above the liner container. The one illustrated requires a total of 25 strips about 290mm (11½in) long.

Reserve enough pieces to produce an evenly spaced base, excluding the end pieces (seven pieces in this example), and drill a hole the same diameter as the chain (or very slightly larger) at each end of all the other pieces.

Paint all the pieces with a suitable wood preservative, ensuring it is brushed well into the holes.

Screw the seven middle pieces to the two base pieces.

Divide the chain into two equal lengths, and thread them through the holes as shown. Thread the chains through alternating rungs until the finished height is reached.

Link the chains to a suitable hook.

Quick and easy wooden basket
1 Cut and drill all the pieces first, and cut the chain to size. Assemble the base.
2 Simply thread the chain through the remaining pre-drilled pieces of wood.
3 Insert a liner to hold the compost. (Above) The finished basket can be used indoors or out.

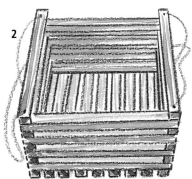
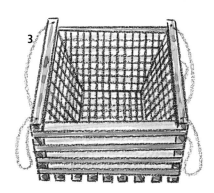

TIERED PLANTER

There are so many good proprietary troughs and simple planters available, some at very reasonable prices compared with buying the materials, that it is only worth making your own if you enjoy carpentry or you want to make something distinctive, like the tiered planter illustrated that you could not buy. This design can be modified very simply to take a supporting trellis for climbing plants in the rear section.

You will require
● Good quality softwood, treated with a timber preservative harmless to plants
● 1 piece 200mm × 18mm × 850mm (7¾in × ¾in × 33½in), for front
● 2 pieces 250mm × 18mm × 850mm (9¾in × ¾in × 33½in), for centre and rear sections
● 2 pieces 268mm × 300mm × 18mm (10½in × 11¾in × ¾in), cut as shown, for ends
● 1 piece 300mm × 18mm × 850mm (12¼in × ¾in × 33½in), for base
● 4 pieces 20mm × 20mm × 850mm (¾in × ¾in × 33½in), for long base braces
● 4 pieces 20mm × 20mm × 80mm (¾in × ¾in × 3¼in), for short (end) base braces
● 4 pieces 20mm × 20mm × 180mm (¾in × ¾in × 7in), for corner braces in front section
● 4 pieces 20mm × 20mm × 230mm (¾in × ¾in × 9in), for corner braces in rear section (only two required if fixing a trellis)
● 1¼in wood screws and woodworking adhesive
Dimensions are actual not nominal sizes. Adjust the 850mm (33½in) dimension to the appropriate length if you want to make it longer or shorter. Follow either metric *or* imperial measurements.

To assemble
Make four rows of large drainage holes in the base with a brace and bit (two rows for each section of the planter), being careful not to split the wood. Stop when the tip of the bit appears at the other side, then turn over the wood and bore from that side – the result will be clean holes without tears.

Cut the end pieces to shape, ensuring a good fit with the three long panels (see diagram).

Treat all the prepared pieces with a wood preservative if not already treated, being especially careful to treat cut surfaces and end grain.

Check that all the pieces fit before assembly.

Glue and screw the four long battens to the bottom of the three long pieces of timber (front, middle, back sections of the planter). Glue and screw the four short battens to the bottom of the end pieces, having checked the position accurately by loosely assembling the planter.

Glue and screw the two end pieces and front, centre and back panels to the base, screwing through the battens. For additional strength, screw the end pieces to the three long sections, from the outside (use brass screws for this, preferably countersunk and hidden with a filler).

If adding a trellis, secure a 75mm × 75mm (3in × 3in) post in each corner, using coach bolts from the back and sides. Don't make the trellis too large, otherwise it will be out of proportion to the planter – for small annual climbers such as *Thunbergia alata*, a trellis about 1m (3ft) high is usually adequate.

How to assemble Use this drawing as a guide to assembly.

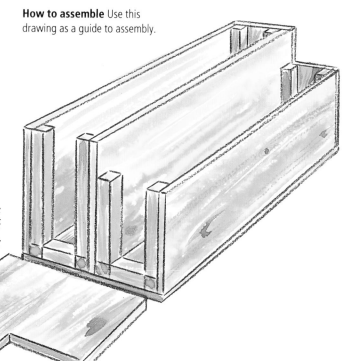

A "STONE" SINK

Old stone sinks are very popular as containers for alpines, but these are difficult to find and are now very expensive. A glazed sink covered with hypertufa (a mixture of cement, sand and peat) is an acceptable substitute, but a shallow concrete trough using the method illustrated produces a sink of more convincing proportions.

Form a bed of moist sand about 2.5cm (1in) thick, slightly larger than the finished sink. Lay bricks on this to provide an inside area of the required size, and cover with a sheet of polythene, tucking it in under the edges.

Mould the damp sand to form a smooth curved channel around the bricks, to form the rim.

Mix three parts coarse sand to one part cement (and a cement dye to give a sandstone colour if you prefer), and

trowel the stiff mix up the sides (if too wet the mix will not stick to the polythene). Cover the top with at least 12mm (½in) of the concrete mix, using a float trowel to make a smooth finish.

Reinforce with wire-netting cut to cover the base and wrap around the sides and ends to a height of about 8cm (3in). It will need to be folded carefully to ensure neat corners.

Add more concrete mix, smoothing the base to a thickness of about 4cm (1½in).

Bore at least five 2.5cm (1in) drainage holes in the base before the concrete sets.

To produce a matt, stone-like finish, brush the surface with a stiff brush after about 24 hours, before the concrete has set too firmly.

After about four days, lift the trough by sliding a spade underneath and raising an edge. If properly set it will lift off the bricks quite easily.

Peel the polythene from the inside, smooth any very rough areas with a coarse file, and clear the drainage holes. Hose down the trough and brush it with a dilute liquid fertilizer to encourage quick weathering. Repeat this operation regularly for a few weeks.

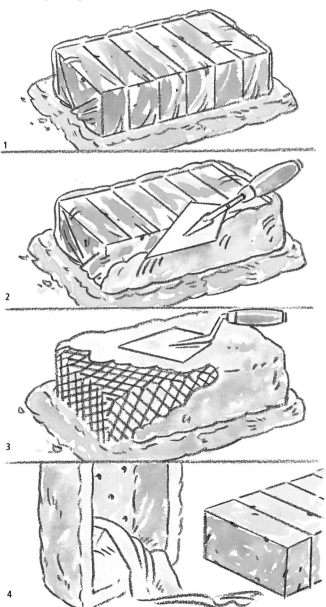

Four steps to a "stone" sink
1 Use an appropriate number of bricks to form a mould of the required size.
2 Spread the special hypertufa mix over the mould.

3 Use wire-netting as reinforcement, then cover with more hypertufa mix.
4 Slide the "sink" off the mould. (Above) The type of sink made by using this technique.

MINIATURE WATER GARDEN

Miniature water gardens are among the easiest features to make, and are generally inexpensive. Many different kinds of containers can be "converted", and the pictures show a few of the possibilities.

Plastic containers are the easiest to use. Most readily available are various kinds of shrub tubs or large indoor plastic plant containers (those intended for indoor use are best as they are less likely to have drainage holes in the base). Some plastic containers have thin sections in the base that can be punched out for drainage but are supplied watertight. This kind of container is ready for immediate use! Simply fill with water and plant.

The size and appearance of a plastic container are important. The surface area should be as large as possible, so bucket-shaped containers are unsuitable. A rectangular container will not only look better, it will probably have a larger surface area to depth ratio (a broad, shallow container is infinitely better than a tall, narrow one). Unless it is to be plunged in the ground, colour should always be considered. Dark brown or even black work well and do not detract from the plants; whites and bright colours seldom look good.

Half barrels Wooden half barrels have more charm than plastic containers, but making them waterproof can be tricky. As genuine barrels were obviously waterproof when they were used for their original purpose there is no reason why they can't be so again even if they have been sawn in half. Unfortunately they may have been allowed to dry out for some time which causes the wood to shrink.

Try to make the barrel waterproof again by keeping it moist. Soak it in a pond for a few days, otherwise fill the barrel with a hose-pipe and keep topping it up periodically. This may be enough to swell the wood to make the barrel waterproof again.

Usually other remedial action is necessary. A caulking material or a mastic sold for sealing aquariums can be used to fill gaps between the staves. Choose a black one, and make sure the barrel is dry first. A combination of this and the natural swelling of the wet wood is usually sufficient to make even a rather poor barrel waterproof.

A really inferior quality barrel may not respond to this treatment, and for these a liner of black butyl rubber is the best solution. To avoid the inevitable severe kinks and folds becoming a major problem in such a small container, make a few slits in the liner to get a better fit, and join the overlap with a butyl liner repair kit (these work rather like a puncture repair outfit). Neatly trim the liner level and staple it to the sides around the rim.

Old glazed sinks can be used as miniature ponds, but they usually look best if fully or partially plunged into the ground, as they are not especially elegant. Above ground, it may be necessary to raise the sink on a couple of bricks to ensure that it is level.

The plug, if still available, can be used to retain the water but it should be glued into position with a suitable waterproof adhesive, such as a PVA glue, and, if necessary, an aquarium sealer too. If there isn't a plug, buy one from a hardware shop. The overflow will need to be blocked if the water level is to be raised to the rim of the sink.

Imitation stone sinks and troughs intended for use as miniature pools are sometimes available and these require no additional preparation.

PLUNGED POOLS

Half barrels, stone sinks and troughs are attractive features that should be displayed in a prominent position. Plastic containers and glazed sinks are best plunged fully or partly into the ground as their beauty lies primarily in the plants. Even an old washing-up bowl can be given a new lease of life this way, perhaps planted with a miniature waterlily.

Making a barrel pool
1 Fill the cut-down barrel with water (or soak it in a pond) to allow the wood to swell and make watertight joints.

2 If after a few days it still leaks, empty the water out, leave the barrel to dry, then fill any areas that leak with a waterproof mastic.
3 If the barrel is in very poor condition it may be necessary to line it with butyl rubber. As this is black it will not be too conspicuous once the barrel is planted.

1

2

Instant pools (left) This type of plastic shrub tub has areas of thin plastic to punch out for drainage holes; leave them intact for an instant pool.

3

A RAISED BED IN BRICK

Brick is an ideal material for making raised beds. The units are small enough to enable a wide range of designs to be created in many shapes and sizes, and they are relatively light and easy to handle. Equally important, bricks blend with plants and the muted colours are often less obtrusive than concrete walling blocks.

Although simple rectangular beds are quick and easy to construct, raised beds will make a better feature if they are a little more imaginative. The two types of brick raised bed illustrated here are simple to construct and both make interesting garden features.

Many clever variations can be created by joining a series of rectangles, perhaps at varying heights to make them more interesting.

Interlocking boxes

As the plan on this page shows, three simple "boxes" were used to form the brick planter illustrated. By altering the height of each box, even by one or two bricks, the effect is made more interesting. Experiment with different proportion and sizes, and adjust the height to create more variations. Lay the bricks loosely on the ground initially to gain a better idea of what the design will look like in the garden.

Simple bricklaying A brick-built raised bed like this is an ideal DIY project for anyone who wishes to acquire simple bricklaying skills. The job can be completed relatively quickly, no complicated bonds are required, the minimum of brick cutting is necessary, and the cost is not prohibitive.

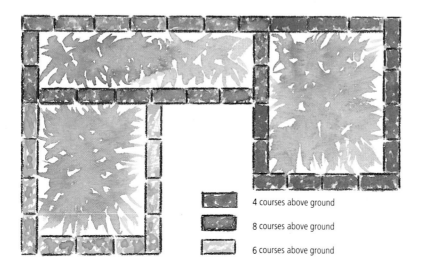

4 courses above ground

8 courses above ground

6 courses above ground

Plan on paper It is always worth drawing out the plan on paper first, as this makes it easier to visualize the proportions of the various boxes and enables the correct number of bricks to be calculated.

PRACTICAL POINTS

Even low raised beds require a firm and level concrete footing. Lay a concrete foundation strip 15cm (6in) thick and 45cm (18in) wide, ensuring it is level. There should be one course of bricks below ground level, so allow for this when calculating how deep to excavate.

Special quality frostproof bricks should be used for garden walls, so always check with the supplier that they are suitable for *garden* walls, otherwise they may crumble after repeated wetting and freezing.

Insert a layer of damp-proof course material (which comes by the roll), and paint the inside of the raised bed with a bitumen-based waterproof paint, otherwise white deposits may become a problem on the outside of the brickwork.

Circular beds

Once the first row of bricks has been laid, circular beds are not as difficult to build as they might appear. First draw a circle of the required radius using two sticks and a length of string (see the illustration below). This will give a reference line on which to lay the bricks out loose. However, minor adjustments will probably be necessary to keep cutting and mortar gaps to a minimum. Then lay the concrete footing and when that has set lay the bricks.

To avoid cutting all the bricks, lay whole bricks with their ends pointing outwards – to create the curve it is necessary to have the inner ends almost touching and a wider wedge of mortar facing outwards.

Cut bricks in half and use them for the final row so that the brickwork does not look too dominant for the size of the bed.

Circular beds (below) Circular beds are more complicated to construct, but well within the scope of most DIY enthusiasts. They can be planted with a tree in the centre or used for seasonal bedding or shrubs – all with equal success.

The illustration shows how the ground is marked out to an accurate circle and the walls constructed on a concrete footing.

mark out a circle to excavate a trench

use a spirit-level on a straight-edge over a series of pegs to ensure an accurate level, then fill with concrete to this level

use cut bricks for the top row (an angle grinder can be used to ensure clean cuts)

1

2

3

45

WOODEN RAISED BEDS

Wood is a material very much at home in the garden and old railway sleepers, rustic logs and planking can all be used to make raised beds.

Railway sleepers

Wooden railway sleepers are ideal for low raised beds. They are strong, long-lasting, and a particularly "sympathetic" material for the garden. They also have a bold profile that can help to give a garden a strength of line and design that is sometimes lacking with other materials. There are two problems: weight and availability (there are firms who supply them; asking the railway which companies buy their old sleepers is often a quick way to track them down).

It takes at least two strong people to lift a railway sleeper, and additional help is advisable. As they are also difficult to cut, it is best to use whole sleepers whenever possible. Some will probably have to be sawn, but working to halves and using a chain saw will minimize the effort.

Because of their weight, beds up to three sleepers high are unlikely to require additional securing or staking, and they can simply be stacked. Stagger the joints at the corners, so that they form a bond (see illustration below). Deeper beds should have strong iron stakes driven either side of the sleepers, to reduce the risk of them toppling.

On a sloping site, sleepers can be used to form a stepped or tiered effect.

Log beds

Logs create a very different atmosphere to railway sleepers. They are much more rustic and informal in appearance, and lack the crisp, neat outline of sleepers. They generally have to be higher to look right (beds just a couple of logs high generally appear insignificant), and the rather bulky appearance means they are more

An integrated approach By using railway sleepers as part of the paving pattern as well as for the raised beds, a more integrated garden design can be achieved. If the area is small, like this, the raised beds should not be too high otherwise the sense of scale and proportion will be destroyed.

Build and bond Stack the sleepers so that they are bonded at the ends, like brickwork. Using full or half length sleepers will save a lot of hard physical work and make bonding easy.

suitable for shrubs and bold herbaceous plants than the less substantial seasonal bedding. They generally look best in an informal garden, perhaps with woodland in the background.

Use logs of even thickness about 15-20cm (6-8in) in diameter.

Different joints produce different visual effects. The halved joints at the ends create a neat, more formal finish that makes the bed more functional with attention focused on the plants. They are also easy to make with a chain saw. The notched and overlapped joints (see illustration below) make the log bed itself a key feature. This kind of construction is very difficult to make from scratch, but kits for self-assembly are available.

There will probably be some gaps where the logs do not meet exactly. This problem is easily overcome by lining the sides with thick polythene, butyl pond liner, or even old carpet. Always ensure that there is free drainage at the base.

A bed for vegetables

A raised vegetable bed like the one shown is a very simple DIY project and provides a much more satisfactory place to grow vegetables on a patio than scattered about in containers. The range of vegetables that can be grown in this way is also much wider, and maintenance is often easier.

A softwood can be used to keep the cost down, but it should be thoroughly treated with a preservative, preferably pressure-treated before purchase. Rough-sawn timber will be slightly less expensive than planed and finished timber.

Planks 230mm × 25mm (9in × 1in) or 300mm × 25mm (12in × 1in) are suitable for the sides (the larger size is more appropriate for a large bed), with 75mm × 75mm (3in × 3in) timber for the corners, supports and anchor posts.

If the bed is to stand on a solid base, make the corner supports the same depth as the planks, but if possible extend them by about 30cm (12in) to anchor them in the ground as shown. Nail the planks to the corner supports. If the bed is more than a couple of metres long, insert additional anchor blocks along the sides and secure with nails.

Low retaining timbers (below and above) Raised beds of limited height can be made from quite modest timbers. The supporting pegs should, however, be well secured in the ground to withstand the pressures created within the bed.

A rustic bed This type of bed can be too dominant for a small garden or for a patio, but can be a fine feature in a more open part of the garden, where the log effect is appropriate to the setting.

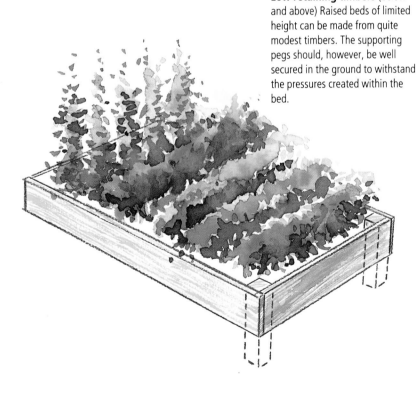

CONTAINER CARE — to get the best from any planting suggestions ensure that compost, container and plants are compatible; the message is plan before you plant.

PLANTING CONTAINERS

The planting schemes starting on page 68 provide plenty of ideas for grouping particular plants, although these may need to be modified according to what is available and the size of the plants. Most of the mixed planting schemes assume starting with small or moderately sized plants. Larger specimens are sometimes available, often with a rootball perhaps 25cm (10in) or so across, but it may be impossible to follow a particular scheme for a moderately sized container with plants of this size. Larger specimens are often best grown in a container on their own, or perhaps with an underplanting of low-growing seasonal plants such as dwarf spring bulbs or impatiens in summer, or with small-leaved ivies to trail over the edge. Do not remove a large part of the rootball in order to cram more plants into a container than is strictly necessary — either choose a larger container or use fewer plants.

Preparing to plant
With the exception of miniature water gardens, all containers must have adequate holes for drainage. A layer of coarse material at the bottom will ensure that water does not stand and stagnate, and prevent the compost being washed through.

Traditionally broken crocks (pieces of old clay flower pots) were used for the drainage layer, but in these days of predominantly plastic pots this is seldom practical. Pieces of broken polystyrene tiles are convenient for covering the actual holes, and a centimetre or so of coarse gravel on top will ensure good drainage. Peat can be used instead of gravel if very good drainage is not particularly important.

It is always tempting to use garden soil for large containers, but permanent plants in containers usually have to cope with less than ideal levels of moisture and nutrients so they should be given every opportunity to thrive. Garden soil in some cases will be a handicap. It may be unsuitable for the plants you want to grow — in an area with alkaline soil *Rhododendrons*, azaleas and *Camellias*, for example, will remain sickly and second-rate if planted in garden soil; given a special ericaceous or acid compost in the container they will flourish.

Advice on composts can be found on page 54, but if it is necessary to economize for large containers, use garden soil at the bottom and fresh potting compost for the top 30cm (12in).

Planting a single specimen
Unless the container is small, it is best to fill and plant in its final position. Firm the compost lightly to about 2.5-5cm (1-2in) below the rim of the container. It may settle further with time, but most woody plants will

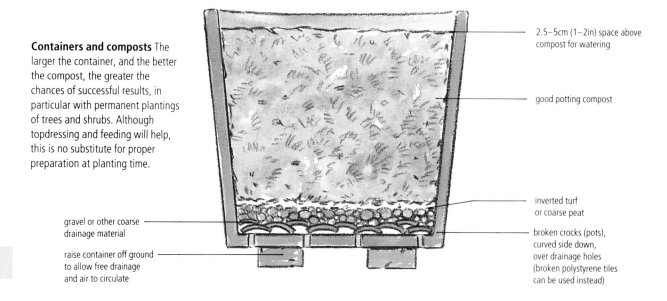

Containers and composts The larger the container, and the better the compost, the greater the chances of successful results, in particular with permanent plantings of trees and shrubs. Although topdressing and feeding will help, this is no substitute for proper preparation at planting time.

2.5–5cm (1–2in) space above compost for watering

good potting compost

inverted turf or coarse peat

broken crocks (pots), curved side down, over drainage holes (broken polystyrene tiles can be used instead)

gravel or other coarse drainage material

raise container off ground to allow free drainage and air to circulate

Height and depth (above) The most successful permanent plantings have both height and depth. In this trough *Aucuba japonica* 'Variegata' and a conifer have been used to provide height, while varieties of *Hedera* (ivies) take the eye downwards. Chrysanthemums have been used to hold interest along the centre with patches of colour.

Planting for balance (left)
1 Use plants of contrasting shapes and colours. In this example a spiky *Phormium*, green and cream variegated *Hebe*, and a silver-leaved *Helichrysum angustifolium* (curry plant) could be used. Arrange them on the surface first to make sure the arrangement works.
2 Remove enough compost to take the rootball easily, starting with the tallest plants at the back.
3 Repeat with the smaller plants in front.
4 Finish off with a decorative and practical mulch of peat, bark or gravel.

benefit from a later topdressing. If the compost is very dry, water it thoroughly then wait a day before planting. Water plants in pots an hour or two before planting. Soak the roots of bare-root plants for an hour or two before planting.

Use a trowel to make a hole large enough to take the rootball. Most plants will have been grown and sold in pots, and adjusting the depth and width of the hole is best done while the plant is still in its pot. Plants in plastic pots can usually be removed by inverting and pulling very gently; clay pots may have to be tapped lightly on the edge of a hard surface.

A few trees and shrubs, especially the less common ones that have to be ordered by mail, may arrive bare-root, in which case the hole should be large enough to spread the roots out as widely as possible and deep enough to bring the final compost level to the same height as it was when planted in the nursery – it is almost always possible to judge the planting depth by the soil mark on the stem.

Some plants, even in garden centres, are supplied as balled plants – *Rhododendrons* and *Daphnes* are sometimes sold like this – with the roots and ball of soil wrapped in hessian or a plastic substitute. Remove the wrapping carefully at the last minute, once the size of the hole has been checked.

Firm the compost gently around the roots before watering thoroughly. If a container-grown plant has been grown in a peat-based compost *make sure the compost in the container covers the surface of the rootball*, even if it means planting slightly deeper. This reduces the chance of the rootball drying out more quickly, especially if a loam-based compost is used for planting.

PLANTING A WINDOWBOX

Lifting a heavy windowbox into position filled with compost and plants is potentially hazardous. It makes sense to plant up with the box in position whenever possible. Fresh compost should be used for new summer seasonal displays, but for autumn-planted bulbs the old compost can be used as these do not require a high level of nutrients.

The planting plans on pages 68 to 113 provide plenty of stimulating ideas, but they will have to be modified to suit the size of windowbox. The distance from front to back, in particular, may cause problems; if there is not enough space to plant the suggested number of rows, either use a box with more generous dimensions or modify the planting plan.

Preparing to plant

To avoid the risk of waterlogging, always ensure that there are drainage holes in the container, and cover these with broken crocks (pieces of old flower pots), or broken polystyrene tiles. In deep containers a layer of gravel is placed over the crocks to ensure good drainage and to prevent the compost washing out, but in a shallow windowbox it is better to use a layer of peat or pulverized bark, which will help to retain moisture while still allowing any excess to drain.

Fill the box with compost to within about 2.5cm (1in) of the top.

A light peat-based (or peat alternative) compost is best for windowboxes in potentially precarious positions, on brackets beneath the window for example, as it will put less strain on supports. A container compost that includes some loam, or a loam-based compost, is a better choice for windowboxes that are absolutely secure and weight is not important (on a broad stone sill on a ground floor window, for example).

PLUNGING POTS

For short-term display, especially in the autumn or early winter, or to provide pockets of fresh interest in a windowbox that has passed its best, plunge pot-plants into vacant spaces for instant results. Ensure the pots are completely covered, and if necessary spread peat or pulverized bark over the top to hide the rims. In the summer, many house and greenhouse pot-plants can be used, but harden them off (acclimatize them) to conditions outside in stages.

Planting

1 Water all the plants thoroughly an hour or so before planting.
2 Arrange the plants on the surface before planting if possible, to make sure the spacing is right.
3 Fill to within about 2.5cm (1in) of the top of the windowbox with a good potting or container compost, and make sure all the rootballs are completely covered (if the tops are exposed they will dry out more quickly).
4 Water thoroughly after planting, and for a decorative effect cover the surface with expanded clay granules (these are sometimes sold for greenhouse benches), fine gravel, or pulverized bark.

Cascading pelargoniums The Balkon or Cascade *Pelargoniums* (geraniums) so popular in countries such as Germany, France and Switzerland, are a distinct type and not the usual ivy-leaved pelargoniums.

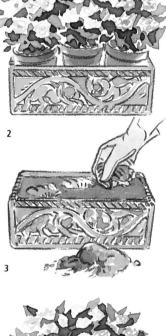

Walls instead of windows

Windowboxes do not have to be placed on windowsills: with suitable brackets they can be used to bring life and colour to an otherwise dull wall. To work well, however, it is best to use lots of windowboxes so that they form a bold design feature (isolated boxes can look a little sparse on a large wall). Staggering them generally helps to break up an expanse of wall much more effectively than arranging them in rows.

PLANTING PRINCIPLES

Bear in mind the following principles when grouping plants:

● In a mixed planting, use some upright plants to provide height. They do not all have to be in a row at the back – perhaps three evenly spaced toward the rear, or a single one in the centre, will be enough to provide punctuation points without looking regimented.

● Bushy or spreading plants should form the backbone of the arrangement, but avoid too many different kinds of plants, otherwise the effect will look fussy and confused. Use mixed colours of one or two types of plants and let

the upright and trailing plants provide the contrast in shape and form.

● Generally trailers planted at the front to tumble over the edge and soften the outline add much to a windowbox, but sometimes it is best to omit them. If the box itself is decorative, make a feature of it by avoiding plants that will obscure its beauty.

● With the exception of single-subject boxes, which can be extremely effective, as the cascading *Pelargonium* boxes so popular in Switzerland, France and Germany prove, choose a relatively small

number of plants but ensure that they contrast in shape, form and colour.

● If seasonal plants are being used, the fewer the types chosen, the more important it is that they have a long flowering period, such as *Impatiens* (busy Lizzie), *Pelargoniums*, and *Fuchsias*. This is less important in a mixed planting where foliage plants or a succession of blooms from different plants, will hold interest.

● Don't overlook foliage plants – green or variegated.

51

PLANTING A HANGING BASKET

Hanging baskets are the most difficult containers to grow well. They demand much more care than tubs, troughs and windowboxes, and being in an exposed position require much more thorough acclimatization before being set in position. Getting the right mix of plants is also more difficult than in a windowbox or tub. Well grown, however, they can be among the most spectacular of all containers.

Planting plans later in the book provide dependable ideas for a range of different planting styles, but these must be adapted to the type and size of container being used. Moss-lined wire baskets are the most versatile, enabling side planting to be achieved easily. Recycled cellulose fibre hanging containers can be planted in the sides by cutting out small triangular holes. Proprietary solid plastic containers are sometimes available that enable plants to be inserted in predetermined positions in the sides, but the vast majority of plastic hanging containers only permit planting in the top.

Trailers are much more important for "baskets" with solid sides, as most are viewed from a low angle. Planting all round the sides of a moss-filled basket can produce a globelike mass of flowers and foliage.

Preparing to plant

Water all the plants, whether in pots or seed trays, a couple of hours before planting. If possible prepare supports in the greenhouse from which the planted basket can be hung – it is inadvisable to put a basket in its summer position straight after planting.

Compost weight is vitally important for hanging baskets. Loam-based composts are generally too heavy. Peat-based composts or their alternatives are more suitable, though they are even more demanding regarding watering and feeding.

Planting

The step-by-step illustrations show the principles of planting a wire basket. For a solid basket, follow the general advice from step four, below.

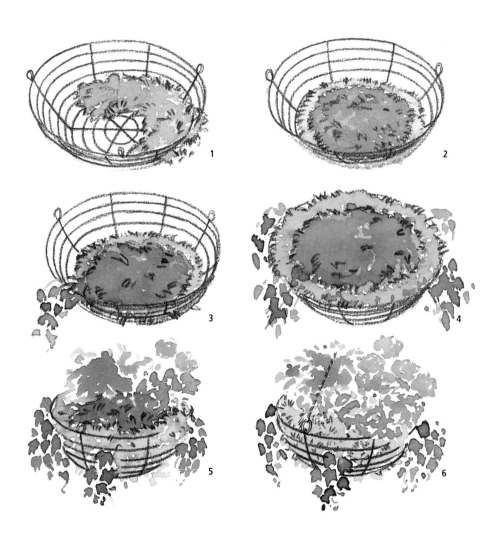

Planting a wire basket

1 Many modern baskets have a flat base, which means they can be stood on a bench for planting.

2 Place sphagnum moss about 2.5cm (1in) thick in the base and up the sides to the first level for side planting.

3 Add compost to this level. Then insert small plants through the sides. Less damage will be done to the plants if the foliage is fed through the mesh from the inside rather than the roots pushed through from the outside.

4 Add more moss to the sides, and bring the compost to the level of the next row of plants.

5 For the top, set the central plant in position first — this is often pot-grown and the rootball should be placed with the minimum of damage before the other plants are set around it. Plant any trailing plants next.

6 Finally infill the top with bushy, plants. Use fingers to pack them between the roots of the other plants; it is generally easier than trying to use a trowel. Finish off the top of the basket with a thick layer of moss (or fine stone chippings).

SMALL HOLE, BIG PLANT

Commercially baskets are often planted with small seedlings in "plugs" (small wedges of compost) that are easily inserted through a small aperture. Plants purchased in late spring or early summer will be much larger and more difficult to plant.

Small-leaved plants can usually be threaded through, but those with larger and perhaps brittle leaves, such as *Begonia semperflorens* (fibrous-rooted begonias), need a different technique. Roll the leaves up in a small square of polythene or paper, rather like rolling a cigarette. The resulting tube will go through quite small holes.

The ball effect An advantage of a wire-mesh hanging basket lined with moss is that it is very easy to plant all round the sides, which helps to produce a ball-like effect even with compact plants such as *Begonia semperflorens* (fibrous-rooted begonia). This basket is particularly interesting, however, as an example of how a planting with two different species can work well if their growth habits are compatible. *Browallia speciosa* has been interplanted with the begonias to provide a much fuller and more interesting texture than would be produced by the begonias alone.

HOOKS AND HANGERS

Decorative wall brackets are commonly used to hang baskets from a wall, but they must be strong. Make sure the arm is long enough to hold the *planted* basket well clear of the wall and strong enough to take the weight (specially important if a large basket is used).

A swivel hook (right) is very desirable to suspend a basket from a beam – it enables the basket to be turned easily every day to even up the growth. To make watering easier there are devices available to raise and lower the basket (see page 56).

THE RIGHT COMPOST

Along with adequate feeding and watering, a suitable compost is crucial for success with container plants. It is tempting to use garden soil, especially for large containers and for shrubs and small trees that normally fend for themselves perfectly adequately in garden soil, but plants in containers are handicapped. Their roots cannot explore new ground freely for nutrients, and they cannot tap reservoirs of water normally held in the lower depths of the topsoil, and perhaps even subsoil. Plants grown close together in a windowbox or hanging basket, for example, are in the same competition for nutrients and moisture as they would be if surrounded by weeds in the ground. In the case of hanging baskets, weight is also an important consideration. So choosing the right compost is vitally important.

Loam composts

Loam-based composts are preferable wherever weight is not a problem. They are easy to keep evenly moist, they have a better natural reserve of nutrients and, for large plants with a lot of heavy top growth, they provide better anchorage and stability. The main problem is one of quality, as loam (the basic ingredient) is variable. In Great Britain loam composts made to the John Innes formula are generally used and this provides some standardization. The potting composts are graded 1 to

COMPOST ADDITIVES

Some compost additives to improve structure or increase water holding capacity, such as vermiculite and perlite, have been used for many years to retain water and open up a heavy soil. Now the super-absorbent polymers are becoming popular. These crystals or gels can absorb and hold water which is then available to the plants for a longer period — theoretically a great advantage for plants in containers. They are available from garden centres so you can mix them into your own compost. However, although possibly beneficial, frequent watering on warm days will still be necessary, so the solution to low-maintenance containers is more likely to lie with some form of automatic watering (see page 56).

3, depending on the amount of fertilizer they contain. For most containers No. 2 is ideal, but for very vigorous plants (such as tomatoes) or for large shrubs and trees No. 3 is appropriate. In other countries proprietary loam-based potting composts are often graded by strength and those with the greatest supply of nutrients, or with slow-release fertilizers, are the best choice for permanent plants.

Peat composts

Peat-based composts have two major advantages: they are clean and easy to use, and they are light. The downside is that once they dry out rewetting them thoroughly is difficult (the water tends to run through them), and nutrients are quickly exhausted.

Peat composts made early headway in the USA with the UC (University of California) range of composts, but various formulations are used everywhere now. Proprietary brands vary considerably but as a general rule it is best to assume that all plants in peat-based composts require feeding after about a month, unless slow-release fertilizers are present (see page 59).

Peat-based composts are not generally suitable for containers planted with large perennial plants, partly because of their inability to sustain good growth over a long period but also because loam provides more stability for bushy plants.

Alternatives to peat

Concerns about the depletion of peat reserves and the effect of peat extraction on wildlife and the landscape, has encouraged the development of alternatives for

Compost decisions These are just some of the compost types that can be used for containers: **1** loam-based (John Innes), **2** organic compost based on animal manure, **3** coconut-fibre compost, **4** hanging-basket compost, **5** peat-based compost, **6** loam-based container compost.

Ericaceous composts (left) Some plants, such as rhododendrons, will not thrive in an alkaline (chalky) soil, and a container may be the best way of growing these plants if the garden soil is not sufficiently acid. Ordinary composts will contain too much lime, but those described as ericaceous are suitable for all lime-hating plants.

Flower colour (below) Hydrangeas react to the amount of lime in the soil by changing the colour of their flowers. On alkaline soils blue varieties may turn pink; for good blues, use an ericaceous (acid) compost.

COMPOST FOR LIME-HATERS

Lime-hating plants require an acid compost. Although peat is acid, peat composts normally have neutralizing agents added, which makes them unsuitable for those plants that prefer an acid compost, such as *Rhododendrons*. Both peat-based and loam-based composts are available for these plants, and are generally described as "ericaceous" mixes.

The home-made organic compost described below can be made suitable for lime-haters by omitting the lime and ensuring that the loam used is acid or neutral.

THE RIGHT COMPOST

soil-less composts. Some of these are based on chipped and treated bark and on products such as coconut fibre. As these become more widely available and more experience is gained with them for a wide range of plants, their strengths and weaknesses will become apparent. They are, however, worth using for seasonal plants.

Container composts

There are proprietary container composts, developed primarily for hanging baskets and windowboxes. These may be loam-based, but they usually have a high proportion of peat or other light products to reduce the weight. They may also have water-retaining products (see Compost Additives) and slow-release fertilizers to maintain steady growth over a long period.

It is worth experimenting with several different brands of these useful composts to see which ones suit the kind of plants that you grow.

Organic composts

Organic composts are available either in organic growing bags or as compost to use in pots or containers.

These are based on products such as peat and cow manure or composted bark and animal manures. They will produce good results but are often more expensive than conventional composts.

An effective home-made organic compost for containers can be made as follows. Mix 7 parts of loam, 3 parts of well-rotted garden compost, manure or leaf mould (or sphagnum moss) and 2 parts of coarse grit. Add 30g (1oz) of garden lime and 150g (5oz) of blood, fish and bone meal to each 9-litre (2-gallon) bucketful of the above mixture, and combine thoroughly.

Bear in mind that plants grown in organic composts still require feeding.

55

WATERING

Slow-release fertilizers can relieve the burden of regular feeding, but watering is a regular and for much of the year a *daily* chore that has to be faced up to as the one major negative aspect of container gardening. Only automatic watering systems can ease the commitment required. A single day of neglect can ruin a hanging basket, and even some of the tougher shrubs in tubs can suffer permanent damage if neglected during a summer holiday.

Automatic or semi-automatic watering systems are generally designed for greenhouses, where plants are conveniently grouped together; containers in the garden are often placed around the garden making it difficult, both practically and visually, to hide their "mechanics". A combination approach is likely to be the most satisfactory solution for most gardeners.

Hose-pipes

A hose that has to be wound and unwound by hand, and fitted to the tap each time, either won't be used regularly or will be left lying around the garden. Investing in a through-feed hose-reel permanently fitted to an outside tap is one of the best investments for anyone with a lot of containers to water. Fold-flat hoses are easy to put away, but less convenient than through-feed reels and some tend to kink badly if taken round a sharp corner.

Hoses are particularly useful for watering hanging baskets, but the main disadvantage is that a forceful jet of water will tend to wash the compost away from the roots. Hose-end attachments often make the spray even more forceful, or alternatively produce a fine spray that

Through-feed hose reel A very convenient way to water several containers. The hose is easily rewound after use.

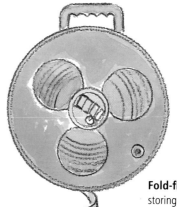

Fold-flat hose reel Useful for storing conveniently, but not as easy to use as a normal through-feed hose and reel. Some of these hoses are liable to kink.

HOLIDAY CARE

The best form of holiday care is a helpful neighbour. Failing that, try arranging a capillary system as shown, or try making a simple temporary drip feed from an old plastic bottle (see illustration). Lift down baskets and treat like other containers. If possible move them to a shady spot.

Various wicks can be improvised, but the best is a piece of capillary matting of the kind sold for greenhouse watering. Cut a broad strip from

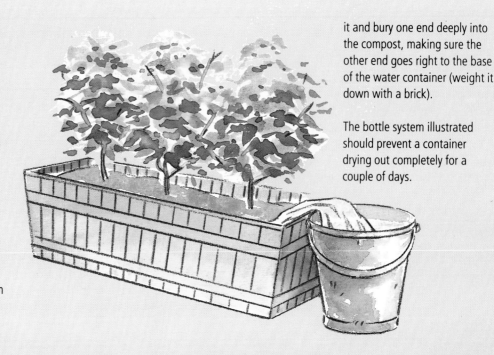

it and bury one end deeply into the compost, making sure the other end goes right to the base of the water container (weight it down with a brick).

The bottle system illustrated should prevent a container drying out completely for a couple of days.

makes it difficult to judge when enough water has been applied. Either use the hose with the tap turned on just sufficiently to produce a trickle, or hold a piece of rag over the end to break the force of the jet.

Basket waterers

Proprietary basket waterers, based on a plastic bottle and tube with a curved end, which work by squeezing the bottle, are convenient for one or two baskets but time-consuming if you have a lot of baskets.

Some compression sprayers have an extension tube with a curved end, designed to make basket watering relatively simple. These work well, but again may be inconvenient if there are many baskets.

Watering-cans

For shrub tubs and troughs at ground level a large garden watering-can is the most practical – there are fewer trips between tap and containers, and it is not necessary to lift the heavy can to any significant height. For window-boxes and other raised containers, a smaller greenhouse watering-can with a long spout is more practical, even though the capacity is less. Always use a rose on the can, even though it takes longer to water.

Self-watering containers

Although intended for indoor use, these provide the real solution for a balcony or verandah. The plastic containers are attractive, and even in the summer they are unlikely to need topping up more frequently than once a week. Plants generally thrive in this kind of container.

Automatic systems

These are most justified when there are a lot of containers in a relatively small area that can be fed from

one source. Drip-feed systems are effective for a long row of hanging baskets for instance, as the supply tubing can be run along the support unobtrusively with small drip tubes leading down into the baskets. They are also useful for tubs and growing bags if the supply tubing can be laid unobtrusively.

With a drip-feed system simply turn on the tap and leave until the containers have received enough water or, better still, use in conjunction with a timer tap to make the system automatic – even while on holiday.

Systems like this require regular checking. Nozzles can become blocked, and if they are adjustable it may be necessary to vary the flow occasionally.

There are various devices for automatically watering growing bags, usually with a suspended bag (sometimes held on an integral frame) which is filled with water and left to drip slowly into the compost. These are acceptable for growing crops like tomatoes or cucumbers in growing bags, but too unsightly to use with ornamentals.

RISE AND FALL OF A HANGING BASKET

A pulley-type fixing, sold specifically for hanging baskets, will enable a basket to be lowered easily to a convenient height to water with an ordinary watering-can. They can be suspended on a bracket or fastened directly to a beam.

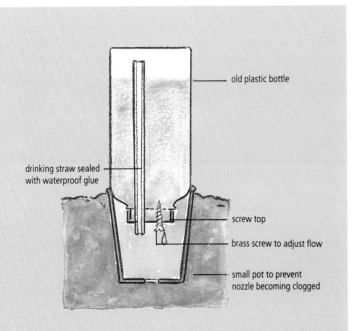

old plastic bottle

drinking straw sealed with waterproof glue

screw top

brass screw to adjust flow

small pot to prevent nozzle becoming clogged

FERTILIZERS AND FEEDING

Anyone who has seen trials of fed and unfed, but otherwise identical, containers, and especially those with limited compost capacity such as hanging baskets, will have no doubt about the importance of feeding. Quite simply it will make the difference between a poor, mediocre display and one that is first-rate with lush, healthy growth. The effects of feeding are most dramatic with seasonal plants in peat-based and peat-alternative composts, but even trees and shrubs in loam-based composts will benefit.

Almost all plants in containers require feeding at some stage but how soon depends very much on the compost. Some peat-based composts, for instance, contain fertilizers which produce very good growth initially but become exhausted rapidly; others contain plant foods that produce less lush growth early on but sustained growth for longer. Increasingly, slow-release and controlled-release fertilizers are being used in composts, and

Healthy growth (below) This example of a well-watered and well-fed container shows vigorous and healthy plants that are clearly growing well. The *Sedum* planted around the base of the *Clematis* shows how containers can be made much more interesting with thoughtful planting.

Sustaining growth (right) Most composts will have started to run out of nutrients long before the plants have filled the basket as well as these violas. The use of slow-release fertilizers, or regular feeding, is crucial to maintain this kind of display.

these may sustain good growth for many months without additional feeding.

You cannot tell how well a particular compost is going to perform simply by looking at it. It makes sense to find one you like, to learn by observation when its food reserves are likely to become exhausted, and then use it regularly. The performance of different feeds can also produce strikingly different results – it's worth trying several, on a range of containers, to see which gives the best results (but bear in mind that some fertilizers may be better for particular plants).

When to feed

The early stages of starvation are not always obvious unless controls are grown alongside. Plants that just don't seem to be growing well or that seem a bit "slow" could be due to the weather, or an unsuitable position. With seasonal summer plants, however, the signs are frequently very obvious even within weeks of planting (some may have become starved in their pots or seed trays beforehand), with small, yellowish leaves and stunted growth. This demands immediate feeding.

Foliar feeds

Some liquid feeds can also be used as foliar feeds (check the label), and applying them to the foliage means they are taken in by the plant more rapidly. Some products sold specifically as foliar feeds contain other substances to stimulate plant growth, and are intended to revive sickly plants. Foliar feeds are best used to give a boost to neglected or ailing plants rather than as part of a routine. Never apply a foliar feed while plants are in strong sunlight.

Liquid feeding

Liquid feeds are generally cheaper than other plant foods, and some provided as powders to dissolve in water are particularly economic. However, having to water them *regularly* is time-consuming if there are a lot of containers and obtaining the correct dilution is an additional chore. Liquid feeding is the best option if you use liquid feeds in other parts of the garden or in the greenhouse, and want to keep costs low.

Pellets, sticks and tablets

There are several products designed to be pushed into the compost, near the plants' roots. The number required depends on the size of the container, but the manufacturer's instructions make this clear. Whether they come in tablet form or as sticks, they must be pushed into the soil with a pencil or piece of dowel.

The products vary widely, not only in formulation – some are intended primarily for flowering plants, others foliage plants – but also in how long they last. Some might require replenishing after a few weeks, others after months, though all are applied much less frequently than liquid feeds. They are the best choice if you are not able to incorporate slow-release fertilizers when planting yet find liquid feeding a bit of a chore to do regularly.

Slow-release fertilizers

These are generally mixed in with the compost, but can be added later when they should be gently worked into the top centimetre or so of the compost. Some are in sachets that are put under the rootball when planting.

Slow-release fertilizers are available from garden centres, who can advise on brand names. Not all work in the same way, though for use in the spring all are satisfactory. Some release nutrients slowly over a period of many months; others only release them when the temperature is warm (useful for autumn application, as it is undesirable to stimulate growth during the winter). In general, one application will provide seasonal plants with nutrients for the whole season – ideal if you want to forget about feeding.

Feeding trees and shrubs Trees and shrubs that are in a container for many years require feeding at least a couple of times a year, preferably with a slow-release fertilizer. If this is not possible use a balanced general purpose fertilizer for the flower garden, either a powder or granules.
1 Sprinkle the fertilizer around the base of the plant, keeping it away from the stem.
2 To ensure that the fertilizer penetrates into the compost, gently fork it into the top 2.5–5cm (1–2in). Always water the container well after adding fertilizer.

1

2

Slow-release sachets Some slow-release fertilizers come in sachets or tablets to put beneath the plant. Because these are used at planting time, they are only suitable for seasonal plants. Make the planting hole, then drop the fertilizer into the bottom before planting. The number required will depend on the size of the container so follow the manufacturer's advice.

WHEN *NOT* TO FEED

A few plants are best grown without too much fertilizer. Some annuals, such as *Tropaeolum* (nasturtiums), may produce so much foliage that the flowers are hidden if too much nitrogen is given. Some *Pelargoniums* are special cases, best grown to discourage too much leafy growth – the famous Balkon or Cascade *Pelargoniums* (the same plants, just different names in different countries) have

to be planted close together and grown with little fertilizer if they are to flower freely.

Alpines and cacti also require less feeding than, say, summer annuals.

Autumn-planted bulbs will not require fertilizer, unless part of a permanent planting and then in spring and not autumn. Avoid stimulating any plant into growth as the cold weather approaches.

AVOIDING PESTS AND OTHER PROBLEMS

Pest and disease control should never be a major problem, and simple precautions should largely eliminate the need for pesticides. Careful choice of plants and varieties, and ensuring that the plants are well fed and not overcrowded, go a long way to eliminating pests and diseases, but it is inevitable that *some* problems will be enountered.

Practical precautions

Even gardeners who don't mind using chemical sprays must prefer to minimize their use, if only to save money and time.

Here are simple precautions that make sense whatever your views on pesticides:

• Grow resistant varieties whenever possible. If growing roses, choose those that show a high degree of disease resistance; if growing *Antirrhinums* (snapdragons) in an area where rust is a common problem, grow rust-resistant varieties. If you live in an area where rust is a common problem on *Althaea* (hollyhocks), grow varieties that can be treated as annuals (by not overwintering the plants you reduce the risk of the disease).

• Avoid plants that are known to be particularly susceptible to pests or diseases, unless you are prepared to spray, for example, *Tropaeolum* (nasturtiums) seldom fail to attract aphids, particularly blackfly. In your area there may be certain plants that always seem prone to particular pests and diseases. Make a point of eliminating these for a simple but effective control.

• Keep the plants well fed. Healthy plants are more able to resist disease.

• Avoid very overcrowded containers. It is usually possible to ensure a full and well-filled display while still allowing enough room for air to circulate around the plants. Overcrowding can lead to the rapid spread of both pests and diseases.

• *Observe.* Make a point of checking for early signs of pests and diseases when you water (or make it a specific job once a week). Picking off affected leaves or shoots at the earliest signs of infection or infestation will often eliminate a problem before it spreads. As an additional precaution, carry a small ready-mixed insecticidal "gun". This is not an economic way to treat a widespread infestation, but it is so much more trouble to mix up an insecticide than to give a single squeeze on a trigger that the chances are you won't bother until the population builds up. Using a small amount of insecticide *early* and confining it to the part affected is both economical and environmentally sensible. For aphids there are comparatively safe and "natural" insecticides that you can use.

ORGANIC REMEDIES

If preventative action has not worked and you want to avoid using the more highly developed chemicals, the following are worth trying.

A soft soap solution should kill most insects on contact but there are insecticidal soaps that have added ingredients to improve the kill of more resistant insects such as whitefly, scale insects and red spider mites

(again there must be direct contact with the pest). Derris is popular for controlling crawling pests such as caterpillars, and pyrethrum can be particularly useful against aphids.

For fungus diseases Bordeaux Mixture (a copper fungicide) can be tried, and green sulphur offers some control against powdery mildew.

Cold protection Plants on the borderline of hardiness can be helped to survive by plunging the pots in the ground and tying straw or dried bracken around them as a protective coat.

Wind shield Some vulnerable evergreens that are not particularly hardy can be damaged by cold winter winds. A sheet of polythene around the sides may offer enough protection.

TROUBLE-SHOOTING

Although there are more potentially harmful insects, diseases and disorders than most gardeners care to think about, control is not as complicated as the masses of chemicals on garden centre shelves would have one believe. Just a handful of garden chemicals will control most problems, and often there are alternative forms of control too.

It is most convenient and practical to summarise the problems and the solutions under a few broad headings to cover the major problems likely to be encountered.

Leaf eaters bite holes in leaves or around the edges. These are most likely to be caused by caterpillars (which will probably be visible), or insects such as weevils or earwigs (which will probably be hiding). Dusting the area with a contact insecticide will usually control them.

Slugs and snails can devastate newly planted seedlings or vulnerable foliage plants such as hostas. Snails will be found on the leaves, slugs will usually leave tell-tale slime trails even if the pests are hiding. Pick off and destroy any that are noticed, and use a slug killer around the base of the plant.

Sap suckers such as aphids and thrips may cause deformed flowers and shoots, and generally weak plants. Aphids, the most common problem, are easily seen as small green or black "flies" (though they don't

always have wings). Apart from spoiling and debilitating the plant directly, they may transmit virus diseases. There are many good insecticides to control aphids, some of which do not harm beneficial insects. A systemic insecticide is the best solution.

Mildews and moulds, rusts and rots cause rotting flowers, fruit and leaves. These and any leaves with brown spots, pimples or blotches are best picked off promptly and burnt. A systemic fungicide such as benomyl will give some control of most fungus diseases except rust and downy mildew – for these try mancozeb.

Problems in the soil can be caused by various grubs and larvae which eat the roots of plants, or chew at the stem at ground level. If this appears to be a problem, a soil insecticide such as bromophos should control them, although established plants are less likely to be severely affected.

Pale, yellowish leaves may be due to a nutrient deficiency. If there are no signs of insects (check with a magnifying glass), try feeding the plants with a balanced feed containing trace elements. If this doesn't work a virus might be the cause.

Viruses could be the cause of stunted plants with mottled or yellowish leaves. They are the most likely

cause if just an isolated plant is affected. If there is no other more likely cause, pull up the affected plant and burn.

The weather, in the form of cold winds and frost, can damage the edges of the leaves on evergreen trees and shrubs which can turn black or brown, particularly in spring. New leaves should be unaffected. The new foliage on vulnerable deciduous plants such as *Acer palmatum* (Japanese maples) may shrivel up shortly after they have opened; this is almost always caused by cold winds, so give them more protection next spring.

Frost and wind damage This *Choisya ternata* (Mexican orange blossom) has been damaged by exceptionally cold winds in a severe winter, but it will recover and produce new leaves.

KEEPING UP APPEARANCES

Plants in containers need routine care like grooming, pruning, and staking just like any other garden plants, albeit on a more modest scale. This is specially important for containers with perennial plants, though even seasonal plants require some attention. Just keeping the containers looking smart will improve appearances.

Container care

Once a year it is worth checking all containers to see whether they require any maintenance. Although gardeners go to great lengths to make a new "stone" container look old, a grubby one may cease to be attractive, and damaged containers can be given a new lease of life with simple repairs.

Cleaning should never be drastic. Plastics and ceramic tiles can be wiped over with a normal non-abrasive kitchen cleaner, but concrete and reconstituted stone containers are best scrubbed with a hard-bristled brush using a mild detergent; if stubborn stains remain try a little diluted bleach on the area.

The white deposit that sometimes forms on terracotta is often acceptable, but to remove it try scrubbing the affected area with a strong solution of vinegar.

Wooden containers can be brightened simply by scrubbing with soapy water; periodically they will need painting again – if the finish is natural wood, use a wood preservative, perhaps one containing a stain.

Repairs can be made to concrete and reconstituted stone containers that have been slightly damaged. If a piece of decoration has been knocked off, it can usually be stuck back satisfactorily with a two-part epoxy resin (make sure both surfaces are clean).

If a concrete container is chipped in an inconspicuous place, try using a fine concrete mix, first using a PVA adhesive to paint the damaged area to ensure a good bond. Some manufacturers of the more expensive reconstituted stone containers can supply a repair kit.

Deadheading

Deadheading will extend the flowering season, and in some cases encourage larger flowers, and is particularly important with some bedding plants. *Bellis*, *Calendulas*, *Petunias*, *Salvias*, and *Mimulus*, for example, all tend to respond well to deadheading. Cut the dead flowers off with scissors or simply pick them off by hand. The plants look tidier for this treatment.

Clearly there are some plants, those with masses of small flowers, such as *Lobelia* and *Alyssum*, where deadheading is not practical without a great deal of time and patience.

Some perennials, such as *Alyssum saxatile* and *Aubrieta*,

look tidier, and the plants remain more compact, if trimmed over with shears after flowering.

Mulches and decorative finishes

Containers with perennial plants ought to be kept looking fresh, and by topdressing and mulching the plants will benefit too. Remove any existing mulch or decorative finish, such as gravel, along with about 2.5-5cm (1-2in) of compost, without damaging the main roots. Replace with a layer of fresh compost (this is sometimes called topdressing), and apply a thick layer of pulverized bark, decorative stone chippings or gravel.

Pruning

Pruning will usually keep shrubs looking attractive. It is as important for shrubs in containers as it is for those in the ground, and should never be neglected. Although many shrubs are pruned in spring, everything depends on the plant concerned (by pruning at the wrong time the season's flowers may be jeopardized). Follow the advice in the individual entries in the *Plant Directory* section of this book (page 114).

Stakes and supports

Whenever possible shrubs and small trees should be grown in containers without supports as it is difficult to secure a large stake in a container, it will simply blow over along with the plant in exceptionally severe weather. It is better to encourage a sturdy plant able to bend with the wind to some extent. But a small temporary stake is a sensible precaution for trees until the plant has filled the container with roots and found a firm anchor.

Some bulbs and herbaceous perennials will bend or flop and spoil the display, specially if near a wall or fence

Deadheading Removing the dead flower heads not only makes plants like this fuchsia look tidier, it also helps many plants, such as *Viola* (pansies) and *Mimulus*, to keep flowering for longer.

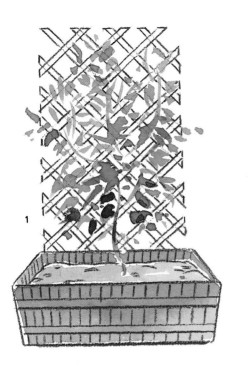

1

2

Supports
1 The most satisfactory support for climbers is a wooden or plastic trellis fixed to the wall. If the container is pushed close enough the plants will climb easily.
2 Plants in growing bags are difficult to support because the depth of compost is so shallow. Proprietary growing-bag supports are the best solution.

3 Plants that are usually self-supporting but may be blown over by winds if shallowly planted in a container, such as daffodils, are best supported with split canes and twine.
4 For tall herbaceous plants, the wire supports sold for use in borders can be used.
5 To produce a wigwam of canes it is best to buy plastic holders that secure the canes at the top.

3

4

5

where wind hitting the wall is forced back against the plants. Proprietary plant supports can be used for large floppy herbaceous perennials, but for plants like *Narcissus* (daffodils) a few split canes inserted near the edge of the container with cotton stretched between them is generally satisfactory.

One of the best ways of supporting a climber is to fix a wooden trellis to a wall or fence, and stand the container at the base.

Tall plants in growing bags definitely need support, especially the tall type of tomatoes (you could grow compact bush varieties instead). If the bag is standing on soil, canes can be pushed through the base, but a growing bag on a patio is likely to be standing on paving and the only practical solution is to use a proprietary growing bag support.

Runner beans in tubs can be supported with a wigwam of bamboo canes tied at the top.

Weeding

If a sterilized loam-based or a peat-based compost has been used, weeds should never be a major problem, but seedlings will appear (sometimes self-sown seedlings of the cultivated plants). Pull them out while still young as they will compete with the cultivated plants for nutrients and moisture.

ACTION PLAN – all outdoor gardening is seasonal. Spring and early summer are the busiest times but container gardening should be a year-round activity if tackled with imagination.

YEAR-ROUND ACTION PLAN

EARLY SPRING

Brighten winter and spring windowboxes and tubs by plunging pots of early bulbs among evergreens. If these have not been grown specially for filling gaps, small pots of bulbs are usually available from garden centres.

Remove winter protection from tender plants in mild areas. In cold areas it may be wise to delay until mid spring.

Finish planting bare-root trees and shrubs, container-grown plants can be planted at any time.

MID SPRING

"Instant" spring displays can be achieved by using pot-grown plants from garden centres. Some small spring-flowering plants such as *Bellis perennis* can be bought in pots in garden centres, and together with pot-grown pansies and pot-grown spring bulbs a very attractive display can be created instantly. If planting a windowbox, knock the plants out of their pots before planting.

Supports for certain plants may be necessary by mid spring – see *Late Spring* for techniques.

Remove winter protection from tender plants if not already done, but don't expose frost-tender plants at night until all risk of frost has passed (not before late spring or early summer in many areas).

Plant evergreens – this is one of the best times.

LATE SPRING

Get supports into position for summer-flowering border plants and others that need support for the summer before growth becomes too advanced. The plants will grow through and hide the supports. Putting supports in too early can make the containers look unattractive while the plants are growing.

Bring containers out of the conservatory once it is safe to do so – if the plants are frost-tender this may not be until early summer.

Apply a balanced fertilizer to trees and shrubs or better still, topdress by removing a few centimetres of compost from the top of the container and replacing it with fresh compost enriched with a little extra fertilizer.

Many vegetables and herbs can be planted now.

Plant hanging baskets but do not hang them out until danger of frost has passed. If possible keep them in a greenhouse for a few weeks to become established.

EARLY SUMMER

Put out hanging baskets and plant summer bedding once risk of frost has passed. This may be in late spring in some areas. A good guide is when the local parks department plants out its summer bedding.

Plant tender vegetables such as runner beans, courgettes, cucumbers and tomatoes.

MID SUMMER

Start feeding seasonal displays if a slow-release fertilizer has not been used.

Deadhead and groom plants wherever this is practical.

Sow biennials such as wallflowers and forget-me-nots in a nursery bed.

LATE SUMMER

Continue feeding and deadheading

Plant autumn-flowering bulbs such as colchicums as soon as they are available. Colchicums are sometimes coming into flower while still in the shop if you wait a little longer, but it is easier to plant them before the flower shoots have emerged.

Take cuttings of pelargoniums (bedding geraniums) if you have somewhere to overwinter them.

EARLY AUTUMN

Continue feeding those plants that still have several weeks or months of display left. In some seasons many summer bedding plants will flower until the first frost, but by this time even composts with a slow-release fertilizer may need supplementary feeding.

Take in tender plants, such as house or greenhouse plants that have been stood out for the summer or used among seasonal displays. Take them in before the nights get cold, and certainly before any risk of frost.

Plant spring-flowering bulbs as soon as there are vacant containers.

Take cuttings of tender perennials if you have somewhere to overwinter them.

MID AUTUMN

Plant spring-flowering bulbs as soon as possible.

Protect slightly tender shrubs and trees in cold areas (see *Late Autumn*). In warmer areas wait for another month as protected containers and plants are not visually attractive.

Plant bare-root plants, container-grown plants can be planted at any time.

LATE AUTUMN

Plant up some bulbs in plant pots to fill in gaps and bring pockets of interest in spring. The main bulb-planting season has passed so it is usually possible to pick up bulbs very cheaply at this time. Put them in half-pots unless the bulbs are very large, as the smaller rootball is easier to accommodate when infilling containers already planted. Keep the pots in a spare piece of ground and set them in position as they come into flower.

Protect containers that are not frostproof by removing the compost and putting the empty containers in a dry place (perhaps a shed).

Protect slightly tender plants that are likely to be killed over winter in your area. The most tender must be taken indoors or into a conservatory, but many that are only likely to be killed by a severe winter, or will survive outside with a little protection, should be covered now.

EARLY WINTER

Check containers, clean them if necessary, and make any repairs.

Check that winter protection is satisfactory and reposition any that has worked loose in autumn winds.

MID WINTER

Check winter containers and pick off any dead or dying leaves.

Sow seasonal bedding plants that require a long growing season, such as zonal pelargoniums and fibrous-rooted begonias. If you do not have a greenhouse, buy plants in late spring.

LATE WINTER

Sow summer bedding plants if you have a heated greenhouse. Just a few plants can often be raised on a light windowledge indoors.

Check over winter and spring containers and remove any dead or dying flowers or foliage.

PLANTING PLANS

An old wheelbarrow makes an interesting and unusual container for this display of mixed summer bedding.

PLANTING PLANS: INTRODUCTION

The planting plans illustrated on the following pages show more than 100 different ways of combining plants beautifully in containers of all types. Some, such as the summer displays, are short term and last but a few months, others will last for several years needing little attention. While most of the displays are full of colour, those in the oriental style are more restrained but create a special atmosphere; others form functional screens or, with herbs and vegetables, are productive. Whatever their style or purpose each one is designed to please.

All the plants used are described in detail in the Plant Directory starting on page 118. A range of plants well suited to growing in containers has been selected to include the best of the new varieties as well as the old favourites: the tried and trusted *Lobelia* and *Fuchsia* to more recent introductions such as *Bidens* and *Verbena*.

Without doubt, summer displays are most popular and a large selection is included. Other sections offer a diverse range of planting themes (including topiary, country style, displays for fragrance and wildlife) to give plenty of scope for creating something different. With a little imagination the ideas from the various sections can be combined effectively. Equally, containers of vegetables, flowers and fruit can be combined to give an attractive and productive display.

Design concepts

Summer displays offer the greatest opportunities for colour combinations, but with all containers it is worth deciding how a colour scheme fits into a given area. Consider how an area is used: a patio for relaxation requires a soft and soothing scheme while an area commanding attention, such as an entrance, would be better served by fiery reds, yellows and oranges.

Consider too the background. In most cases the display should provide a contrast. The plants within the display should also contrast with one another – in colour, where subtle blends or stark clashes will give very different effects; in texture, where size and shape of leaf and flower all of a similar colour can look very

effective; in form, where the different plant shapes of upright, bushy, weeping and trailing can combine to give extra visual excitement. The colour, texture and form of the container, as well as any accessories, should also be considered along with the plants as part of the overall design.

The growth rate of the plants is also an important consideration. Plants need to be positioned correctly otherwise a very vigorous plant could create an imbalance or, worse still, smother smaller plants.

The illustrations of the planting patterns show the designs in their prime. However, emphasis has been put on creating designs which will be attractive over as long a period as possible. For example, most of the winter and spring displays list flowering bulbs which are not illustrated but will extend the season of interest beyond that shown.

Developing the designs

These designs are an excellent starting point to achieve a wonderful display. They can also be easily modified to establish a personal touch. Learn through experience and experiment – it is sometimes frustrating but usually there are rewards. Don't be afraid to be adventurous. Try several new plants or varieties of plants each year. This could well bring improvement or, if not, it is reassuring to know the original choice was best. In any year the weather will play its part, so note which plants thrive in a hot summer and which cope with rain and dull conditions – the plant directory also gives guidance.

Much can be learned from other people's gardens, so make a note and take photographs of any displays that appeal. Consider why they look good or how they could be improved upon. Many gardeners are easily enticed into discussion about their horticultural efforts and only too pleased to pass on their experiences.

Finally, don't become a slave to your garden by taking on too many containers to begin with. The numbers can be increased over the years. In this way their care will be a joy, not a chore.

Indicates the type of plant shown in the illustration and the suggested number of plants to be used in the size of container indicated. Where a number is not specified, a single plant is used.

Botanical names have been used to identify the plants for easy reference to the Plant Directory on page 118, with any widely used common names following in brackets. The exceptions to this are the fruit, vegetables and herbs where the reverse applies.

The suggested number of plants will create a very "full" effect. A reduced number of plants can be used but will not be quite as effective. If larger plants are used, a reduced number will be required.

In order to simplify buying plants in some cases a colour rather than a variety is specified. This applies to bedding plants in particular. Where varieties are specified they have been chosen to achieve a particular effect.

A scented pot for late spring (below) Ingredients for a 45cm (18in) pot:
1 *Narcissus* white 'Cheerfulness' × 12
2 *Myosotis alpestris* (forget-me-not) × 5
3 *Convallaria majalis* (lily of the valley)
4 *Primula polyantha* (polyanthus) × 5
5 *Dianthus barbatus* 'Giant Auricula Eyed' (sweet William) × 5
6 *Cheiranthus cheiri* (wallflower) × 5.

Scent at a pinch A group of plants with aromatic leaves. Ingredients for a 50cm (20in) pot:
7 *Thuya plicata* 'Zebrina'
8 *Salvia rutilans* (pineapple sage)
9 *Thymus × citriodorus* 'Aureus' (golden lemon-scented thyme)
10 *Lavandula stoechas* (French lavender)
11 *Pelargonium tomentosum* (peppermint geranium)
12 *Eucalyptus citriodora* (lemon-scented gum).

Summer scents Ingredients for a 38cm (15in) pot:
13 *Lantana camara*
14 *Heliotropium peruvianum* (cherry pie) × 3

15 *Alyssum maritimum* × 10
16 *Verbena* 'Silver Anne' × 3
17 *Matthiola bicornis* (night-scented stock), sow a few pinches of seed after pot is planted.

Sweet summer perfumes
Ingredients for a 50cm (20in) pot:
18 *Hedychium gardnerianum* (ginger lily)
19 *Lilium auratum*
20 *Nicotiana alata* white (tobacco plant) × 5
21 *Heliotropium peruvianum* (cherry pie) × 3
22 *Lathyrus odoratus* 'Bijou Mixed' (sweet pea) × 5.

Heady evening scent
Ingredients for a 60cm (24in) pot:
23 *Datura* 'Grand Marnier' will fill the evening air with its delicious fragrance
24 *Alyssum* 'Wonderland' × 12 adds colour and daytime scent at low level.

Fresh vegetables and herbs are one of the great joys of gardening and many can be raised successfully in containers.

VEGETABLES AND HERBS

L imited space is no excuse for not growing edible crops. Here are some attractive ideas which can be adapted to suit your own requirements, ranging from small pots, to a large raised bed.

To maximize on available space it is advisable to choose varieties which can be harvested over as long a period as possible. For instance, a winter cabbage will occupy a large space over a long period, whereas a courgette plant will yield heavily over four months.

While herbs virtually look after themselves, the successful vegetable gardener must be prepared to supply ample water and feed, undertake pest control, and work to a programme of successional planting, in order to give continuity of cropping.

Pot-grown runner beans
(*Phaseolus coccineus*) (right)
Originally grown as an ornamental, this vegetable is very productive over a long season. Some kinds are particularly attractive in flower. A free-standing 60cm (24in) pot with four support canes makes an attractive feature.

Trough with runner beans (left)
Runner beans (*Phaseolus coccineus*) trained up a trellis or similar support, will screen an unsightly area, wall or fence. Sow three seeds per cane and thin to leave the strongest plant.

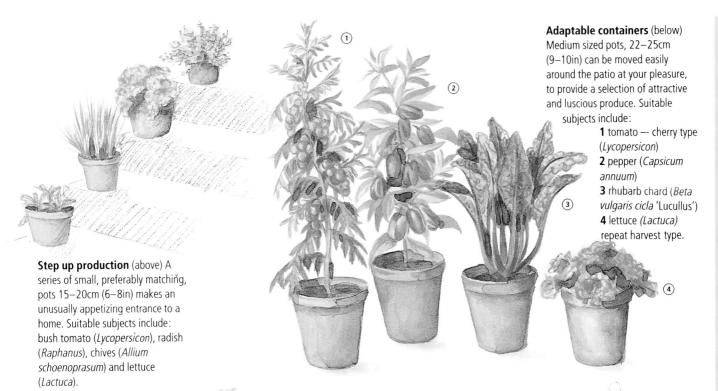

Step up production (above) A series of small, preferably matching, pots 15–20cm (6–8in) makes an unusually appetizing entrance to a home. Suitable subjects include: bush tomato (*Lycopersicon*), radish (*Raphanus*), chives (*Allium schoenoprasum*) and lettuce (*Lactuca*).

Adaptable containers (below) Medium sized pots, 22–25cm (9–10in) can be moved easily around the patio at your pleasure, to provide a selection of attractive and luscious produce. Suitable subjects include:

1 tomato –- cherry type (*Lycopersicon*)
2 pepper (*Capsicum annuum*)
3 rhubarb chard (*Beta vulgaris cicla* 'Lucullus')
4 lettuce (*Lactuca*) repeat harvest type.

Eye-catching vegetable pots (left) Some vegetables and herbs are particularly showy as pot-grown specimens.
1 Fennel (*Foeniculum vulgare*) grown in a 38cm (15in) pot gives a lovely feathery texture – green- and bronze-leaved kinds are available
2 tuberous-rooted vegetables such as the Jerusalem artichoke (*Helianthus tuberosus*) do well in large pots. Varieties such as 'Dwarf Sun Ray' also provide a bright display of flowers at no extra cost. Given frost protection, a good early crop of new potatoes (*Solanum tuberosum*) can be achieved at a time when shop prices are still high.

Herbs in a trough (below) The subtle variations of leaf colour and shape, with the occasional flower, give this arrangement its own particular charm.

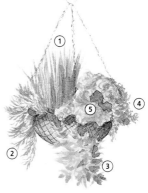

Hanging herb basket (above) A 35cm (14in) basket will supply fresh herbs from spring to autumn and looks most effective when suspended near the kitchen door.
1 chives (*Allium schoenoprasum*) × 3
2 trailing rosemary (*Rosmarinus lavandulaceus*)
3 spearmint (*Mentha spicata*)
4 thyme (*Thymus*) × 2
5 parsley (*Petroselinum crispum*).

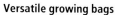

Versatile growing bags
Convenient and productive, many mouthwatering crops can be grown in a limited space.

(Far left) courgette (*Cucurbita pepo*) plants × 3, one green- and one yellow-fruited, give a colourful variation. Marrows, squashes (*Cucurbita maxima*) and, in a sunny spot, melons (*Cucumis melo*) are also suitable.

(Below centre) tomatoes (*Lycopersicon*) × 3 are a most popular subject for growing bags;

standard varieties, beef-steak and cherry types are superior but need training on a cane. Bush types are less demanding.

(Below right) salad bag – a wide range of juicy salads are suitable. The illustration shows:
1 bush tomatoes (*Lycopersicon*) × 2
2 row of radish (*Raphanus*)
3 parsley (*Petroselinum crispum*) × 6
4 row of chives (*Allium schoenoprasum*)
5 lettuce – repeat harvest type (*Lactuca*) × 4.

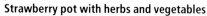

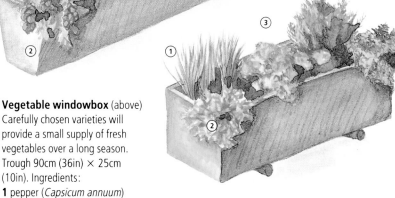

Strawberry pot with herbs and vegetables
(below) Herbs in side pockets are semi-permanent residents, while short-term salad crops are grown in the top. Ingredients:
1 lettuce (*Lactuca*) × 5
2 chive (*Allium schoenoprasum*) × 3
3 alpine strawberry (*Fragaria vesca* 'Semperflorens') × 3
4 parsley (*Petroselinum crispum*) × 3
5 mint (*Mentha*);
6 thyme (*Thymus*).

Vegetable windowbox (above)
Carefully chosen varieties will provide a small supply of fresh vegetables over a long season. Trough 90cm (36in) × 25cm (10in). Ingredients:
1 pepper (*Capsicum annuum*)
2 tomato – bush variety (*Lycopersicon*)
3 a patch of salad onion 'Ishikuru' (*Allium cepa*)
4 a patch of radish (*Raphanus*)
5 lettuce (*Lactuca*) × 4
6 rhubarb chard (*Beta vulgaris cicla* 'Lucullus') × 6

A terracotta herb collection
(above) Trough 75cm (30in) × 25cm (10in).
1 chives (*Allium schoenoprasum*) × 3
2 Spearmint (*Mentha spicata*)
3 parsley (*Petroselinum crispum*) × 5
4 thyme (*Thymus*)
5 rosemary (*Rosmarinus officinalis*).

72

Formal bay trees (below) The culinary way to add a touch of elegance to a garden or patio. Bay trees (*Laurus nobilis*) are available in many interesting shapes,

excellent as focal points or in pairs to highlight entrances. Other herbs can provide a softening effect to the container. Shown here:
1 thyme (*Thymus*)
2 lavender (*Lavandula*).

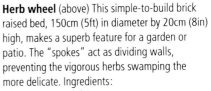

Herb wheel (above) This simple-to-build brick raised bed, 150cm (5ft) in diameter by 20cm (8in) high, makes a superb feature for a garden or patio. The "spokes" act as dividing walls, preventing the vigorous herbs swamping the more delicate. Ingredients:
1 bay (*Laurus nobilis*)
2 chive (*Allium schoenoprasum*) × 10
3 spearmint (*Mentha spicata*) × 3
4 thyme (*Thymus*) × 6
5 parsley (*Petroselinum crispum*) × 12
6 prostrate rosemary (*Rosmarinus lavandulaceus*) × 3
7 apple mint (*Mentha rotundifolia*) × 3.

A raised bed of vegetables and herbs An area 1.8m × 3m (6ft × 10ft) allows a wide selection of goodies to be grown. The seat is a welcome place to relax and browse through the recipe books.
Ingredients:
1 lavender (*Lavandula*)
2 bay (*Laurus nobilis*)
3 garlic chives (*Allium tuberosum*)
4 apple mint (*Mentha rotundifolia*)
5 parsley (*Petroselium crispum*)
6 sweet basil (*Ocimum*)
7 mint (*Mentha*)
8 chives (*Allium schoenoprasum*)
9 thyme (*Thymus*)
10 rosemary (*Rosmarinus*)
11 kohl rabi (*Brassica caulorapa*),
12 carrot (*Daucus carota*)
13 Swiss chard (*Beta vulgaris cicla*)
14 tomato – bush type (*Lycopersicon*)
15 lettuce (*Lactuca*)
16 strawberry (*Fragaria*)
17 radish (*Raphanus sativus*)
18 Japanese onions (*Allium* 'Ishikuru')
19 pak choi (*Brassica chinensis*).

73

Autumn is the time to cheer up containers for the winter – then just sit back and wait for spring to enjoy a spectacular riot of colour.

WINTER AND SPRING DISPLAYS

For half the year we rely on autumn-planted displays to brighten up the dullest months; some careful planning is therefore very worthwhile. Designs should include bright evergreen plants to provide instant impact and form a solid framework. Some may be flowering shrubs but most winter and spring blooms will come from bedding plants and bulbs. Traditionally these have more or less limited any floral display to spring. However, recent developments have seen the introduction of winter-flowering pansies which have added another dimension to winter displays. They produce their flowers in all but the hardest weather and in profusion during the spring. In addition a shrewd choice of bulbs will vary the colour and height of the display, supplying a succession of new interest every few weeks.

Some shrubs and ivies can be left *in situ* for several years, being equally suitable companions for the summer-flowering subjects as they are to those of winter and spring. However, after a period of glorious summer display, it is easy to underestimate the value of autumn plantings, but they are very worthwhile as these treasures will warm the cockles of the heart in winter.

Evergreen shrubs give a backbone to a display (below and right) Two 90cm (36in) troughs illustrated in late winter/early spring. Ingredients:
1 *Skimmia japonica* 'Rubella' × 3
2 *Hebe × franciscana* 'Variegata' × 2
3 *Viola* 'Universal Mixed' (winter-flowering pansy) × 12
4 *Narcissus* 'February Gold' (daffodil) × 12
5 *Hedera helix* 'Buttercup' (yellow-variegated ivy) × 4
Other bulbs: *Tulipa* 'Colour Cardinal' (mid-spring tulip).

1 *Aucuba japonica* 'Crotonifolia' × 2
2 *Hebe × franciscana* 'Variegata'
3 *Solanum capsicastrum* (winter cherry) × 6
4 *Crocus* 'Whitewell Purple' × 30
5 *Hedera helix* 'Glacier' (silver-variegated ivy) × 3
6 *Viola* 'Universal Red Wing' (winter-flowering pansy) × 12.
Other bulbs: *Tulipa* 'Princess Irene' (tulip) × 12.

A colourful yet simple urn (above) Ingredients for a 50cm (20in) container:
1 *Chamaecyparis pisifera* 'Boulevard' forms an evergreen centre-piece

2 *Tulipa turkestanica*, a low-growing tulip flowering in early spring × 20
3 *Viola* 'Universal Orange' (winter-flowering pansy) × 15.

Winter shiner (above) Illustrated in late winter. Ingredients for a 40cm (16in) pot:
1 *Skimmia japonica* 'Rubella' forms the centrepiece
2 *Euonymus fortunei* 'Emerald 'n' Gold' × 6 forms a bright carpet
3 *Iris reticulata* × 20 peeps through the carpet
Other bulbs: *Tulipa* 'Princess Irene' (tulip) × 12.

Brimming with colour (above) Illustrated in late spring. Ingredients for a 45cm (18in) pot:
1 *Thuja plicata* 'Zebrina' gives the display height
2 *Anemone coronaria* De Caen × 25 in mixed colours provides an abundance of bloom
3 *Primula polyantha* (polyanthus) in mixed colours × 12
4 *Myosotis alpestris* (forget-me-not) × 18.

A subtle blend of purple and pink (above)
A display at its best in winter and early spring. Ingredients for a 40cm (16in) pot:
1 *Phormium* 'Dazzler' (New Zealand flax) forms a visually strong centre-piece
2 *Erica carnea* 'Springwood Pink' creates a low carpet beneath.
Any of a wide variety of bulbs could be included to provide colour later in the season.

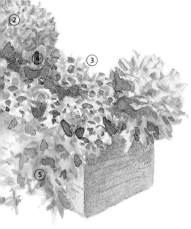

Busy little pots (right) Many plants can be squeezed into a small space to provide plenty of interest and a feeling of energy. Included here are *Hyacinthus*, *Narcissus* (daffodil), *Primula*, *Hedera* (ivy), *Euonymus* and *Erica* (heather). Some may consider this display too fussy, but many will appreciate being able to see the various plants develop through winter into spring.

Elaborate but informal (left)
Illustrated in early spring.
Ingredients for a 1m (3¼ft) trough:
1 *Chamaecyparis lawsoniana* 'Ellwood's Gold' (golden Lawson cypress)
2 *Skimmia japonica* 'Rubella'
3 *Hebe × franciscana* 'Variegata'
4 *Hedera helix* 'Glacier' (silver-variegated ivy)
5 *Juniperus sabina* 'Tamariscifolia'
6 *Erica carnea* 'Springwood Pink'
7 *Primula vulgaris* (primrose) in mixed colours × 10
8 *Viola* 'Universal Yellow' and 'Universal Blue' (yellow and blue winter-flowering pansies) × 12
9 *Hyacinthus* 'Pink Pearl' (hyacinth)
10 *Erica carnea* 'Springwood White'.
Other bulbs: *Narcissus* (daffodil), *Tulipa* (mid-season tulip), *Muscari armeniacum* (grape hyacinth).

An elaborate formal scheme (below left) Illustrated in early winter. Ingredients for a 1m (3¼ft) trough:
1 *Chamaecyparis lawsoniana* 'Ellwood's Gold' (golden Lawson cypress) × 2
2 *Skimmia japonica* 'Rubella' × 3
3 *Erica carnea* 'Springwood Pink' × 4
4 *Hedera helix* 'Glacier' (silver-variegated ivy) × 3
5 *Euonymus fortunei* 'Emerald 'n' Gold' × 3
6 *Juniperus sabina* 'Tamariscifolia' × 2
7 *Solanum capsicastrum* (winter cherry) × 2
8 *Viola* 'Universal Light Blue' (winter-flowering pansy) × 12
9 white-flowered *Cyclamen persicum* × 6.
Other bulbs: *Hyacinthus* (hyacinth).

Well-furnished for spring (right) Ingredients for a 50cm (20in) pot:
1 *Thuja plicata* 'Zebrina' set towards back of pot
2 *Skimmia japonica* 'Rubella'
3 purple-flowered *Erica* (heather)
4 *Hedera helix* 'Buttercup' (ivy) × 3
5 *Juniperus sabina* 'Tamariscifolia'
6 *Erica carnea* 'Springwood Pink'
7 *Tulipa* 'Apricot Beauty' × 12
8 *Euonymus fortunei* 'Emerald 'n' Gold'
9 *Cheiranthus cheiri* 'Scarlet Bedder' (wallflower) × 6.
Other bulbs.

Substantial and imposing
(left) An extra-wide trough – 1m × 0.3m (3¼ft × 1ft) illustrated in spring. Ingredients:
1 *Chamaecyparis lawsoniana* 'Ellwood's Gold' (golden Lawson cypress)
2 *Aucuba japonica* 'Crotonifolia'
3 *Skimmia japonica* 'Rubella'
4 *Juniperus sabina* 'Tamariscifolia'
5 *Euonymus fortunei* 'Emerald 'n' Gold'
6 *Iberis sempervirens* (candytuft)
7 *Rosmarinus lavandulaceus* (prostrate rosemary)
8 *Erica carnea* 'Springwood Pink'
9 *Hedera helix* 'Glacier' (silver-variegated ivy)
10 *Erica carnea* 'Springwood White'
11 *Solanum capsicastrum* (winter cherry)
12 *Alyssum saxatile*
13 *Narcissus* 'Minnow' × 15
14 *Viola* 'Universal Blue' (blue winter-flowering pansy) × 6
15 *Vinca major* 'Variegata' (variegated periwinkle)
16 white *Hyacinthus* (hyacinth) × 10
Other bulbs: pink *Tulipa* (tulip) × 12.

Massed shrubs, bulbs and bedding (left) Heaps of colour and interest are packed into a king-size 80cm (32in) tub. Ingredients:
1 *Chamaecyparis lawsoniana* 'Green Pillar' (Lawson cypress) set towards the back of the container
2 *Camellia* 'Inspiration'
3 *Aucuba japonica* 'Crotonifolia'
4 *Hedera helix* 'Glacier' (silver-variegated ivy) × 5
5 *Euonymus fortunei* 'Emerald 'n' Gold' × 5
6 *Juniperus sabina* 'Tamariscifolia' × 2
7 *Solanum capsicastrum* (winter cherry) × 5
8 *Erica carnea* 'Springwood Pink' × 5
9 *Viola* 'Universal Blue' (winter-flowering pansy) × 5
10 *Narcissus* (daffodil) × 15
11 *Skimmia japonica* 'Rubella'.
Skimmia japonica 'Rubella'.
Other bulbs: *Iris reticulata*, *Anemone coronaria*, *Hyacinthus* 'Anne Marie' (hyacinth), *Crocus* 'Whitewell Purple'.

A distinguished winter combination (right) Ingredients for a 60cm (24in) tub:
1 *Camellia reticulata* 'Zaotaohung'
2 *Skimmia japonica* 'Rubella'
3 *Coronilla glauca*
4 *Ilex aquifolium* 'Handsworth New Silver' (silver holly)
5 *Nandina domestica* 'Firepower' (dwarf sacred bamboo)
6 *Juniperus squamata* 'Blue Star'
7 *Cytisus* × *kewensis*
8 *Hedera helix* 'Goldheart' (ivy)
9 *Aubrieta deltoidea* × 3
10 *Erica carnea* 'Springwood Pink'
11 *Rosmarinus lavandulaceus* (prostrate rosemary)
12 *Viola* 'Universal White' (winter-flowering pansy) × 6
13 *Eranthis hyemalis* (winter aconite) × 15
Other bulbs: *Anemone coronaria* De Caen mixed, *Narcissus* (daffodil), *Iris reticulata*.

As the doyennes of container gardening, summer baskets are immensely popular, terrific fun and give great pleasure wherever you choose to position them.

SUMMER BASKETS

There are few more glorious floral spectacles than a well-grown hanging basket. Yet there are few more disappointing sights than its parched remains in mid August. Such disappointment is avoidable if you follow the instructions on page 52–53.

As well as the traditional hanging basket, wall baskets, corners baskets and mangers all provide the opportunity to lift colour above ground level and add an extra dimension to almost any area.

Many plants make suitable basket subjects, a few are almost indispensable. Trailing varieties are particularly valuable as they greatly contribute to the character and charm of a hanging container.

The following designs offer a range of ideas which can, of course, be adapted to suit individual tastes. The suggested numbers of plants per basket will provide a very full effect. Where possible choose plants which have been grown in small pots, 10cm (4in) or less, so as to allow enough room for their roots as well as plenty of fresh compost. If larger plants are used reduce the numbers but still fill in between with smaller plants such as lobelia.

Before planting a basket remember it will need to be watered regularly until disfigured by frost or cold winds. This effort will be well rewarded with a lovely display lasting for five months or more.

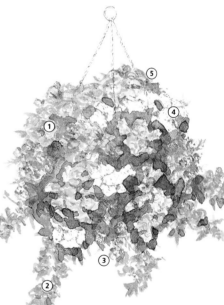

Simply bright This combination of startling contrasting colours presents an eyecatching, almost dazzling effect. Ingredients for a 35cm (14in) basket:
1 10 *Verbena* 'Sissinghurst' × 2
2 Yellow pendulous *Begonia* × *tuberhybrida* × 5, planted in top only.

Softly softly Subtle effects are soothing to the eye, particularly if used in an area intended for relaxation. Ingredients for a 35cm (14in) basket to create a ball effect:
1 *Brachycome iberidifolia* (Swan River daisy) × 8
2 *Impatiens* 'Salmon Blush' (busy Lizzie) × 8, alternately planted.

Blue 'n' pink A small but well-chosen range of colours using several different plants can provide a delicate effect. Ingredients for a 35cm (14in) basket:
1 pink *Impatiens* (busy Lizzie) × 5
2 red- and white-flowered ivy-leaved *Pelargonium* × 2
3 blue trailing *Verbena* 'Blue Knight' × 5
4 white *Alyssum* × 10
5 blue *Petunia* × *hybrida* × 5.

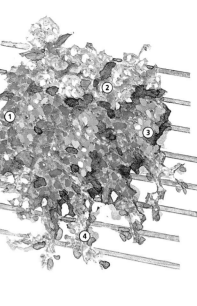

Lighting up a wall
Planted in a 35cm (14in) half basket and suitable for a shady spot.
1 *Begonia* 'Illumination' × 3
2 *Pelargonium* Sensation 'Lavender' × 3
3 blue trailing *Lobelia* × 10
4 silver-leaved *Helichrysum petiolare* × 2.

Subtle blend (right) The white flowered 'L'elegante' ivy-leaved *Pelargonium* and the lilac blue *Brachycome iberidifolia* (Swan River daisy) combine wonderfully to produce an air of romance and tranquility.

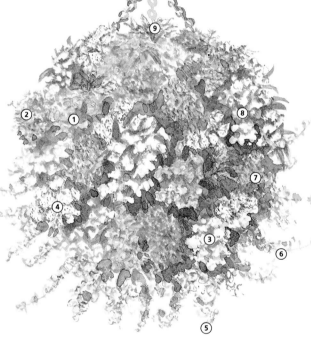

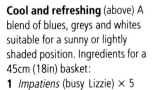
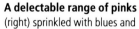

Cool and refreshing (above) A blend of blues, greys and whites suitable for a sunny or lightly shaded position. Ingredients for a 45cm (18in) basket:
1 *Impatiens* (busy Lizzie) × 5
2 *Felicia amelloides* × 3
3 *Mimulus* 'Malibu Ivory' × 6
4 white *Alyssum* × 10
5 *Glechoma hederacea* 'Variegata' (variegated ground ivy) × 3
6 *Helichrysum microphyllum* × 3
7 light blue trailing *Lobelia* × 10
8 white pendulous *Begonia* × 3
9 *Senecio* 'Silver Dust' × 5.

A delectable range of pinks (right) sprinkled with blues and silver. Ingredients for a 45cm (18in) basket:
1 *Lobelia* 'Lilac Cascade' × 10
2 *Impatiens* 'Salmon Blush' (busy Lizzie) × 5
3 *Lotus berthelotii* × 5
4 *Pelargonium* 'Rose' × 3
5 pink trailing *Fuchsia* × 3
6 *Brachycome* 'Tinkerbell' × 5
7 pink *Diascia* × 5
8 lilac *Petunia* × 6.

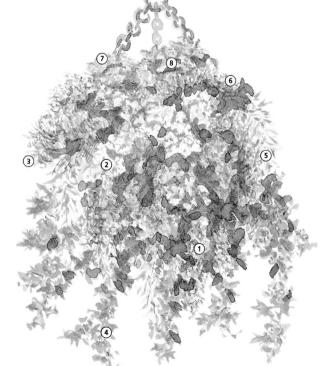

79

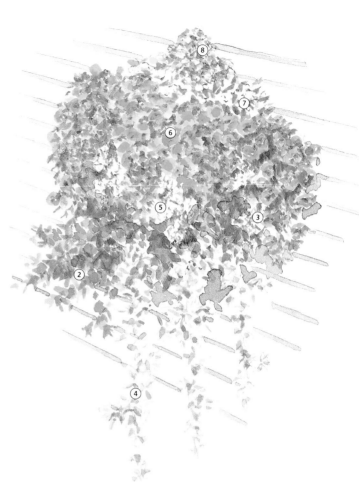

A traditional design (above)
Only the top is planted making this
display suitable for the solid type
of basket. Trailing plants take the
eye away from the hard lines of
the container. Ingredients for a
35cm (14in) basket:
1 purple *Impatiens* (busy Lizzie)
× 2

2 *Lobelia* 'Sapphire' × 5
3 red- and white-flowered ivy-
leaved *Pelargonium* × 2
4 *Helichrysum petiolare*
'Limelight' × 2
5 white *Begonia semperflorens*
× 3
6 *Petunia* 'Sky Blue' × 3
7 *Pelargonium* Sensation
'Lavender'.

Colourful cascade (above) The
sprawling plants used in this
design will allow a container to
furnish quite a large area of wall.
Ingredients for a 40cm (16in) wall
basket:
1 pink *Diascia* × 3
2 *Verbena* 'Sissinghurst' × 3
3 white-flowered ivy-leaved
Pelargonium × 2

4 *Plectranthus hirtus* 'Variegatus'
× 2
5 trailing white *Lobelia* × 8
6 *Petunia* Daddy Mixed × 5
7 white *Impatiens* (busy Lizzie)
× 3
8 variegated *Pelargonium*.

**A semi-drought resistant
scheme** (above) Although still
requiring water to flourish, the
plants included here are more
tolerant of sporadic watering than
most – but don't get complacent.
Ingredients for a 40cm (16in)
basket:
1 *Pelargonium* Sensation Mixed
× 5
2 *Convolvulus mauritanicus* × 3
3 *Bidens* × 3
4 *Hedera helix* 'Glacier' (ivy) × 2
5 white-flowered ivy-leaved
Pelargonium × 2
6 *Sedum lineare* × 5.

A basket for dry shade (right)
Several houseplants are suitable
for outdoor use in summer. Most
of these are tolerant of shade and
inconsistent watering, although in
a fairly light position and given
copious water, this design will
produce a luxuriant display.
Ingredients for a 35cm (14in) wall
basket:
1 *Impatiens* mixed (busy Lizzie)
× 5
2 *Asparagus sprengeri* × 2
3 *Chlorophytum comosum* (spide
plant) × 2
4 *Hedera helix* (ivy) × 2
5 *Tradescantia* (wandering Jew)
× 3

Sunshine collection (left) This mixture of yellows and oranges will certainly stand out from the crowd. Ingredients for a 40cm (16in) basket:
1 *Tagetes* Star Fire Mixed (French marigold) × 8
2 *Sanvitalia procumbens* (creeping zinnia) × 8
3 orange pendulous *Begonia* × *tuberhybrida* × 3
4 *Bidens* × 3
5 *Helichrysum petiolare* 'Variegatum' × 3
6 orange *Impatiens* (busy Lizzie) × 5
7 *Calceolaria rugosa* 'Sunshine' × 5
8 *Thunbergia alata* (black-eyed Susan) × 2.

The blues (right) Some very delicate effects can be achieved by using a selection of shades and textures in blue. A careful choice of background is important to display this type of design to the full. Ingredients for a 40cm (16in) three-quarter or corner basket:
1 *Brachycome iberidifolia* 'Tinkerbell' × 3
2 dark blue trailing *Lobelia* × 12
3 *Impatiens* 'Blue Pearl' (busy Lizzie) × 5
4 variegated *Glechoma* × 2
5 mauve-flowered ivy-leaved *Pelargonium* × 2
6 *Verbena* 'Blue Knight' × 5
7 blue *Petunia* × 6
8 *Felicia amelloides* × 3.

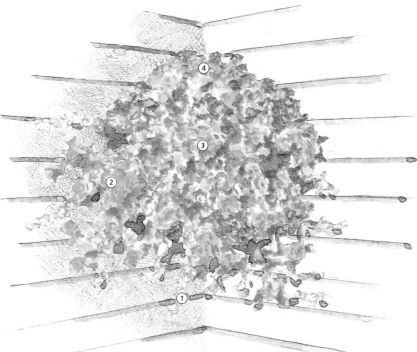
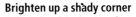

Brighten up a shady corner (left) A cheerful selection of mixed colours, but water generously for good results. Ingredients for a 50cm (20in) quarter- or hay basket:
1 silver-leaved *Helichrysum petiolare* × 6
2 rose-pink-flowered ivy-leaved *Pelargonium* × 10
3 *Mimulus* 'Malibu Mixed' × 12
4 *Pelargonium* Sensation Mixed × 5.

81

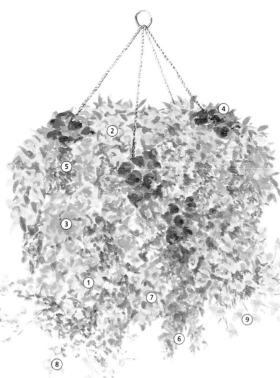

Tone it down (left) Bright yellow and oranges are diluted by pastel shades to give a soft appearance. Ingredients for a 40cm (16in) basket:
1 *Lobelia* 'Lilac Fountain' × 12
2 yellow pendulous *Begonia* × *tuberhybrida* × 3
3 *Mimulus* 'Malibu Orange' × 8
4 blue *Petunia* × 5
5 *Brachycome iberidifolia* 'Tinkerbell' × 5
6 trailing blue *Verbena* 'Blue Knight' × 8
7 *Impatiens* 'Salmon Blush' (busy Lizzie) × 5
8 silver *Helichrysum petiolare* × 2
9 *Bidens ferulifolia* × 2

Anything goes! A blitz of colour with no particular theme. Ingredients for a 40cm (16in) cauldron:
1 *Verbena* 'Sissinghurst' × 8
2 pink trailing *Fuchsia* × 3
3 *Impatiens* mixed (busy Lizzie) × 8
4 *Petunia* 'Daddy Mixed' × 8
5 mixed trailing *Lobelia* × 12
6 *Brachycome iberidifolia* 'Tinkerbell' × 5
7 *Calceolaria rugosa* 'Sunshine' × 5
8 *Bidens ferulifolia* × 3
9 ivy-leaved *Pelargonium* × 3
10 *Felicia amelloides* × 5
11 *Helichrysum petiolare* 'Limelight' × 3
12 *Cordyline australis*.

PRACTICAL TIPS

Watering is the key to success:
● Ensure there is a convenient water supply nearby.

● Ensure the lining of the basket is high at the edges and the compost surface slopes down towards the centre, as this makes watering much easier.

● The more the plants grow, the more water they'll consume. Towards the end of summer they get very thirsty!

● Walls and other buildings shelter baskets from rain. Remember to water these baskets even in wet weather.

● Consider installing an irrigation system for your baskets — it will make an amazing difference.

Uplifting colour (right) Without hanging baskets, this display of pots would seem rather flat; however, in combination they provide a stunning 2.1m (7ft) high extravaganza. An abundance of blue trailing *Lobelia* helps to link the *Petunias* at the lower level with the ivy-leaved *Pelargoniums* in the baskets. A common colour theme throughout unifies the display.

Windowsill gardening can feature anything from tomatoes to conifers, but colourful floral displays are always admired.

SUMMER BOXES AND TROUGHS

For some people the windowbox or veranda trough is their only opportunity to garden out of doors. For others, boxes and troughs are used on a large scale for massed effect. Whatever the situation this type of container provides the scope to use a very wide and exciting range of plants.

Most of the designs shown here follow a simple formula using a generous helping of trailing plants to hang over the edge. Upright plants are used towards the back and the more spreading subjects fill in between. "Architectural" or "dot" plants are sometimes incorporated to add emphasis. These basic principles aside, the designs can be simple or complex as desired.

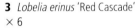

Brighten up a dull spot (below)
Yellows and oranges certainly stand out from the crowd, blue tones down the overall effect. Ingredients for a 75cm (30in) trough:
1 yellow *Tagetes erecta* (African marigold) × 2
2 mixed *Tagetes patula* (French marigold) × 15
3 *Bidens ferulifolia* × 2
4 *Convolvulus mauritanicus* × 3.

Tried and trusted (bottom)
Three good "doers" used in a simple design of mixed colours. Ingredients for a 90cm (36in) trough:
1 *Impatiens* (busy Lizzie) × 9
2 *Pelargonium* Sensation Mixed × 9
3 mixed trailing *Lobelia* × 12.

A predominance of red and pink Toned down with whites and a blue, this is a collection of reliable varieties (above). Ingredients for a 75cm (30in) trough:
1 mixed *Begonia semperflorens* (fibrous-rooted begonia) × 8
2 *Pelargonium* 'Apple Blossom' × 2

3 *Lobelia erinus* 'Red Cascade' × 6
4 *Brachycome iberidifolia* × 2
5 ivy-leaved *Pelargonium* 'Sugar Baby' × 2
6 white *Petunia* × 2.

Foliage finesse (below) *Fuchsia*, *Tropaeolum* (nasturtium) and *Pelargonium* (geranium). Effective displays can be created by carefully combining plants with striking leaves. Although most will produce flowers these are normally regarded as a bonus but beware, they might spoil the colour scheme or steal the show.

A window framed (above) A conventional windowbox is complemented by trelliswork at each end allowing climbing plants to furnish either side of the window. Ingredients for a 1m (3¼ft) trough:
1 *Petunia* 'Express Plum' × 6
2 bush *Fuchsia* × 2
3 *Lobelia* 'Lilac Fountain' × 10
4 white-flowered ivy-leaved *Pelargonium* × 2
5 *Plectranthus* × 3
6 trailing *Fuchsia* × 2
7 *Braychycome iberidifolia* × 4
8 *Ipomoea Rubrocaerulea* 'Heavenly Blue' × 4
9 *Impatiens* 'Salmon Blush' (busy Lizzie) × 6.

A two-tiered trough The arrangement gives the display increased height and depth to create a more striking effect than that on one level. The trailing ivies in this design could be left *in situ* and the flowering plants changed seasonally. Ingredients for a 90cm (36in) pair of troughs:
1 *Salvia splendens* × 6
2 mixed *Impatiens* (busy Lizzie) × 12
3 *Petunia* 'Daddy Mixed' × 8
4 *Hedera helix* 'Glacier' (silver-variegated ivy) × 5
5 *Begonia* × *tuberhybrida* 'Non-Stop White' × 6.

Golden sunshine (left) Brighten up even the dullest spots with the riotous yellow of *Tagetes* and trailing *Bidens*. This red brick wall provides an ideal contrast to the flowers.

85

Floral waterfall (above) Trailing *Fuchsia, Lobelia* and *Bidens* lead the way in this cascade of floral delight. The trough from which they grow has long been obscured.

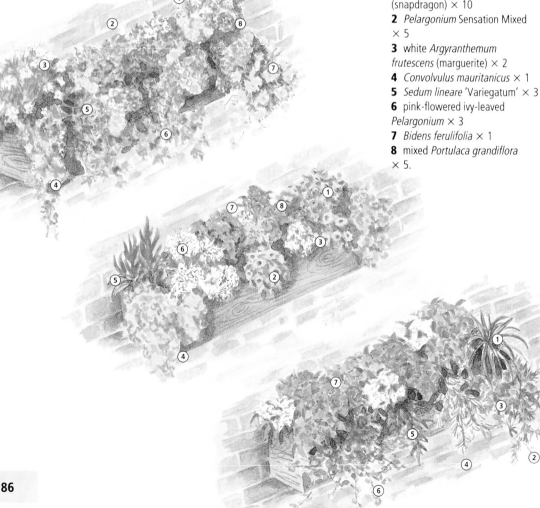

Design for a hot spot (top left) The plants used are more tolerant of dry compost than most – but they still need regular watering to do well. Ingredients for a 1m (3¼ft) trough:

1 *Antirrhinum* 'Floral Showers' (snapdragon) × 10
2 *Pelargonium* Sensation Mixed × 5
3 white *Argyranthemum frutescens* (marguerite) × 2
4 *Convolvulus mauritanicus* × 1
5 *Sedum lineare* 'Variegatum' × 3
6 pink-flowered ivy-leaved *Pelargonium* × 3
7 *Bidens ferulifolia* × 1
8 mixed *Portulaca grandiflora* × 5.

Cheap and very cheerful (middle left) All these plants are grown from seed sown directly into the compost. Designs can be simple or complex as desired. Ingredients for a 1m (3¼ft) trough:

1 mixed *Calendula officinalis* (pot marigold)
2 *Sanvitalia procumbens* (creeping zinnia)
3 *Alyssum maritimum* (sweet alyssum)
4 *Tropaeolum majus* 'Alaska' (nasturtium)
5 *Amaranthus* 'Foxtails'
6 *Nicotiana* 'Domino White'
7 *Tagetes tenuifolia* 'Tangerine Gem'
8 *Antirrhinum* 'Floral Showers' (snapdragon).

Selected for shade (bottom left) Many bedding plants will perform reasonably well in shade but this selection will do better than most. Ingredients for a 75cm (30in) trough:

1 *Chlorophytum comosum* 'Vittatum' (spider plant)
2 *Asparagus sprengeri*
3 ivy-leaved *Pelargonium*
4 *Tradescantia* (wandering Jew)
5 *Hedera* (ivy)
6 silver-leaved *Helichrysum petiolare*
7 mixed *Impatiens* (busy Lizzie) × 10.

Distinctive and elegant (left) This 4.2m (13ft) long set of troughs makes a real impact. Ingredients:

1 *Cordyline* × 3
2 mixed *Impatiens* (busy Lizzie) × 20
3 *Pelargonium* Sensation Mixed × 16
4 mixed *Petunia* × 16
5 trailing *Fuchsia* × 4
6 mixed pendulous *Begonia* × *tuberhybrida* × 4
7 blue trailing *Lobelia* × 25
8 *Brachycome iberidifolia* × 8
9 *Plectranthus* × 4
10 *Lotus berthelotii* × 4
11 *Verbena* 'Sissinghurst' × 4
12 *Calceolaria* 'Sunshine' × 12.

Multi-tiered troughs (right) A number of containers is combined to create a bank of colour supplied by *Alyssum*, *Petunia* and *Hedera* (ivy). The display is in scale with the buildings, whereas a single run of troughs would have been too insignificant to make an impact.

A luxuriant display (right) This large box or raised bed features a wide variety of foliage and flowering plants blended together. Ingredients for a 2.1m (7ft) × 90cm (36in) container:

1 *Canna* × *generalis*
2 white *Nicotiana* × 3
3 *Lobelia cardinalis* × 3
4 *Salvia farinacea* 'Victoria' × 6
5 Bush *Fuchsia*
6 pink *Osteospermum* × 5
7 *Begonia* × *tuberhybrida* 'Non-Stop Mixed' × 7
8 trailing *Verbena* 'Blue Knight' × 3
9 *Heliotropium peruvianum* (cherry pie) × 3
10 *Convolvulus mauritanicus*
11 *Diascia* 'Ruby Field' × 6
12 white *Argyranthemum frutescens* (marguerite) × 3

13 *Felicia amelloides* × 3
14 mixed *Impatiens* (busy Lizzie) × 8
15 *Amaranthus* 'Foxtails' × 3
16 blue *Plumbago capensis*
17 *Tanacetum ptarmiciflorum* × 5.

Flower-filled pots, timber barrels and stately urns provide some of the most sumptuous of summer displays to brighten the dullest garden corner.

SUMMER POTS, TUBS AND URNS

Easy to plant and tend, all but the biggest of these containers are movable making them very versatile in a yard or patio.

A pot or urn can be found to suit nearly every situation and a planting scheme chosen to match. Tall plants will add height; place them in the centre of a free-standing container, towards the rear if it is positioned against a wall.

In ornate pots trailing plants can be used sparingly so as only to slightly obscure the pattern – otherwise standard containers can be virtually concealed by flowers and foliage.

Timber half barrels can also be put to good use as sturdy containers for plants whose foliage and flowers show up well against the barrel's stained wood. Always ensure there are drainage holes drilled in the base of barrels before planting them up.

Architectural shapes Urns can enhance hard features such as steps or walls.
(Far left) A *Cordyline* in a raised urn forms a fine silhouette against the sky; a mixture of red ivy-leaved *Pelargonium* × 8 and blue trailing *Verbena* × 8 form the low carpet.
(Mid left)
1 white-flowered *Argyranthemum* × 3
2 Red ivy-leaved *Pelargonium* × 8
(Near left)
1 *Tanacetum ptarmiciflorum* (silver feather) gives height and colour contrast
2 *Pelargonium* 'Sensation' × 10
3 *Plectranthus* × 6.

Summer shiner (below) The competition created by dense planting encourages long trailing growth. This has been so successful here that the half-barrel is completely hidden by its own plants: *Bidens*, trailing *Lobelia*, *Begonia* and *Mimulus* do the job superbly. A contrast in height is provided by *Abutilon*, *Fuchsia* and *Argyranthemums*.

Small pots with simple designs (left) These can be as impressive as larger displays as long as they are in scale with their surroundings.

(Far left) Ingredients for a 50cm (20in) diameter pot:
1 *Tagetes* Starfire Mixed × 12
2 *Amaranthus* 'Foxtails' × 3 in a tight group.

(Near left) Ingredients for a 45cm (18in) diameter pot:
1 variegated *Pelargonium* × 3 in a tight group
2 *Brachycome* × 12.

A stately purple-leaved *Cordyline* (right) The *Cordyline* is underplanted with a vigorous mixture of *Verbena* 'Sissinghurst' and *Helichrysum petiolare* whose silver foliage contrasts superbly with the pink flowers. They are of similar vigour so neither gets swamped by the other. Use six plants of each in a 70cm (28in) diameter tub.

Contrasting foliage (above) The large bronze leaves of a *Canna × generalis* are set off against the fine blue-green foliage of *Argyranthemum gracile* 'Chelsea Girl' which produces only the occasional flower. Use six plants in a 75cm (30in) diameter half barrel.

89

Sophisticated pot on a pedestal (below) This gives the opportunity to use the luxurious effect of long trailing plants. In this design a predominance of yellow is toned down by blues and white. Ingredients for a 50cm (20in) diameter pot:

1 *Calceolaria* 'Sunshine' × 5
2 *Begonia* × *tuberhybrida* 'Non-Stop Apricot' × 3
3 *Alyssum* × 10
4 *Hedera helix* 'Buttercup' (golden-leaved ivy) × 2
5 yellow pendulous *Begonia* × *tuberhybrida* × 3
6 *Bidens* × 3
7 *Petunia* 'Light Blue' × 5
8 *Felicia amelloides* × 3
9 *Phygelius aequalis* 'Yellow trumpet'.

Reliable combination (above) The central conifer is practically smothered by *Impatiens* (busy Lizzie), *Pelargonium* (geranium) and *Helichrysum petiolare* 'Limelight' while mixed trailing lobelias spill over the edge of this wooden half-barrel. Regular watering and feeding is the secret of such success.

PRACTICAL TIPS

● Allow at least a 2.5cm (1in) gap between the top of the container and the top of the compost to allow water to be applied easily.

● Remove dead flowers and seedheads; as well as tidying the plants this will also promote extra flower production.

● Renew the top 30cm (12in) of compost each spring as planting schemes are changed.

● Ensure that the compost and containers are free draining.

● Use only fresh, weed-free compost.

● Control vigorous varieties which may swamp smaller plants.

A well-furnished half barrel
(left) The dark-stained wood sets off a vigorous skirt of silver-yellow *Helichrysum*, with a decorative display of deep blue and pink blue. Ingredients for a 60cm (24in) barrel:
1 a tight central group of *Salvia farinacea* 'Victoria' × 3

2 *Brachycome* 'Purple Splendour' × 12
3 *Impatiens* 'Salmon Blush' (busy Lizzie) × 8
4 variegated *Helichrysum* × 6.

Fuchsia centrepiece (left)
Plenty of water will help this combination to flourish. Ingredients for a 45cm (18in) barrel include:
1 bush *Fuchsia*
2 pendulous *Begonia* × *tuberhybrida* 'Chanson Mixed' × 5
3 trailing *Lobelia* × 10 to soften the edge.

Two designs for a shady spot
(right) All but the deepest shade will allow these two pots to thrive, provided the compost is kept moist. (near right) Ingredients for a 60cm (24in) diameter tub:
1 a tight group of *Lobelia cardinalis* × 3 as a centrepiece
2 mixed *Impatiens* (busy Lizzie) × 10
3 silver-leaved *Helichrysum petiolare* × 5.
(far right) A more elaborate arrangement to brighten a dark corner. Ingredients for a 65cm (26in) diameter tub:
1 white *Nicotiana*
2 *Begonia* × *tuberhybrida* 'Non-Stop White' × 3
3 pink *Impatiens* (busy Lizzie) × 5
4 *Lysimachia nummularia* 'Aurea' × 5
5 white ivy-leaved *Pelargonium* × 3
6 *Mimulus* 'Malibu Ivory' × 5
7 mixed *Begonia semperflorens* × 5
8 *Senecio bicolor cineraria* 'Silver Dust' × 5.

91

The busy gardener with precious little time to spare can use pot plants to achieve colourful and dramatic effects in an instant.

CONTAINERS FOR ALL SEASONS

Flowering or foliage pot plants are now obtainable through many outlets such as supermarkets and filling stations. Rather than buy a number of plants to fill a container at one time, why not purchase a new pot plant every two weeks or so to replace older plants as they fade?

The designs shown on these two pages feature two permanent residents, a conifer and an ivy, around which the displays are formed. Although six seasonal designs are shown, there would be interim stages as the individual plants are exchanged. It is preferable to remove the pots before planting as this makes it easier to keep the roots moist. Arrange the plants as desired, firming the compost around them to aid stability. During the summer months many houseplants are suitable for inclusion in these designs. In winter, or during cold spells, this type of display only succeeds in a protected site.

Autumn into winter (below)
1 *Chamaecyparis lawsoniana* 'Green Pillar' (Lawson cypress)
2 *Hedera helix* 'Glacier' (ivy)
3 Pot chrysanthemums
4 *Erica gracilis* (Cape heath)
5 *Solanum capsicastrum* (winter cherry).

Early winter and Christmas (below)
1 *Chamaecyparis lawsoniana* 'Green Pillar' (Lawson cypress)
2 *Hedera helix* 'Glacier' (ivy)
3 *Narcissus* 'Paper White'
4 *Primula vulgaris* (primrose)
5 *Cyclamen persicum* (florists' cyclamen)
6 *Euphorbia pulcherrima* (poinsettia)
7 *Hyacinthus orientalis* (hyacinth).
Some tinsel could be added for seasonal effect.

Mid winter (below)
1 *Chamaecyparis lawsoniana* 'Fletcheri' (Lawson cypress)
2 *Hedera helix* 'Glacier' (ivy)
3 *Primula vulgaris* (primrose) × 3
4 *Senecio multiflora*
5 *Hyacinthus orientalis* (hyacinth)
6 *Calceolaria herbeohybrida* (slipper flower).

A collection of houseplants
(right) These make a fine display for the doorstep or patio and a spell out of doors in summer will often rid a plant of pests. Most houseplants are tolerant of shade, but avoid cold winds. Ingredients:

1 *Yucca*
2 *Cyperus alternifolius* (umbrella plant)
3 *Chlorophytum comosum* 'Vittatum' (spider plant)
4 *Coleus blumei*
5 *Asparagus sprengeri*
6 *Plectranthus*.

Winter glow (left)
The red buds of *Skimmia* (centre) and the orange-red *Erica* are illuminated by the sun. When past their best both could be planted in the garden, while the background conifer remains *in situ*.

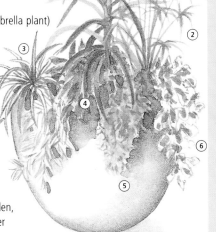

Spring and Easter (below)
1 *Chamaecyparis lawsoniana* 'Green Pillar' (Lawson cypress)
2 *Hedera helix* 'Glacier' (ivy)
3 *Narcissus* (daffodil) × 5
4 *Saxifraga stolonifera* (mother of thousands)
5 *Senecio* × *hybridus*
6 *Hydrangea macrophylla* 'Blue Wave'
7 *Lilium longiflorum* (Easter lily).

Spring into summer (below)
1 *Chamaecyparis lawsoniana* 'Green Pillar' (Lawson cypress)
2 *Hedera helix* 'Glacier' (ivy)
3 *Campanula isophylla alba* (white bellflower)
4 *Pelargonium* 'Sensation'
5 *Browallia speciosa*
6 *Rosa* (patio rose)
7 *Campanula isophylla* (bellflower)
8 *Tolmiea menziesii* (pick-a-back plant).

Summer and into autumn (below)
1 *Chamaecyparis lawsoniana* 'Fletcheri' (Lawson cypress)
2 *Hedera helix* 'Glacier' (ivy)
3 *Asparagus sprengeri*
4 *Argyranthemum frutescens* (marguerite)
5 *Celosia plumosa*
6 *Impatiens* 'Tango' (busy Lizzie).

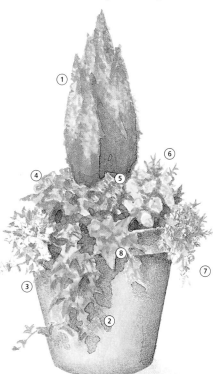

93

Many of these most charming plants are at home in containers,

needing only a tiny area in which to flourish and display their exquisite beauty.

ALPINES AND MINIATURES

The term alpine is these days seldom used in its true sense – plants on a mountain which naturally occur between the tree line and the zone of permanent snow. The popular definition encompasses these alpine species as well as many other plants of a similar type. True alpines or not, this group contains some choice plants, nearly all of which will thrive in a container.

The term miniature is used here to describe both small plants and others which can be used to create wonderful little landscapes. A selection of these small plants can be grown in a limited space, to provide interest over a long period.

Alpines and miniatures are best grown where they can be viewed at close quarters so that their exquisite beauty can be fully appreciated.

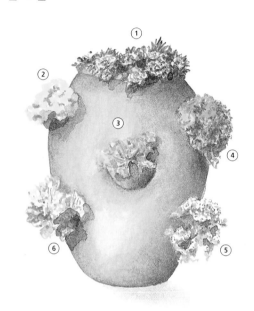

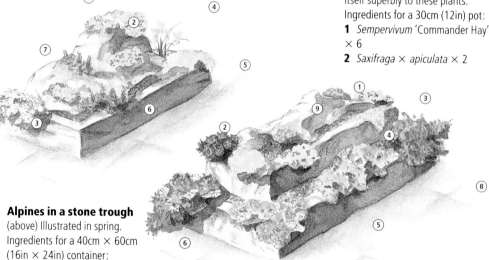

Alpines in a strawberry pot
(above) This type of container lends itself superbly to these plants. Ingredients for a 30cm (12in) pot:
1 *Sempervivum* 'Commander Hay' × 6
2 *Saxifraga* × *apiculata* × 2
3 *Lewisia* Cotyledon Hybrid
4 *Saponaria ocymoides*
5 *Erigeron mucronatus*
6 *Saxifraga* × *urbium* (London pride). Varieties of *Trifolium*, *Sedum*, *Phlox*, *Armeria* and *Arabis* could be planted in the pockets at the rear of the pot.

Alpines in a two-tiered trough (left) This system allows the more vigorous plants to be grown at a lower level, so they are less likely to smother the slower growers above. Illustrated in early summer. Ingredients for a 60cm × 90cm (24in × 36in) trough:
1 *Saxifraga burseriana* × 2
2 *Sempervivum* 'Commander Hay' × 3
3 *Sedum spathulifolium* 'Cape Blanco' × 2
4 *Raoulia australis* × 2
5 *Aubrieta deltoidea* × 2
6 *Iberis sempervirens*
7 *Phlox douglasii* × 2
8 *Juniperus squamata* 'Blue Star'
9 tufa rock.

Alpines in a stone trough
(above) Illustrated in spring. Ingredients for a 40cm × 60cm (16in × 24in) container:
1 *Dionysia tapetodes* × 2
2 *Sedum acre* 'Aureum' (golden stonecrop) × 2
3 *Saxifraga burseriana*
4 *Narcissus triandrus albus* (angel's tears) × 5
5 *Raoulia lutescens* × 3
6 *Sempervivum montanum* (mountain houseleek) × 3
7 tufa rock.

Turn to stone (right) A group of containers and a raised bed are able to host a large number of plants in a small area. The blue-flowered *Campanula* and the white *Gypsophila* form a distinct contrast to the smaller species. This arrangement helps to ensure that the former more vigorous plants do not smother the latter. The gravel and natural rock provide the perfect setting.

Alpine window box

(left) Illustrated in early summer. Ingredients for a 100cm × 30cm (40in × 12in) trough:

1 tufa rock
2 *Sempervivum* 'Commander Hay'
3 *Raoulia lutescens*
4 *Linum arboreum*
5 *Chamaecyparis obtusa* 'Nana Aurea'
6 *Diascia cordata*
7 *Gypsophila repens*
8 *Arabis albida*
9 *Armeria caespitosa* (thrift)
10 *Phlox subulata*
11 *Helianthemum* 'Raspberry Ripple'
12 *Saponaria ocymoides*
13 *Erigeron mucronatus*
14 *Polygonum vacciniifolium*.

A miniature garden (right) Pebbles, rock and water form the hard landscape for a 75cm (30in) bowl. Ingredients:
1 *Sorbus reducta*
2 *Chamaecyparis lawsoniana* 'Green Pillar'
3 *Abies balsamea hudsonia*
4 *Cryptomeria japonica*
5 *Rhododendron calostrotum keleticum*
6 *Salix hastata* 'Wehrhahnii'
7 *Chamaecyparis pisifera* 'Aurea Nana'
8 *Jasminum parkeri*
9 *Pratia pendunculata*
10 *Cotoneaster microphyllus thymifolius* × 2
11 *Thymus* × *citriodorus* 'Silver Queen'.

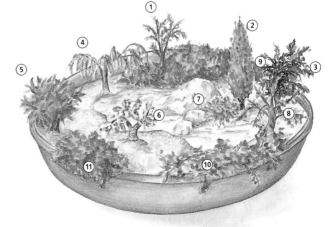

Container plants can be functional and pleasing; use them to mark boundaries beautifully, highlight good views or screen unsightliness.

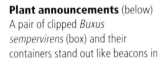

FUNCTIONAL CONTAINERS

As well as brightening up daily life plants are often used for practical purposes. They make a pleasant alternative to visually hard features such as fences or walls, and usually prove less expensive. Unsightly boundary screens are often inherited and need to be softened or disguised. On the other hand, it may be desirable to highlight certain areas or features such as an entrance-way or vista. The following designs demonstrate how container-grown plants can be used effectively to perform these functions. Whatever the requirement or situation there is nearly always the opportunity to introduce some attractive and functional plantings.

Plant announcements (below)
A pair of clipped *Buxus sempervirens* (box) and their containers stand out like beacons in this herbaceous border. A clear statement that something of interest lies within. In this case a paved area and seat.

Highlight an entrance (top)
A pair of narrow growing conifers gives this door a more inviting appearance. Ingredients for each 50cm (20in) tub:
1 *Juniperus scopulorum* 'Skyrocket'
2 *Hedera helix* 'Goldheart' (ivy) × 5.

A well-framed window
(above) Two *Pyracantha atalantioides* (firethorn) in 50cm (20in) tubs. Two main stems from each plant, one vertical and one horizontal, are trained along wires or canes. Regular pruning maintains their formal shape.

Two schemes for large troughs and a matching windowbox (above). These contrasting styles are both effective methods of separating different areas.

A formal design (above left) *Buxus sempervirens* (box) and *Taxus baccata* (yew) are both particularly suited to clipping into a formal hedge. With care and patience more elaborate shapes can be created (see *Topiary* right).

An informal design (above right) Ingredients shown in summer:
1 *Chamaecyparis pisifera* 'Boulevard' makes a strong feature
2 *Hedera helix* 'Goldheart' (ivy)
3 *Choisya ternata* (Mexican orange blossom)
4 *Hebe* × *franciscana* 'Variegata'
5 *Fuchsia* 'Mrs Popple'
6 *Senecio* 'Sunshine'
7 *Aucuba japonica* 'Crotonifolia'
8 *Ceanothus* 'Puget Blue' (Californian lilac)
9 *Hedera helix* 'Glacier' (silver-variegated ivy) × 6.

Topiary (left) The clipping of plants into fantastic shapes is an age-old art. Being by nature very eye-catching, topiary is of great value in landscape design. Ideal as a focal point it can be used to attract people to a certain area or lure them around a desired route. Growing a specimen from scratch takes time and patience; for the less patient there is now available a good range of "ready-grown" shapes. Specimens range from the very formal (illustrated) to birds, ships and even giant chess pieces. A suitable contrasting background will show off the shapes to the full. *Buxus sempervirens* (box) and *Taxus baccata* (yew) are excellent for topiary work.

PRACTICAL TIPS

● Rain water is naturally shed from the perimeter of the plants, so very little gets into the compost. Be sure to check compost moisture levels even during wet weather.

● Feeding benefits most plants. The bigger a container-grown plant becomes the more nutrients it will require. So apply a general feed in spring but, better still, apply a slow-release fertilizer which will last all season.

● Prune and clip flowering shrubs and fruit bushes to shape, and to promote healthy growth. Precise timing differs from species to species.

Screening a fence or wall

(right) A run of troughs is planted with climbers which are supported by a wire fence or trelliswork. As climbers are, by nature, sparsely clad at the base, lower growing plants are used to furnish this area. The illustration shows a recently planted scheme during mid summer. After two more growing seasons this will be a dense wall of intermingled plants. Ingredients for a 3m (10ft) set of troughs:

1 *Lonicera × brownii* (scarlet trumpet honeysuckle)
2 *Clematis armandii*
3 *Solanum jasminoides* 'Album' (white-flowered potato vine)
4 *Passiflora caerulea* (blue passion flower)
5 *Hedera helix* 'Glacier' (silver variegated ivy) × 3
6 *Hebe × franciscana* 'Variegata' × 2
7 *Diascia cordata* × 5.

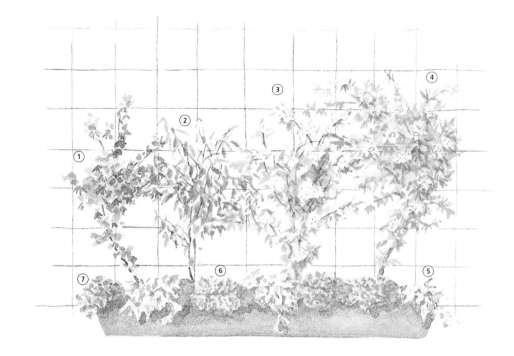

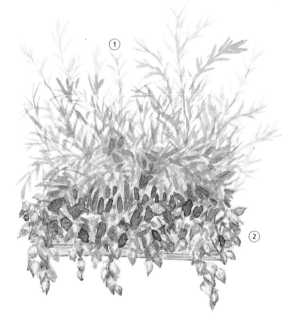

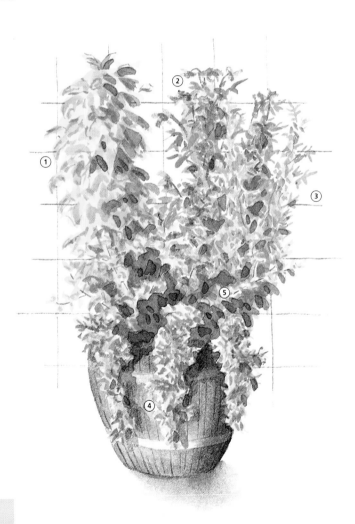

A free-standing screen (left)

A large wooden barrel, 80cm (32in) across, with the top removed and a trellis supported by a central post. Ingredients:

1 *Hedera colchica* 'Dentata Variegata' (variegated elephant's ear ivy) × 2
2 *Clematis* 'Jackmanii × Superba'
3 *Eccremocarpus scaber* (Chilean glory flower) × 3
4 *Vinca major* 'Variegata' (variegated greater periwinkle) × 6
5 *Lonicera japonica* 'Aureo-reticulata' (variegated Japanese honeysuckle).

Bamboo curtain (above) A

windowbox provides some privacy for a large room. Ingredients for a 1.2m (4ft) trough:

1 *Phyllostachys nigra* (bamboo) is sparse enough to allow light into the room × 3
2 *Hedera helix* 'Goldheart' (gold-variegated ivy) visually softens the container × 4.

Cover up (right) This well-fitted square tank disguises a manhole cover superbly. The container can easily be moved to allow access for maintenance.

Plants for a purpose (below)
1 *Vitis* 'Brant' (grapevine) spreads over the trellis to provide dappled shade on a hot summer's day
2 *Convolvulus cneorum* × 3 spilling over the edge of the 50cm (20in) pot, is also a sun lover
3 *Juniperus scopulorum* 'Skyrocket' forms a strong pillar completing the archway started by the vine. Between them they define the entrance clearly
4 *Diascia cordata* × 5 flow out of the pot
5 *Fremontodendron* 'California Glory' makes a floriferous yet open and airy screen
6 *Convolvulus mauritanicus* × 3 has a lax habit and blue flowers which contrast superbly
7 *Hedera helix* 'Goldheart' (gold-variegated ivy) forms a visually solid corner to the area while its irregular growth habit "breaks up" the strong outline of the structure.

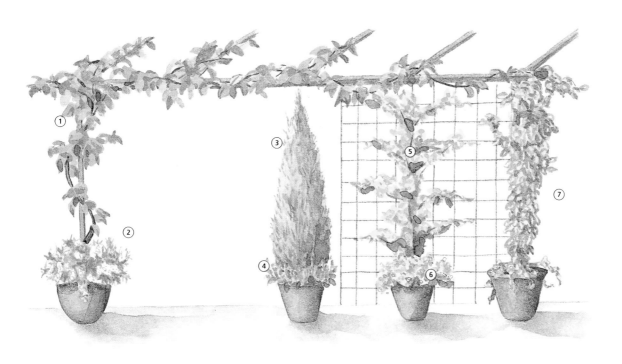

The soothing effect of water will give any garden a relaxing atmosphere and extra interest. Container plants and water features can be combined to good effect.

WATER DISPLAYS

As one of the basic needs of life, water has an almost magnetic attraction to all living things. Huge waterfalls, cascades and fountains have for centuries formed magnificent central features in many a grand garden. Yet even in the smallest garden it is quite possible to experience the magical effects of water. Reflected images or the cool and refreshing feel of water are just two experiences offered.

Some plants are particularly fond of water and flourish when their roots are waterlogged – a characteristic which can be put to good use in the container garden.

A simple water feature accompanied by some well-chosen plants will enrich virtually any garden, whatever its size.

Focal point (above) An ornamental birdbath is the dominant feature in this raised water garden. White-flowered arum lilies thrive with their "feet" in water, while ivy softens the hard stone .

A living umbrella (far left)
1 The huge rhubarb-like leaves of *Gunnera manicata* form a marvellous spreading canopy to provide shelter from rain or sun
2 *Myosotis palustris* (water forget-me-not) × 10 spills over the edge of the large full barrel. Both plants are lovers of moist soil so drainage from the container should be minimal .

A miniature water garden (left) Ingredients for a 40cm (16in) half-barrel:
1 *Carex oshimensis* 'Evergold'
2 *Iris laevigata* 'Variegata'
3 *Nymphaea pygmaea* 'Alba' (miniature water lily)
4 *Myosotis palustris* (water forget-me-not).

A patio pool (above) Water creates a refreshing centre-piece to this split-level paved area. Container-grown plants such as white *Astilbe* provide a "splash" of colour, while the grasses are a perfect complement to the brickwork.

Floating flowers (left) *Passiflora caerulea* (blue passion flower) twines around a pink-flowered *Camellia*. The flowers of both plants resemble water lilies when floated on the water of the adjacent stone pool.

Summer plunge pot (left) For standing in margins of a larger water feature such as a pond. Ingredients for a 50cm (20in) pot:
1 *Canna* × *generalis* (Indian shot)
2 *Cyperus alternifolius* (umbrella plant)
3 *Carex elata* 'Aurea' × 2
4 *Myosotis palustris* (water forget-me-not) × 5
5 *Carex oshimensis* 'Evergold' × 3.

101

Get closer to nature by attracting wildlife to your patio and windowsills.
A pot will attract bees and butterflies,
provided its contents are carefully selected.

ATTRACTING WILDLIFE

Water is vital to the survival of all living things, plants and animals alike. A small water feature is therefore the ideal centre-piece for an area aimed at attracting birds, butterflies and bees. The colour, movement and sound of these creatures introduces an extra dimension to any garden. A good choice of plants is important. Many fruit- and berry-bearing plants are particularly attractive to birds, while plants whose flowers produce copious nectar will entice butterflies and bees. Suspended nets full of nuts are an additional attraction for birds. Endeavour to maintain a water supply, especially in very hot or very cold conditions, as the birds will come to rely on it. Position wildlife containers carefully to provide good growing conditions for the plants, and to allow them to be viewed clearly from window or garden.

A pot-grown wildlife garden (below) The stone bird bath acts as a centre-piece for a collection of plants selected to attract butterflies, birds and bees over a long period. This design, shown in autumn, creates a relaxed and peaceful atmosphere. Ingredients:
1 *Malus* 'Red Jade' (crab apple)
2 *Sorbus aria* 'Lutescens'
3 *Ilex* 'Handsworth New Silver' (silver holly)
4 *Ilex aquifolium* 'Bacciflava' (a yellow-berried holly)
5 *Aucuba japonica* 'Crotonifolia'
6 *Hebe Franciscana* × 'Blue Gem'
7 *Hebe* 'Midsummer Beauty'
8 *Aster amellus* 'King George' (Michaelmas daisy)
9 *Mahonia aquifolium* (Oregon grape)
10 *Pyracantha angustifolia* (firethorn)
11 *Cotoneaster salicifolius* 'Gnom'
12 *Ribes uva-crispa* (gooseberry)
13 *Pyracantha atalantioides* (firethorn)
14 *Lonicera periclymenum* (common honeysuckle).

A living bird table (above) This 40cm (16in) hanging basket, customized for wildlife, is especially useful where space is limited. Shown in early summer. Ingredients:
1 *Lavandula stoechas* (French lavender)
2 *Fragaria vesca* 'Semperflorens' (alpine strawberry) × 5
3 *Cotoneaster salicifolius* 'Gnom'
4 *Alyssum maritimum* (sweet alyssum) × 10
5 *Iberis sempervirens* (evergreen candytuft) × 2
6 *Hedera helix* 'Glacier' (silver variegated ivy)
7 A dish of water.

The butterfly bush (left) Small tortoiseshell butterflies feast on the nectar of *Buddleia davidii*. This easily-grown shrub certainly lives up to its reputation.

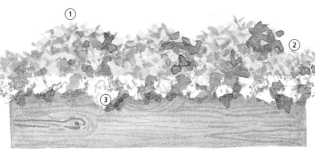

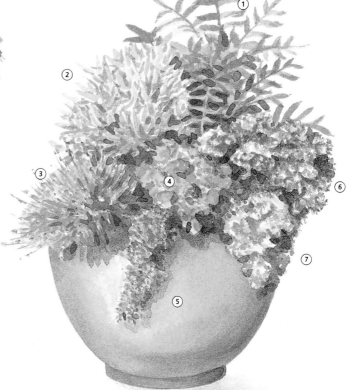

A nectar feast for butterflies and bees (above) This simple combination is attractive to both insects and humans alike. Ingredients for a 90cm (36in) trough:
1 *Lantana camara* × 3
2 *Tagetes* 'Starfire Mixed' × 15
3 *Alyssum maritimum* (sweet alyssum) × 15.

Bees and butterflies galore (right) A design to attract these useful insects over a long period with a succession of nectar-filled blossom. Ingredients for a 70cm (28in) pot:
1 *Mahonia* 'Charity'
2 *Hebe* 'Midsummer Beauty'
3 *Lavandula stoechas* (French lavender)
4 *Sedum spectabile*
5 *Thymus* (thyme)
6 *Aster amellus* 'King George' (Michaelmas daisy)
7 *Aubrieta deltoidea*.

Container grown fruit bushes will not only provide delicious produce, but carefully trained plants and their glorious blossoms are of great ornamental merit.

FRUIT IN CONTAINERS

The thought of picking and biting into a juicy home grown peach is ecstasy for many gardeners. If it were only that simple – fruit probably requires more time, effort and knowledge than any other type of gardening, but consequently it can be also one of the most rewarding.

It is advisable to grow only a single fruit plant in a container, as additional plants would compete for food and water. Therefore the designs below demonstrate the various shapes and forms in which a range of fruits can be grown. There is more than one way of training each type; so choose the method most suited to the situation.

There are many factors to consider when buying a fruit tree so it is advisable to consult the fruit expert at the nursery or garden centre. A poor choice initially is certain to lead to problems and frustration later on.

It is only fair to point out that great commitment is required from the fruit gardener, but time and patience will bring success and great satisfaction.

Fruit to perfection (right) This delicious-looking 'Jester' apple superbly demonstrates how fruit can be successfully grown in containers.

1 Fan-trained nectarine (*Prunus persica*) A method ideally suited to growing this sun-loving fruit against a wall, although most fruit will benefit from the extra warmth afforded by such a position. As well as improving the flavour of peaches, apricots and pears, their early blossom will be protected from crop-depleting frosts as the wall acts as a storage heater giving off warmth accumulated during the day during the night.

2 Standard gooseberry (*Ribes uva-crispa*) This method of training is particularly suited to this thorny subject for the container is easily accessible for watering, weeding and feeding.

3 Triple-cordon redcurrant (*Ribes rubrum*) 'Red Lake' Triple cordon refers to the three vertical growths; double (two uprights) and single cordons are also popular. This method allows intensive production in a small area. Many different fruits can be grown in this way including apples, pears, gooseberries, cherries and plums.

4 Bush blueberry (*Vaccinium corymbosum*) This up and coming fruit is related to the rhododendron, the bush shape being its normal habit of growth. Most soft fruit will assume a bush form if left unattended although correct pruning will lead to greater productivity.

5 Espalier pear (*Pyrus*) Along with cordons this is one of the classic forms of training fruit. Unlike cordons the growth is horizontal although the principles involved in training and pruning are the same; so too are the types of fruit suited to this method (see Triple-cordon redcurrant).

6 Dwarf peach (*Prunus persica* 'Garden Lady') This and other specially bred varieties are not quite as flavoursome as the standard types, but offer an option for growing in very small areas and are easier to protect in winter.

7 Bush apple (*Malus*) Apples are also available as dwarfs, in this case the flavour and quality are not sacrificed as the best varieties are grafted onto a dwarfing rootstock, such as M9 or M27. 'Pixie' is a dwarfing rootstock which offers a similar advantage to plums, apricots, peaches and nectarines.

8 "Stepover" apple (*Malus*) Using a dwarfing rootstock (M27), apple trees are particularly suited to this form. Branches are trained horizontally as near to the ground as possible. They look most attractive lining either side of a path.

9 Alpine strawberries (*Fragaria vesca* 'Semperflorens') These will fruit over a long period when grown in a windowbox. They are at a convenient height to be picked and eaten fresh.

10 Grape vine (*Vitis*) Revelling in a sunny position a vine can be left to its own devices, but is less productive than if pruned and trained correctly when it can fruit prolifically. Kiwi fruit (*Actinidia chinensis*) requires similar conditions but detests an exposed site. In addition both are first-class ornamental plants.

*Add an extra delight to any display by
including some plants with scented flowers
or aromatic foliage.*

CONTAINERS FOR SCENT

The presence of scent in the garden is often undervalued. Many plants can offer at least a hint of perfume, but carefully chosen varieties will provide some delightful effects. The scent of spring hyacinths wafting in through an open window, or the fragrance of summer honeysuckle as the front door opens are always welcome, if often unexpected.

Flowers are by no means the only purveyors of scent. The leaves of numerous plants provide some most pleasant aromas when crushed between the fingers or merely brushed against. Some plants have a scent so strong it fills a garden on a still evening, but most perfumes are intimate and are best when encountered at close quarters. For this reason scented plants should be thoughtfully positioned, so that they can be easily and regularly appreciated. The windowsill, the patio and, in particular, the entrance area are prime sites.

Our designs show some seasonal schemes and some which will provide different scents over most of the year. Scented leaves and flowers can be combined effectively and the addition of some bright and colourful bedding plants will complete the effect.

Patio perfumes (above) The central lily flanked by pot-grown *Daturas* creates a deliciously fragrant combination. The aroma of the silver-leaved *Helichrysum italicum* (curry plant) will also enrich the evening air.

A scented doorway (left) This design will provide a succession of different and very desirable scents intermittently throughout the year. Illustrated at its peak in early summer. Ingredients for a pair of 50cm (20in) tubs:
1 *Lonicera periclymenum* (common honeysuckle)
2 *Jasminum polyanthum*
3 *Thymus × citriodorus* 'Aureus' (golden lemon-scented thyme)
4 *Daphne odora* 'Aureo-marginata'
5 *Lavandula angustifolia* 'Munstead' (lavender)
6 *Mahonia aquifolium* (Oregon grape)
7 *Choisya ternata* (Mexican orange blossom)
8 *Trachelospermum jasminoides* (star jasmine)
9 *Rosa* 'Albéric Barbier'.
Bulbs: *Hyacinthus*, *Narcissus* 'Cheerfulness', *Convallaria majalis* (lily of the valley).

A scented pot for late spring
(below) Ingredients for a 45cm
(18in) pot:
1 *Narcissus* white 'Cheerfulness'
× 12
2 *Myosotis alpestris* (forget-me-
not) × 5
3 *Convallaria majalis* (lily of the
valley)
4 *Primula polyantha* (polyanthus)
× 5
5 *Dianthus barbatus* 'Giant
Auricula Eyed' (sweet William) × 5
6 *Cheiranthus cheiri* (wallflower)
× 5.

Scent at a pinch A group of
plants with aromatic leaves.
Ingredients for a 50cm (20in) pot:
7 *Thuya plicata* 'Zebrina'
8 *Salvia rutilans* (pineapple sage)
9 *Thymus* × *citriodorus* 'Aureus'
(golden lemon-scented thyme)
10 *Lavandula stoechas* (French
lavender)
11 *Pelargonium tomentosum*
(peppermint geranium)
12 *Eucalyptus citriodora* (lemon-
scented gum).

Summer scents Ingredients for a
38cm (15in) pot:
13 *Lantana camara*
14 *Heliotropium peruvianum*
(cherry pie) × 3

15 *Alyssum maritimum* × 10
16 *Verbena* 'Silver Anne' × 3
17 *Matthiola bicornis* (night-
scented stock), sow a few pinches
of seed after pot is planted.

Sweet summer perfumes
Ingredients for a 50cm (20in) pot:
18 *Hedychium gardnerianum*
(ginger lily)
19 *Lilium auratum*
20 *Nicotiana alata* white (tobacco
plant) × 5
21 *Heliotropium peruvianum*
(cherry pie) × 3
22 *Lathyrus odoratus* 'Bijou Mixed'
(sweet pea) × 5.

Heady evening scent
Ingredients for a 60cm (24in) pot:
23 *Datura* 'Grand Marnier' will fill
the evening air with its delicious
fragrance
24 *Alyssum* 'Wonderland' × 12
adds colour and daytime scent at
low level.

Simple, subtle arrangements for a garden where the elements of nature can be appreciated in quiet contemplation.

THE ORIENTAL INFLUENCE

The Chinese and Japanese have for centuries used their gardens for contemplation and repose. We in the West have learned much from their style which has developed from using basic natural materials. Much thought, however, goes into positioning all the elements within the arrangement to give a well balanced and meaningful display. The gardener can adjust these ingredients to reflect his or her feelings at a particular time. The gravel, for instance, which is usually used to represent water, can be raked into different patterns. The stones and plants, which may represent islands, can also be rearranged.

A careful choice of materials is vital for full effect. Look for plants, containers and stones with a particular character of their own.

A miniature oriental landscape In a simple raised bed 3m × 1.8m × 0.25m (10ft × 6ft × 10in) deep the rocks provide the backbone, while the gravel represents a stream running down into a pond. The Oki-Gata lantern leaves little doubt that this arrangement is inspired by the Orient. Ingredients:

1 *Pinus parviflora* 'Adock's Dwarf'
2 *Aucuba japonica* 'Crotonifolia' × 2
3 *Camellia japonica*
4 *Acer palmatum*
5 *Rhododendron* (azalea)
6 *Juniperus sabina* 'Tamariscifolia'
7 *Soleirolia soleirolii* (mind your own business) × 20

Bonsai (left) A style of gardening practised in Japan over many centuries. The plants are given only a very restricted root run in small, often ornate containers. Hollow rock or wood is sometimes used. Some highly prized specimens are known to be hundreds of years old but the inexperienced bonsai gardener should not be over ambitious. Care of bonsai, although not difficult, is an acquired skill. Learn your trade on smaller plants and gradually become more adventurous.

Ornamental pot Pot and shrub perfectly complement each other in this attractive arrangement.

A pot of bamboo (left) The simple combination of *Phyllostachys nigra* (black bamboo) and a carefully chosen ornate pot creates an oriental atmosphere.

A timeless scene of the Orient (below) A gravel base with rocks provides the setting for a simple but meaningful display. Ingredients:

1 *Acer palmatum*
2 *Pinus mugo* (mountain pine)
3 *Phyllostachys nigra* (black bamboo)
4 *Rhododendron* (azalea)
5 *Soleirolia soleirolii* (mind your own business).

The charm of a country garden can be enjoyed even in the city with rustic containers overflowing with cottage-garden flowers.

COUNTRY CONTAINERS

A sense of fun and an apparent lack of organization are the hallmarks of the country garden. An atmosphere of a cottage garden on a warm summer's afternoon can easily be introduced to a small, town patio or country residence by way of a few simple planters, in fact the simpler the better. A hotch-potch of well worn containers gives an ideal framework, while a soft style of planting completes the picture. Beyond these guidelines readers can experiment to their hearts' content. There is infinite scope but try to include some scented plants, and some varieties which will extend the display beyond the summer months.

A summer barrel (far left)
Ingredients for a 60cm (24in) barrel:
1 *Althaea rosea* (hollyhock) × 3
2 pink *Penstemon*
3 *Nicotiana* 'Domino Mixed' × 6
4 *Alchemilla mollis* (lady's mantle)
5 *Fragaria* (strawberry)
6 pink *Diascia*
7 *Saxifraga stolonifera* 'Tricolor'
8 *Aster amellus* 'King George'
9 *Lilium auratum* 'Apollo' × 3
10 *Foeniculum vulgare* (fennel).

An old terracotta pot in summer (near left) A small and simple combination of plants can be very effective. Ingredients for a pot 40cm (16in) in diameter:

1 Yellow *Argyranthemum*
2 *Gypsophila repens* 'Rosea'
3 *Lavandula stoechas*
4 *Alchemilla mollis* (lady's mantle)
5 pink *Penstemon*.

Windowbox with picket fence (above) Give a hint of country fun to a town house. Ingredients for a window box 1m (3¼ft) long:
1 *Amaranthus caudatus* × 3
2 *Alyssum* × 12
3 *Lathyrus* (sweet pea) × 6
4 *Tropaeolum majus* (nasturtium) × 10
5 *Viola* (pansy) × 5
6 *Nicotiana* 'Domino Mixed' × 5
7 mixed *Antirrhinum* (snapdragon) × 10.

Colour bonanza (left) Vibrant flowers spring from every conceivable fitting. Ivy-leaved *Pelargoniums*, *Tropaeolum* (nasturtiums) and *Petunia* dominate the scene and thrive on this sunny wall.

Watering can (bottom) Blue trailing *Lobelia* acts as a floral substitute for the usual contents.

A basket full of London pride
Saxifraga × *urbium* (London pride) (centre) The contents can be changed for different potted plants as they come into flower.

An old chimney pot (top)
This provides a raised position from which *Convolvulus mauritanicus* cascades down.

An old-style wooden wheelbarrow (far right) This makes a fine feature by a front door. Wooden barrels and other rustic containers play an important part in creating a country atmosphere. Ingredients:
1 *Tagetes pumila* Star Fire Mixed × 5

2 *Erigeron mucronatus* × 6
3 *Petunia* 'Mirage Velvet' × 3
4 *Convolvulus mauritanicus* × 2
5 *Tropaeolum majus* 'Alaska' (nasturtium) × 6
6 variegated *Pelargonium*
7 *Fuchsia* 'Mrs Popple'.

111

Chosen with care a handful of carefully selected container-grown plants can bring a sunny holiday atmosphere to any garden, patio or poolside.

THE EXOTIC LOOK

The popular definition of "exotic" conjures up images of South Sea islands and tropical forests, although, strictly speaking, an exotic plant could be an uninspiring specimen from the Arctic.

By introducing two or three carefully chosen specimens it is well within anyone's grasp to simulate these most desirable effects, automatically associated with sunny climes. So it could be said that these are "warm" plants, as opposed to many conifers which tend to suggest a cold, snowy mountain top.

All of the plants included in the following designs have a very strong outline which helps give them their "exotic" character. For this reason, the designs are simple and use low growing plants to "set off" these shapes, rather than taller plants which would detract from them. These strong shapes also make the designs most suitable to act as focal points within the garden.

Going bananas (far left) The huge and wonderful leaves of *Musa ensete* (Abyssinian banana). Here a large container, 90cm × 90cm (36in × 36in) supports a good sized specimen. Intermingled *Helichrysum petiolare* 'Limelight' and *Felicia amelloides* form a colourful base and soften the hard lines of the container.

The Canary Island palm (left) *Phoenix canariensis.* Slower growing than the banana but the classical palm shape is of great landscape value. Here the basal planting is white-flowered *Argyranthemum frutescens* (marguerite) in a 75cm (30in) pot.

Large-scale exotica (left) Big container-grown *Trachycarpus fortunei* (Chusan palm) dominate the area and create a warm sub-tropical atmosphere. The scene is further enhanced by white walls and terracotta pots.

Bold and upright (below left) This *Phormium tenax* in a 60cm (24in) pot, is set off by the blue sea of *Convolvulus mauritanicus* × 10 beneath.

The Chusan palm (below centre) *Trachycarpus fortunei* has a truly exotic flavour. The underplanting of this 60cm (24in) pot with the succulent *Portulaca grandiflora* 'Sundance' × 20 accentuates the arid feel of this container.

A carefully chosen group (below right) Plants with varying growth habit and leaf texture contrast exquisitely with one another to create a sub-tropical atmosphere. Ingredients for three 60cm (24in) pots:
1 *Arundinaria murielae* (bamboo)
2 *Fatsia japonica* (Japanese aralia)
3 *Phormium* 'Dazzler' (mountain flax)
4 *Hedera helix* 'Glacier' (silver-variegated ivy) × 5.

THE PLANT DIRECTORY

Nerium oleander *forms the centrepiece of this mixed collection of container-grown plants.*

THE PLANT DIRECTORY: INTRODUCTION

This section is intended to be an easy reference to almost 1,000 of the most suitable plants for container growing outside.

The list of plants was carefully chosen by the authors to have as wide an appeal as possible.

We hope that through our careful selection you will be able to grow the best plants to the highest standards.

Plant hardiness and zone ratings

All plants are hardy in their natural habitat because there they have evolved to cope with a particular climate. However, many of the house and garden plants now so widely grown originate from abroad. The ability of a plant to overwinter in a foreign climate is a very complex matter and, as yet, there is no scientific formula to

Botanical (or Latin) name This is international and the form given is the one most widely used in nurseries and garden centres.

Second botanical name In improving plant classification botanists may rename a plant. Where appropriate these are given in brackets.

Common name This is only given if it is widely recognized and does not apply to several different plants.

Height The average height after five years growth in a container is given. A container restricts roots and slows plant growth, more so than in an open border. Also when a plant outgrows its container most people prune it or replace it with another.

Zone See zone maps on page 184. A caption is only provided when the plant illustrated differs from that in the main description.

Characteristics A brief description drawing attention to seasonal variation and other details that cannot be illustrated.

Position The best place to position the container plant to obtain optimum results.

Uses Examples of good visual associations with other plants and containers are given. Where relevant, the overall effect and any particular uses are mentioned.

Compost Brief notes for each plant are provided. These link in with the information on composts and feeding given on pages 54-55, 58-59.

Special maintenance Since container plants are often at eye level, regular attention and, in some cases, special maintenance is worthwhile to keep them looking good.

Other kinds to try A small selection of related plants which are distinct but also of special merit for containers are described briefly.

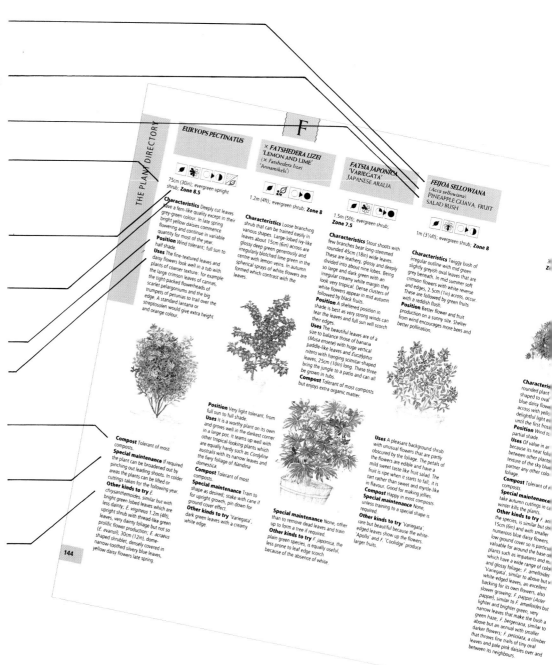

SYMBOLS

These appear below the name of each plant to enable the fast and efficient selection of suitable plants at a glance. They indicate when a plant is effective by showing the season when the leaves and flowers are present. The symbols for the amount of sunlight the plant prefers, and whether it needs to be taken inside for the winter in areas where frost occurs, provide a quick check to the conditions necessary for success.

Deciduous plant – normally loses all its leaves in the winter. It may have different coloured spring or autumn foliage.

Evergreen plant – normally retains most of its leaves throughout the year. Evergreens are effective visually all year round and are useful as a permanent screen or shelter.

Semi-evergreen plant – normally retains some leaves during a typical winter or dormant season.

These symbols give a general indication of when the plant blooms. Since there is some seasonal variation from year to year it cannot be precise but is a useful guide.

Seasons are given rather than months since the former apply worldwide.

blooms mid winter

blooms late winter

blooms mid spring

blooms late spring

blooms mid summer

blooms late summer

blooms mid autumn

blooms late autumn

This symbol indicates that the plant is grown primarily for its foliage or fruit rather than its flowers.

Plants vary in their requirement of direct sunlight: some have a wide tolerance, others have precise needs. Generally the middle of the range shown will give the best results. The shaded section shows the proportion of daylight hours that the plant should be without direct sun.

Direct sunlight all day.

No direct sun for a quarter of the day.

No direct sun for half the day.

No direct sun for three-quarters of the day.

No direct sun.

House in winter to protect plant from severe frost damage. Move the plant into a greenhouse, or near a window for light in the house, shed or garage.

ZONES CHART

Zones designate the lowest range of temperatures in which a plant will normally survive. Thus a plant in Zone 8 will normally survive between −12°C and −6°C (10°F and 20°F).

Zone	°Centigrade	°Fahrenheit
1	below −45	below −50
2	−45 to −40	−50 to −40
3	−40 to −34	−40 to −30
4	−34 to −29	−30 to −20
5	−29 to −23	−20 to −10
6	−23 to −18	−10 to 0
7	−18 to −15	0 to 5
7.5	−15 to −12	5 to 10
8	−12 to −6	10 to 20
9	−6 to −1	20 to 30
10	−1 to 5	30 to 40

MELLOIDES
'ITA'
celestis 'Santa

en shrublet;

FICUS CARICA
FIG

2.1m (7ft); deciduous large shrub;
Zone 7.5

Characteristics Robust twigs support 15cm (6in) palm-shaped leaves with three to five deep lobes. The tops of the shoots can bear a few flowers in each leaf axil. No petals are visible and they look like tiny green figs. In warm climates there can be three crops a year but in cool climates the fruits do not start to turn a pinkish grey until autumn when their softness indicates picking time.

Position A sunny wall is the best site to ripen fruit, but if fruit is not important a shady spot will do.

Uses The large leaves are quite attractive but the production of fresh fruit is the delight of the connoisseur.

Compost Very well drained and not too rich, consequently they do very well in containers such as half barrels.

FOENICULUM VULGARE
'PURPUREUM'
PURPLE FENNEL

1.2m (4ft); herbaceous perennial;
Zone 7

Characteristics Erect smooth light green robust stems branch and give rise to thousands of extremely fine hair-like leaflets of a bronzy copper colour. When pinched or brushed they exude a scent reminiscent of aniseed. From the top of the stem in summer many tiny yellow flowers appear arranged in an open flat head.

Position Does well in full sun to full shade.

Uses An attractive foliage plant to trail down over the edge of windowboxes and hanging baskets.

Compost Tolerant of most composts provided they have adequate organic matter.

Special maintenance Young plantlets in excess can be cut off and rooted.

FRAGARIA x ANANASSA
'VARIEGATA'
STRAWBERRY

12cm (5in); semi-evergreen herbaceous plant; **Zone 7**

Characteristics This is the variegated form of the familiar fruiting plant. Tufts of leaves each divided into three saw-edged leaflets which produce long horizontal runners by which the plant spreads. White flowers in clusters in late spring are followed by the delicious conical red fruit. In this kind the leaves have broad white edges, an attractive background for the red fruit. It is slower growing than the green-leaved kinds, an advantage between other plants, but this also means fewer and smaller fruits.

Position Does well in full sun to full shade.

Position Tolerant of salt winds. Does well in full sun or partial shade.

Uses Well known flavouring particularly suited to fish dishes. Grown in a pot on its own set by the kitchen door or in association with the broad-leaved *Beta vulgaris cicla*, rhubarb or Swiss chard, its dainty foliage is charming.

Compost Tolerant of all composts.

Special maintenance Remove the dead flowers and stems if desired, but they have great form and texture even when dead.

Other kinds to try *F. vulgare*, the green-leaved species, may fit better in some colour schemes in the garden and on the plate!; *F.v. dulce* 'Finnochio' (Florence fennel), similar except the leaf bases swell up to form a "bulb" with a taste between celery and aniseed.

al maintenance Thinning ots allows the sun to ripen the nd fruit better, so train fanned nst a wall or as an open-ush.

nds to try 'Brown Turkey', st kind, fruit brownish flesh; 'Black Ischia', ler fruit, purplish black, flesh; 'White Marseilles', medium pale green,

Uses An attractive foliage plant to trail down over the edge of windowboxes and hanging baskets.

Compost Tolerant of most composts provided they have adequate organic matter.

Special maintenance Young plantlets in excess can be cut off and rooted.

Other kinds to try 'Rabunda' perpetual, fruits from summer to mid autumn; *F. vesca* 'Semperflorens' (Alpine strawberry), 7cm (3in) high, this little trailing evergreen is a useful short ground cover and also bears its tiny 14mm (½in) fruits from mid summer to late autumn. Never a huge crop but nearly always of delicious flavour; *F.v.* 'Alexandria', a newer kind than 'Baron Solemacher'. Both have fruits about 2cm (¾in) long.

 deciduous

 semi-evergreen

evergreen

flowering period

foliage/ fruiting plant

full sun

¼ shade-¾ sun

½ shade-½ sun

¾ sun-¼ shade

full shade

needs winter protection

categorize plant hardiness. Trials and experience over many winters give some indication of survival through an average winter, but even within a small garden, a plant may succeed in one area but die in another; and, of course, winters can vary enormously. Cold winds, moisture levels, snowcover and soil fertility are just a few of the complex interacting influences. The United States Department of Agriculture has devised a map which shows zones of hardiness in the USA; this is a positive help for selecting suitable plants. Using the American system as a guide and applying knowledge that I have gained growing and observing plants in the British Isles for over 40 years, I have produced a similar map but, since most of Britain would fall into one zone, I have included an extra zone – Zone 7.5 – to give more guidance. I have also compiled zone maps for Western Europe, Australia, New Zealand and South Africa. These are based on growing plants from these zones in Britain. Other sources have produced zone maps based solely on mean minimum isotherms for the coldest month. The zone grades on this page and the maps on pages 184-185 do not claim to provide a foolproof system, however they do offer the best guidance that can be given at this time. If the reader's experience should prove different from that given here please write to the author, for it is only by disseminating information that further knowledge can be gained.

ABIES BALSAMEA HUDSONIA 'NANA'
DWARF BALSAM FIR

30cm (12in); evergreen conifer; **Zone 6**

Characteristics This bushy conifer has an irregularly rounded outline and smooth grey bark to older branches. The needles are grey-green, narrow, flat and leathery.

Position Although small the plant is quite tough. Place in full sun to half shade.

Uses Most useful for a miniature landscape such as in a windowbox where a little mountain scene can be created with a few rocks and a contrasting ground-hugging carpet of bright green *Soleirolia soleirolii* or *Sedum album* 'Coral Carpet'; both provide complementary colour and texture.

Compost Very tolerant provided drainage is good.

Special maintenance None directly but do not let other plants grow into and cover this dwarf fir or else its foliage will turn brown.

Other kinds to try *A. concolor* 'Glauca Compacta', slow growing 60cm (24in) conifer with steel blue foliage; *A. koreana* (Korean fir), conical shape with fairly open branches. This slow growing tree with dark green needles can produce very attractive violet-blue cones that sit on the branches like candles when it is only a few years old.

ABUTILON × HYBRIDUM
TREE MALLOW

2.4m (8ft); evergreen upright tree or shrub; **Zone 9**

Characteristics Slim stems bear green maple-shaped leaves and 7cm (2–3in) long bell-like flowers, complete with "striker" formed by the fused projecting stamens, flowers almost continuously.

Position Avoid drying winds that cause flowers to drop and leaves to scorch.

Uses Can be trained to any shape. In a hanging basket stop the side-shoots to develop a wide bushy shape. In an urn or pot stop the main shoot low down to allow about five shoots to fan out into a screen or, alternatively, gradually nip out the side-shoots to make a standard like a parasol hung with coloured bells.

Compost Tolerates most composts but an enriched loam-based type is best for stability of the plant.

Special maintenance Continuous growth and flowering can be maintained by regular feeding and watering. Stop shoots and tie in growth to achieve the required shape. Repot annually for good growth. If the plant gets too big, prune hard back in winter. Whitefly may need controlling under glass, preferably by biological means. In zone 8 or below, wrap hessian around the base of the plant in winter to protect it from frost. It will regrow again if cut back to just above the compost.

Other kinds to try 'Canary Bird', extra-large primrose yellow flowers; 'Ashford Red', soft red bells; 'Boule de Neige', white flowers with yellow "striker"; 'Souvenir de Bonn', orange bells, white-edged leaves, very vigorous; 'Cannington Peter', dark crimson flowers, contrasting yellow mottled leaves; 'Cannington Carol', scarlet flowers, yellow mottled leaves, the neatest bush for baskets; 'Orange Glow', the most floriferous of the tall types; 'Louis Marignac', tall growing with light, delicate silvery pink bells; 'Cannington Sally', yellow mottled leaves, bright orange-scarlet flowers in profusion; *A. megapotamicum*, yellow and crimson flowers, slim leaves. In a basket will creep down; *A. suntense* 'Violetta', grey-green leaves, violet-blue bell-like flowers in late spring to mid autumn, sunshine encourages flowers, Zone 7.5.

Abutilon × hybridum 'Canary Bird'

ACACIA PRAVISSIMA
FISH-TAIL MIMOSA

2.4m (8ft); evergreen multi-stemmed small tree; **Zone 8**

Characteristics Young plants have upright shoots with astonishing fin-shaped grey-green leaves, much sought by floral arrangers. As it matures the branches at the top of the vertical stems bush out and produce delicate clusters of scented yellow powder-puff flowers from mid to late spring.

Position Tolerant of wind. Prefers full sun but will grow in light shade.

Uses The unique foliage makes this small tree a great attraction for a patio. It can also be fan-trained against a sunny wall.

Compost Tolerates most composts but a loam-based type gives weight and stability.

Special maintenance Can be pruned to produce a single trunk or to fan out. Wrap straw or bubble plastic around the base in winter for zones 7 or less; this may enable it to survive winter frost. Otherwise take it inside for the winter if space permits.

Other kinds to try *A. rhetinodes* (*A. retinoides*) (four-seasons mimosa), deliciously scented, primrose yellow flowers all four seasons of the year, grey-green willowy leaves, Zone 9; *A. dealbata* (silver wattle), feathery divided grey-green leaves. A very vigorous late-winter flowering tree only for the biggest container, Zone 8; *A. baileyana* (Cootamundra wattle), finely divided blue-grey leaves, needs more wind shelter, Zone 9.

ACER PALMATUM
JAPANESE MAPLE

1.2m (4ft); deciduous shrub or tree; **Zone 7.5**

Characteristics Dainty slim branches bear attractive smooth palm-shaped leaves, so thin that when the sun shines behind them they illuminate like stained glass; fresh green in spring, when the bunches of green flowers appear, yellow and orange in autumn. After some years small propeller-like fruits will be produced.

Position Choose a shaded spot out of the wind, as the leaves and young shoots will become desiccated and die back. This may allow entry of coral spot disease which will cause further dieback. Very tolerant of shade.

Uses Associates well with other shade-tolerant plants, like hostas, which will grow beneath its delicate network of branches. It gives a light and airy feel to dark places and is most appropriate for oriental themes.

Compost Tolerates most composts provided they have adequate organic matter to retain moisture, otherwise the foliage will scorch.

Special maintenance Ensure regular watering, a mulch of leafmould in spring aids young growth. Carefully prune out any twigs that die back.

Other kinds to try 'Ozakazuki', leaves turn brilliant scarlet in autumn; 'Senkaki', young shoots of coral red look superb in winter; 'Butterfly', leaves white-edged with a pink flush, slow growing; 'Dissectum', leaves finely cut into feathery fringes; *A. negundo* 'Flamingo', 2.1m (7ft), upright tree, leaves divided into three to five leaflets each with a broad white margin and a pink flush.

Acer palmatum 'Ozakazuki'

ACTINIDIA CHINENSIS
(*A. deliciosa*)
CHINESE GOOSEBERRY, KIWI FRUIT

3m (10ft); deciduous vigorous twining climber; **Zone 7.5**

Characteristics Dark green heart-shaped leaves, 18cm (7in) long. Reddish hairs on the veins and shoots give interesting texture. In late spring to mid summer ivory-buff flowers open beneath the leaves. These are 4cm (1½in) across and waft a gentle scent in the breeze. Female plants of five years old or more may produce hairy brown fruit, 2.5–6.5cm (1–2½in) long, in late autumn depending on cultivation and variety. Remember both male and female plants are needed to produce the fruit.

Position Grow in half sun to full shade away from strong winds which will shred leaves and deter pollinating insects. Wind shelter is essential for fruit and good visual effect.

Uses An excellent quick-growing screen for summer. The fruit when properly ripe is delicious, rich in vitamin C, and the green, delightfully patterned slices are superb for cake decoration. Fruit will keep several months in a cool place.

Compost Tolerates most composts but extra organic matter and nitrogen is needed to maintain fruit development and fruit size.

Special maintenance Ensure regular watering when the fruits are swelling; a mulch will help retain moisture. For fruit production, maintain an open branch framework on a pergola or trellis and prune off all side growths that have fruited to a new basal replacement shoot.

Other kinds to try 'Hayward', large, broad fruits, the best keeper of all, very late flowers miss frost damage; 'Bruno', earlier to flower and longer slimmer fruits, a heavy cropper; 'Monty', the most fruitful but rather small; *A. kolomikta*, 2m (6ft), on mature plants, oval heart-shaped leaves show white ends flushed with pink which cover one third or more of the leaf – a brilliant effect, deliciously scented, early summer flowers and small yellowish fruit.

ADIANTUM PEDATUM
MAIDENHAIR FERN

40cm (16in); semi-evergreen fern slowly creeping habit; **Zone 7.5**

Characteristics Very dainty bright green finger-like divisions to its fronds make an attractive contrast to the shiny black stems.

Position Strong sun and wind will cause dieback, so plant in the shade of other plants or similar shaded sheltered position.

Uses A delicate contrast for large-leaved plants, such as *Hosta* and *Bergenia*. Looks good around the base of shrubs.

Compost Prefers neutral to acid (lime-free) compost with adequate organic matter.

Special maintenance Remove from frost spots and, in colder areas, a mulch of leafmould in late autumn will help to protect the roots and crowns from exceptionally hard frosts and also encourage new fronds to develop.

Other kinds to try var. *aleuticum*, from the Aleutian Isles, only 10cm (4in) high, limy compost; var. *japonicum*, young fronds a delicate rose pink in spring; 'Laciniatum', finely divided fronds look like green foam; *A. venustum*, less hardy fern best taken inside for the winter, Zone 9. Triangular fronds with minute segments look like green raindrops.

deciduous

semi-evergreen

evergreen

flowering period

foliage/ fruiting plant

full sun

¼ shade-¾ sun

½ shade-½ sun

¼ sun-¾ shade

full shade

needs winter protection

119

AEONIUM ARBOREUM

60cm (24in); evergreen shrubby succulent; **Zone 9.5–10**

Characteristics The thick occasionally branching stems have a snakeskin-like pattern caused by leaf scars. Each stem is crowned with a rosette of shiny green leaves, flower-like in form and up to 15cm (6in) across. In late spring a pyramid of tiny yellow star-shaped flowers is produced but the flowers reduce the vigour of the plant.

Position Sun is important for sturdy growth otherwise the plant can become drawn up and topple over. The purple-leaved forms only colour well in full sun.
Uses The unusual habit of this plant makes it invaluable as a contrast with other succulents and cacti. The purple-leaved kinds provide an amazing background for silver-grey *Sedum spathulifolium* 'Cape Blanco', *Agave americana*, *Echeveria glauca* and the pink *E.* 'Metallica Rosea'.
Compost Tolerant of most composts but needs added grit for good drainage.
Special maintenance Make sure invading worms do not block the drainage holes of the container with their casts. A mulch of stone chippings aids surface drainage and looks good. To be safe, house in winter in Zone 9 or above.
Other kinds to try 'Atropurpureum', leaves dark purple in sun; 'Schwarzkopf', very similar to above but black-purple foliage; *A. tabuliforme*, leaf rosette like a flat green plate.

AGAPANTHUS CAMPANULATUS
BELL AGAPANTHUS

75cm (30in); deciduous hardy herbaceous perennial; **Zone 7.5**

Characteristics Green strap-shaped leaves emerge in spring to form a dense tuft from which arise shiny green succulent stems topped with a rounded shower of bright sky-blue bell-shaped flowers in summer.
Position They are amazingly accommodating provided their compost is suitable and grow well in full sun or full shade. They will also stand exposure to salt winds.
Uses A tub or urn of this plant standing alone looks superb; the robust spray of basal leaves balances the flowers to perfection. However, it is a seasonal plant best put on display during summer but replaced by another container for other seasons.
Compost Since these plants grow in moist valleys in the wild, an enriched moisture-retentive compost is best, but good drainage is important too.
Special maintenance Dividing a plant normally prevents flowering the following year so, if possible, leave them undisturbed. Try to have a spare tub for plants split in rotation every few years. Divide in spring and water in well, then water sparingly until the new shoots show.
Other kinds to try *A. campanulatus albus*, the same but white flowers; *A. praecox orientalis* evergreen, 1.2m (4ft) high, bright mid blue flowers, less hardy, Zone 8.5; *A. praecox orientalis pallidus*, light blue flowers; *A. praecox orientalis* 'Variegatus', white-edged leaves contrast with mid blue flowers.

Agapanthus praecox orientalis

AGAVE AMERICANA
CENTURY PLANT

45cm (18in); perennial evergreen succulent; **Zone 9**

Characteristics Thick succulent grey-green leaves form a dramatic rosette. Each bulky leaf has a horny toothed margin reminiscent of a crocodile's jaw. Since the tall flower stem with spikes of cream flowers only forms in spring to summer when the plant is large and mature, it rarely flowers in a container.
Position Tolerant of salty winds, maximum light and a sunny position ensures a hardier plant. Shade produces overplump leaves that break off if knocked!
Uses Its geometric and dramatic shape is perfect for surmounting a pillar; a living finial. Its natural defences are also useful and it can be placed to keep people away.
Compost Tolerant of many composts but add a good proportion of stony grit to ensure good drainage.
Special maintenance If winter rain is high in Zone 9, a transparent cover over the top (not the sides) of the plant keeps it dry and helps to prevent rotting. In colder zones, bring inside for the winter.

Agave americana 'Variegata'

Other kinds to try 'Variegata', leaves broadly margined with creamy white; 'Mediopicta', leaves with bright yellow centre; 'Mediopicta Alba', leaves with pure white centre; *A. sisalana* 'Variegata', white-edged leaves lack the tough teeth of *A. americana* and are more flexible – a kinder plant alongside a path.

AGERATUM HOUSTONIANUM
FLOSS FLOWER

45cm (18in); tender hummock-shaped annual; **Zone 10**

Characteristics The rounded 2.5cm (1in) green leaves form a rounded bushlet which becomes covered with powder-puff-like light blue flowers with a hint of mauve. The flowers retain their clear colour for a long time from summer through to autumn.
Position Flowers best in a sunny place.
Uses The shorter kinds are normally used as an edging to a container to "cushion" the taller plants, but they can also look well in a trough as a carpet through which taller open-textured plants like the marguerites (*Argyranthemum*) can spring.
Compost Grows well in loam- or peat-based compost.
Special maintenance Apart from regular watering, just pick off any flowerheads that go brown.
Other kinds to try 'Blue Mink', extremely popular, dense-flowered, 25cm (10in); 'Blue Danube', early-flowering dwarf, 25cm (10in); 'Tall Blue', tall enough at 45cm (18in) to fill in between popular bedding plants like *Antirrhinum* and China aster (*Callistephus*).

Ageratum houstonianum 'Blue Mink'

ALCHEMILLA MOLLIS
LADY'S MANTLE

50cm (20in); clump-forming herbaceous perennial; **Zone 7**

Characteristics Rounded pale green leaves about 7.5cm (3in) across, each one slightly folded at the veins, rather like a reversed umbrella, and covered with short fine silky hairs. They look most attractive after a shower since the raindrops are held on the fine hairs. Sprays of tiny greenish yellow flowers occur in mid summer.

Position Tolerant of some shade and full sun.
Uses It makes an excellent ground cover beneath *Acer palmatum* 'Dissectum Atropurpureum' or *Leptospermum scoparium* 'Red Damask', its wide leaves with silvery silky hairs a perfect foil for the crimson shrubs.
Compost Tolerant of loam- or peat-based compost.
Special maintenance No special treatment is necessary apart from removing dead leaves and flower-heads.
Other kinds to try *A. conjuncta*, 30cm (12in), small dainty leaves have several leaflets reminiscent of horse-chestnut foilage; *A. alpina*, 15cm (6in), similar to above.

ALLIUM CEPA
ONION

30cm (12in); loosely-tufted biennial bulb; **Zone 7**

Characteristics The decorative value of this well-known vegetable is often forgotten. The leaves are hollow and round in cross section. When young, as in salad onions, they stand upright and are a glossy mid green.
Position Only sow on the light sunny side of a container, so the leaves are not shaded by neighbouring plants.
Uses In texture and form onions contrast well with the flat rounded rosettes of lettuce (*Lactuca sativa*) and the fluffy humps of curled parsley (*Petroselinum crispum*). The fine leaves and dainty flowers of *Lobelia erinus* trailing down over the edge of a container of salad onions also look delightful.
Compost A well-drained and enriched compost gives fast growth and crisp foliage.
Special maintenance Sow a succession of salad onions. Sow in a large container in rows 10cm (4in) apart and use an onion hoe to thin the plants to 2.5cm (1in) to achieve about 30 plants per 0.1 sq m (1 sq ft).

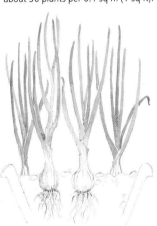

Other kinds to try 'White Lisbon', quick growing, silvery skin, mild flavour; 'White Lisbon Winter Hardy', can be sown in late autumn; 'Ishikura', like thin leeks with no basal bulb, they can be used over a long period; *A. schoenoprasum* (chive), a perennial grass-like herb from the *Allium* family; carries purple flower balls.

ALTHAEA ROSEA
(*Alcea rosea*)
HOLLYHOCK

2.1m (7ft); tall spike-shaped biennial; **Zone 7**

Characteristics The rounded rough 12.5cm (5in) leaves form a green base for the towering flower spike. The bell-like flowers of rose, pink, cream or yellow are each up to 7.5cm (3in) across and open from summer to autumn. The centre of the flower is often darker and the column of yellow stamens that spring from within gives further contrast.
Position Plant in full sun for strong stems, but hollyhocks will tolerate a little shade.
Uses This is a key plant for creating a cottage-garden effect. There can be no equal to frame a doorway or fill a corner between two walls. It complements the delicate-flowered billowing plants such as *Gypsophila*, *Heliotropium* or white marguerites (*Argyranthemum*).
Compost A loam-based compost gives greater stability for the huge spikes.
Special maintenance It is wise to stake the tall stems and remove dead flowers to maintain vigour. Should any leaves develop rust disease remove them from the garden and consider a different variety for the following year.
Other kinds to try Single Rust-resistant Mixed, 2.1m (7ft), mixed colours, practically immune to rust disease; 'Chater's Double', 1.8m (6ft), mixed colours, peony-form doubles; 'Summer Carnival', 1.8m (6ft), mixed colours, double, can be grown as an annual; 'Powder Puffs', 1.8m (6ft), mixed colours, very double flowers densely packed; 'Silver Puffs', 60cm (24in), silver-pink doubles.

ALYSSUM MARITIMUM
(*Lobularia maritima*)
SWEET ALYSSUM

15cm (6in); spreading hardy annual; **Zone 7**

Characteristics The quick-spreading growth is a mass of tiny oval grey-green leaves which soon becomes almost completely covered with heads of white flowers with a gentle scent. These are on display from summer to autumn.
Position Choose a sunny spot for maximum number of flowers.
Uses Invaluable as a low edging to containers and a good foil for strong coloured neighbours, such as petunias and scarlet-flowered pelargoniums. Sweet alyssum is also very attractive to butterflies.
Compost Happy in most composts provided drainage is reasonable.
Special maintenance No special treatment required.
Other kinds to try 'Little Dorrit', 10cm (4in), white, compact habit; 'Snow Carpet', 7.5cm (3in), white, ground hugging; 'Royal Carpet', 7.5cm (3in), rich purple and ground hugging; 'Wonderland', 15cm (6in), pinky purple; *A. saxatile* (*Aurinia saxatilis*), perennial evergreen alpine, 20cm (8in) with grey-green leaves and golden yellow flowers, a good edging plant for spring; 'Citrina', soft lemon yellow, a gentler colour contrast for associating with *Aubrieta*.

Alyssum maritimum 'Little Dorrit'

deciduous

semi-evergreen

evergreen

flowering period

foliage/fruiting plant

full sun

¼ shade-¾ sun

½ shade-½ sun

¼ sun-¾ shade

full shade

needs winter protection

AMARANTHUS CAUDATUS
LOVE-LIES-BLEEDING

1m (3¼ft); bushy annual; **Zone 10**

Characteristics Strong branching growth with oval pointed slightly corrugated light green leaves. During summer and autumn towards the tips of the branches hang 45cm (18in) tassels of crimson-red flowers.
Position Choose a light and sheltered position as strong winds can damage the tassels.
Uses A high container, such as an urn on a pedestal or a large windowbox, shows this plant off best since it allows the dark tassels to hang down. Amaranthus looks well with plants of upright habit and dainty daisy flowers such as *Argyranthemum frutescens*.
Compost Tolerant of most composts.
Special maintenance Remove brown tassels if desired, but they are quite nice in form and texture.
Other kinds to try 'Viridis', similar with green tassels; *A. hybridus erythrostachys* 'Red Fox' (prince's feather), leaves purplish green, the crimson plumes are upright and about 15cm (6in) long; *A. hybridus* 'Green Thumb', similar to above but green plumes; *A. hybridus* 'Illumination', similar but grown for its foliage which is rich crimson-scarlet, marked yellow and bronze.

ANAGALLIS ARVENSIS CAERULEA
PIMPERNEL

30cm (12in); annual; **Zone 7**

Characteristics This forms a dense spreading cover of tiny lance-shaped leaves. In summer the plant is covered with star-shaped deep blue flowers. In the centre of each flower are five small yellow stamens which, although small, provide an attractive contrast to the petals.
Position Fairly wind tolerant but they prefer a light place in full sun or dappled shade.
Uses A valuable summer ground cover plant for a windowbox. It looks attractive around the base of spiky *Cordyline australis* with an edging of *Alyssum maritimum* 'Snow Carpet'.
Compost Tolerant of most composts.
Special maintenance None.

Other kinds to try *A. tenella* 'Studland', 12mm (½in) carpet of tiny round to oval leaves on stems which will trail down over the edge of a hanging basket, star-shaped bright pink flowers. Plant at the edge of a tub pond as it likes moisture.

ANEMONE BLANDA
MOUNTAIN WINDFLOWER

10cm (4in); spreading perennial tuber; **Zone 7**

Characteristics The leaves are made up of three deeply divided leaflets. This dainty foliage makes an attractive carpeting background for the dainty daisy-like spring flowers. Each flower measures 5cm (2in) across with 10 or more petals held on an upright stem.
Position Best in sun but they tolerate light shade from other plants.
Uses The ferny foliage and dainty flowers give an informal display for spring unmatched by tulips or daffodils. However, they can be used as a carpet beneath white or lemon yellow *Narcissus* of modest size, such as 'Cheerfulness', 'Niveth' and 'Tresamble', which do not clash in colour or obscure the anemones with over-lush foliage.
Compost Most composts are acceptable provided drainage is good and there is an adequate supply of organic matter.
Special maintenance Leave permanently in position or, if the container requires regular replanting for summer, the tubers may be saved and replanted in autumn provided the leaves have time to yellow naturally.
Other kinds to try 'Atrocaerulea', dark blue; 'Radar', reddish carmine; 'White Splendour', white; *A. coronaria* similar to above but 25cm (10in) high and with 5–8-petalled buttercup-like flowers, 7.5cm (3in) across; *A.c.* De Caen 'Hollandia', brilliant scarlet; *A.c.* De Caen 'Mr Fokker', bright blue; *A.c.* De Caen 'Mixed', purples, reds, blues, pinks.

Anemone blanda 'Atrocaerulea'

ANTHEMIS NOBILIS
(*Chamaemelum nobilis*)
CHAMOMILE

10cm (4in); evergreen mat-forming perennial; **Zone 6**

Characteristics Very finely divided moss-like leaves spread to form a deep emerald green carpet. Daisy flowers, 5 to 7mm (¼in) across, white with yellow centres open in late summer to contrast with the dark rippling mat of foliage.

Position Although it will grow in light shade, full sun is best for a healthy tread-tolerant carpet.
Uses Widely grown as a scented carpet of foliage, there is no reason why chamomile cannot be used in a container to form a green cushioned seat or even a bed on which to lie and enjoy the aroma. It has the advantage of being more tolerant of drought than most lawn grasses. In a container it can form a small alpine lawn surrounded by rock-garden plants. It is the ingredient for tonics and hair washes, and the flowers can be picked to make a tea.
Compost It will tolerate most composts provided they are well drained.
Special maintenance Chamomile can be clipped to achieve a level surface, but many people prefer a naturally rippling surface dotted with little white flowers.
Other kinds to try 'Treneague', non-flowering and less invasive, a better neighbour for small alpines and for reduced maintenance, but it does need full sun; 'Flore Pleno', double flowers like dainty white buttons.

ANTIRRHINUM MAJUS
SNAPDRAGON

75cm (30in); perennial sub-shrub but grown as an annual; **Zone 8**

Characteristics Erect and branched from the base, the stems are clothed with smooth lance-shaped green leaves up to 5cm (2in) long. Arranged in spikes, the flowers are tubular, up to 5cm (2in) long, with two lips. The lower lip is pouched and has a flexible hinge which insects can push back to gain access – amusing for children to watch. Antirrhinums flower almost continuously during the summer.
Position They need sun for at least half the day to flower well.
Uses The taller types spear through flat-topped bedding plants like *Tagetes* or *Ageratum*, while the dwarf kinds form a carpet.
Compost Tolerant of most composts but young seedlings dislike being dry, so choose one with good moisture-retentive properties or water regularly.
Special maintenance When all the flowers on a spike have died pick it off to encourage replacements to form. At the end of the season burn or remove all old plants to get rid of spores of rust disease.
Other kinds to try Madame Butterfly Series, 75cm (30in), double, mixed colours for a massed display; 'Coronette', 60cm (24in), mixed colours, a well-packed spike of two-lipped flowers followed by a coronet of secondary spires. Some resistance to rust: Princess Series, 38cm (15in), single-flowered bush plants, at present the most rust-resistant kind, mixed or sometimes in separate colours; Floral Showers Series, 20cm (8in), compact, mixed colours, can be used as edging.

Antirrhinum majus 'Coronette'

ARABIS ALBIDA
(*A. caucasica*)
WHITE ROCK CRESS

15cm (6in); evergreen mat-forming perennial alpine; **Zone 6**

Characteristics Loose cushions of slightly greyish green oval leaves. In spring it becomes covered with clusters of white flowers.
Position Quite wind tolerant; flowers best in full sun.
Uses It makes an excellent snowy white carpet for a spring container. Mixed with blue winter-flowering pansies it is a brilliant foil for hyacinth 'Pink Pearl', or early-flowering tulips 'Peach Blossom' or 'Brilliant Star', since all three bulbs are short stemmed.

Compost Tolerant of most composts provided drainage is good. Some additional lime will deter club-root disease.
Special maintenance It is wise to replace the plants every year to prevent a build-up of pests.
Other kinds to try 'Plena', double white flowers which last longer than the species; 'Variegata', leaves edged creamy white which form an attractive carpet even when not in flower; 'Rosabella', single pink flowers; *A. blepharophylla*, 10cm (4in) high plant similar to above but with stiff hairs on leaf edges and purplish pink flowers.

ARGYRANTHEMUM FRUTESCENS
MARGUERITE

60cm (24in); evergreen sub-shrub; **Zone 9**

Characteristics The attractive branches are smooth and grey-green as most plants are propagated annually so the shrubby habit has not had time to develop. The leaves are deeply divided into thin segments 3–5mm (⅛–¼in) long. Overall the effect is of a grey-green feathery dome. The dainty daisy flowers appear in summer and are about 4cm (1½in) across with sparkling white rays and yellow centres.
Position Sun and shade tolerant, but less flowers form in shade.
Uses Perhaps the most adaptable container plant, it can be used as a natural dome or trained to any shape – ball, pyramid or standard. It will brighten any dull doorway and is a superb alternative to a standard bay tree.
Compost Any compost is suitable provided drainage is good and feeding is consistent to give continuous growth and flowering.
Special maintenance Pinch back shoots to achieve the desired shape, remove flowerheads from double-flowering kinds for perfect effect. Fine-leaved kinds are less prone to leaf miner damage.
Other kinds to try *A. gracile* 'Chelsea Girl', white flowers, leaves like fine grey-green hair; *A. foeniculaceum* 'Royal Haze', sparse white flowers, fine blue-grey foliage; *A. coronopifolium*, white flowers, 30cm (12in) spreading broader, grey-green leaves; *A.* × 'Sark', white, double; 'Edelweiss' and 'Quinta White' are similar; *A. callichrysum* 'Penny', yellow flowers, more compact and floriferous than the widely available 'Jamaica Primrose'; *A. callichrysum* 'Prado', many bright yellow flowers, 50cm (20in), floriferous; *A. maderense*, primrose flowers, 30cm (12in), spreading grey-green foliage; *A.* × 'Vancouver', rich pink, double, a deeper coloured more compact form of 'Mary Wooton'; *A.* × 'Wellwood Park', deep pink, single; *A.* × 'Powder Puff', fine grey-green foliage, small double feathers tufts of pale pink flowers; *A. haematomma* 'Rollason's Red', the darkest coloured marguerite of them all, a spreading plant with crimson-rose single flowers, fading to deep pink in full sun.

Argyranthemum × 'Vancouver'

 deciduous

 semi-evergreen

 evergreen

 flowering period

 foliage/fruiting plant

 full sun

 ¼ shade-¾ sun

 ½ shade-½ sun

 ¼ sun-¾ shade

 full shade

 needs winter protection

ARMERIA MARITIMA 'VINDICTIVE'
SEA PINK, THRIFT

10cm (4in); evergreen dwarf sub-shrub; **Zone 6**

Characteristics Forms a hummock of greyish dark green grassy leaves which is attractive at all times. In summer stiff wiry stems are topped with round clusters of many bright pink flowers.
Position Tolerates full wind and salt-laden gales, requires full sun to half shade for good flowering.
Uses The attractive green domes contrast well in a windowbox with a coarser-textured carpet of *Sedum spathulifolium* 'Cape Blanco', with its silvery spoon-shaped leaves, or the russet red rosettes of *Sempervivum tectorum* (common houseleek).
Compost Adequate drainage is needed otherwise tolerant of most composts.

Special maintenance Avoid overfeeding and do not let other plants overshadow thrift plants or they will turn brown.
Other kinds to try
A. pseudarmeria 'Bees Ruby', 30cm (12in) a bigger version of the above with flatter, longer and greener leaves, ruby red flowers; *A. juniperifolia* (*A. caespitosa*), densely cushioned, 7.5cm (3in) grey-green leaves.

ARUNDINARIA VIRIDISTRIATA
(*Pleioblastus auricoma*)
GOLD STRIPED BAMBOO

1.5m (5ft); evergreen slow spreading bamboo; **Zone 6**

Characteristics The canes are mainly clump forming but spread slowly. They are pale creamy yellow when young gradually becoming purplish. The leaves are bright green with broad yellow stripes although the pattern varies. Each leaf is about 15cm (6in) long and 4cm (1½in) across.

Position It colours best in sun. It will tolerate half shade although the variegation disappears.
Uses One of the best bamboos for a tub for its medium stature allows its use on patios of modest size where it gives an oriental effect all year. Good partners are *Fatsia japonica*, with big evergreen palm-shaped leaves, and *Euonymus fortunei* 'Silver Queen', prostrate and silvery.
Compost Enriched loam-based compost with extra organic matter ensures good growth and bright leaf colour.
Special maintenance Ensure adequate moisture during drought. Stand the container in a saucer kept full of water to provide a useful small reserve. Remove old canes with poor foliage.
Other kinds to try *A. variegata* (*Pleioblastus variegatus*) (dwarf white-striped bamboo), 1.2m (4ft) canes which are pale green and slender, leaves dark green with brilliant white stripes which vary in width; *A. murielae* (*Thamnocalamus spathaceus*), 3m (10ft), apple green leaves, makes a good screen.

ARUNDO DONAX
GIANT REED

4.8m (16ft); deciduous, giant grass; **Zone 8.5**

Characteristics A giant grass that looks very much like a bamboo, with thick vertical stems, and floppy blue-green lance-shaped leaves. The whitish yellow flower panicles of summer are not its chief beauty.
Position Despite its height the plant is wind tolerant and the leaves give a fluttering sound in the breeze. Place in full sun to half shade.
Uses Provides an excellent "tropical" background in the summer as it contrasts well with other exotic looking subjects such as the red rhubarb, *Rheum palmatum* 'Atrosanguineum', whose broad rounded leaves and foamy pink flowers look well against a tall blue-green background.
Compost Tolerates most composts provided they have adequate organic matter to retain the moisture the plant needs. It will tolerate wet soils.
Special maintenance Ensure regular watering or place the container in a shallow saucer of water. In early winter, after the first hard frosts, the plant can be cut down to ground level and stored in its container in a cool shed or garage until it shoots again in spring.
Others kinds to try 'Versicolor' ('Variegata'), leaves with broad creamy white stripes, 2.1m (7ft), slower growing than the species, therefore much more useful for containers.

Arundo 'Versicolor'

ASPARAGUS SPRENGERI
(*A. densiflorus*)
SPRENGER'S ASPARAGUS FERN

60cm (24in); evergreen trailing perennial; **Zone 9**

Characteristics This bushy and trailing foliage plant has slim somewhat wiry stems covered with very narrow bright green "leaves". Small insignificant white flowers in summer are sometimes followed by red berries.
Position Extremely hot drying winds can cause it to defoliate but new shoots will form. It prefers a well shaded place.
Uses Flowers and fruit are not reliable and it is the trailing stems with their mass of fine bright green "foliage" that is of great value in hanging baskets and windowboxes. The light texture balances such large bright heavy heads as African marigolds (*Tagetes*).
Compost Tolerates most composts.
Special maintenance Remove stems if most of the leaves have turned yellow.

ASTER AMELLUS 'KING GEORGE'
MICHAELMAS DAISY

50cm (20in); deciduous herbaceous perennial; **Zone 7**

Characteristics Clumps of round to oval rough green leaves covered in late summer and autumn with 4cm (1½in) diameter blue-violet, yellow-centred daisy flowers.
Position Flowers best in sun which is also a good position to attract butterflies.
Uses It is an outstanding autumn-flowering plant for attracting butterflies, equalled only by *Sedum spectabile*, whose fine-textured pink flowers will provide a good contrast.
Compost Happy in most composts.
Special maintenance Prevent branches of other plants from casting shadows which will deter flower-bud formation. Unlike the common Michaelmas daisy, *A. amellus* 'King George' is not susceptible to mildew.

Other kinds to try 'Violet Queen', deep violet; 'Pink Zenith', mauvy pink; *A. thomsonii* 'Nanus', dainty blue flowers, 40cm (16in), long flowering season through most of summer and autumn.

ASTILBE CHINENSIS 'PUMILA'

30cm (12in); herbaceous perennial; **Zone 7**

Characteristics The mound of attractive deeply toothed divided leaves is topped by fluffy spikes of fine raspberry red flowers in summer and early autumn.

Position Given moisture at the roots, these plants are very tolerant of a wide range of conditions, including full sun and some shade.
Uses They like wet soil and so thrive at the edge of a pool where the fine leaves and fluffy flowers look superb with the round leaves and clear-cut flowers of white waterlilies.
Compost Tolerates a range of composts but extra organic matter is very important to hold water.
Special maintenance The flowers are quite attractive even in winter when they have turned brown, so leave until snow or heavy rain breaks them down. If possible, leave plants undisturbed and top dress with well-rotted compost in spring rather than repot.
Other kinds to try 'Fanal', crimson-red, 60cm (24in); 'Sprite', shell pink, 50cm (20in); 'Irrlicht', white, 50cm (20in).

AUBRIETA DELTOIDEA
PURPLE ROCK CRESS

5cm (2in); evergreen perennial alpine; **Zone 6**

Characteristics The ground-hugging trailing stems are covered with tiny greyish green leaves. The flowers, each about 1cm (¾in) across, have four petals which are violet-blue to purple. They open in mid spring.
Position The plant will survive in cold and windy places but needs full sun to produce plenty of flowers.
Uses Forms a good short carpet beneath tiny bulbs like *Crocus chrysanthus* 'Snowbunting' or early double tulip 'Peach Blossom'. Aubrieta will also trail over the edge of the container to soften the outline.
Compost Tolerates most composts provided there is good drainage.

Special maintenance After flowering the plant can look bedraggled, therefore cut back the trailing growth and a neat cushion of new foliage will form.
Other kinds to try 'Dr Mules', semi-double, purple; 'Red Carpet', purplish red; 'Argenteo-variegata', violet-pink with white-edged leaves, slower growing.

AUCUBA JAPONICA 'PICTURATA'
SPOTTED LAUREL

1.5m (5ft); evergreen shrub; **Zone 7**

Characteristics Rounded to upright bush with thick green branches well covered with smooth shiny laurel-like leaves. This variety is relatively new but is becoming popular and deservedly so, because each leaf has a bright green margin with some yellow spotting and the centre of the leaf is a brilliant clear yellow. Some forms of this are female and if pollinated by a male plant will bear attractive clusters of shiny red fruit in winter.
Position Although very tolerant of most conditions including full sun and deep shade, extremely cold drying winds or hot dry wind will brown the leaf tips.
Uses Although hardy in most areas it is decidedly tropical in appearance and is a fine background to the brilliant red winter twigs of *Acer palmatum* 'Senkaki'. It is tolerant of atmospheric pollution.
Compost Tolerant of most composts.
Special maintenance Once the plant is mature and growth has slowed down, reduce some of the branches and feed the compost to produce the larger brilliant-coloured leaves of growth again.
Other kinds to try 'Variegata', the most common form. It has yellow-spotted leaves but there are different forms available, some better than others, some male and others female so fruiting is possible; 'Crotonifolia', heavily mottled yellow and normally male, so will not fruit.

deciduous

semi-evergreen

evergreen

flowering period

foliage/fruiting plant

full sun

¼ shade-¾ sun

½ shade-½ sun

¼ sun-¾ shade

full shade

needs winter protection

125

B

BALLOTA PSEUDODICTAMNUS
FALSE DITTANY

60cm (24in); evergreen sub-shrub; **Zone 7.5**

Characteristics Woolly grey-green rounded leaves on woolly grey upright and spreading stems form an attractive rounded shrub of soft colour and texture. In summer whorls of small pale mauve-pink flowers are produced. Each of these is backed by a grey-green rosette of sepals which persist through autumn and winter.
Position Tolerant of dry and windy places. Best in full sun as it becomes straggly in deep shade.

Uses It has a wonderful softening effect and looks good with the large shiny purplish leaves of *Bergenia* or the pink and bronze leaves of *Phormium tenax* 'Sundowner' at its base. It also associates well with fuchsias and chrysanthemums.
Compost Tolerant of most composts provided drainage is good.
Special maintenance If the plant does become thin and straggly cut back to about half its height in spring. It will reshoot to become a denser shrub.
Other kinds to try *B. acetabulosa*, similar leaves not quite so grey and with slightly crimped edges.

BEGONIA SEMPERFLORENS
FIBROUS-ROOTED BEGONIA

30cm (12in); fleshy tender evergreen grown as an annual; **Zone 10**

Characteristics Deep green glistening leaves, 8cm (3in) long, are oval to rounded and slightly cupped. Single pink flowers with rounded petals and a little ball of yellow stamens arise from each leaf axil. They will flower continuously from mid summer to late autumn if growth can continue.
Position Cold tender so avoid frost pockets, low positions where freezing air cannot drain away. Hot dry winds can turn leaves brown. Do not plant where people or animals might tread.
Uses An excellent long-flowering filler, its shiny leaves contrast well with feathery silver-leaved foliage plants such as *Senecio cineraria*.
Compost These soft succulent plants should not be allowed to dry out, so extra organic matter in the compost is important.
Special maintenance Handle with care as these plants are brittle. If need be protect with strands of cotton to keep off animals. During very dry weather water each evening.
Other kinds to try 'Olympia Red', green foliage, scarlet-red flowers, 15cm (6in); 'Olympia White', green foliage, white flowers, 15cm (6in); 'Olympia Pink', green foliage, pink flowers, 15cm (6in); 'Ambra Red', bronze foliage, vivid red flowers, 15cm (6in); 'Ambra White', bronze foliage, white flowers, 15cm (6in); 'Ambra Pink', bronze foliage, pink flowers, 15cm (6in); 'Pendula Mixed', trailing habit, pink, red and white flowers, 15cm (6in).

BEGONIA × TUBERHYBRIDA MULTIFLORA
TUBEROUS BEGONIA

30cm (12in); tender herbaceous perennial; **Zone 10**

Characteristics Triangular leaves of green, off-centred, about 15cm (6in) long, form a fairly bushy plant. Rosette-like flowers, 5cm (2in) diameter, some double some semi-double, open during summer to mid autumn. Colours vary with variety.
Position Avoid corners where the plant would be singed by drying wind. Enjoys full sun but tolerates shade.
Uses These very colourful flowers can form the main planting in a container. They can be grown from seed or tubers and look good with *Argyranthemum*.
Compost Tolerant of most composts provided organic matter is adequate to hold the necessary moisture.
Special maintenance Ensure adequate water is given; dead flowers lodged on the plant can be removed.
Other kinds to try 'Non-Stop Red', red double flowers in a long succession; also 'Non-Stop Rose', rose pink, 'Non-Stop Apricot', 'Non-Stop Yellow' and 'Non-Stop White' – all have double flowers over a long season; 'Chanson Mixed', a range of flower colours, pendulous stems up to 60cm (24in) long – superb for hanging baskets; 'Apricot Cascade', double orange-apricot flowers, pendulous habit; 'Illumination' similar but salmon-pink.

Begonia × *tuberhybrida multiflora* 'Apricot Cascade'

BELLIS PERENNIS
'RED CARPET'
DOUBLE DAISY

15cm (6in); hardy perennial herbaceous plant; **Zone 6**

Characteristics A tight rosette of rounded green leaves gives rise in spring to red double button-like flowers, 2.5cm (1in) across. Normally grown as a biennial.

Position Very tolerant of all positions from full sun to half shade.
Uses A good carpet for tulips such as the yellows 'Westpoint' and 'Golden Melody', or the white 'Kansas'.
Compost Tolerant of most composts.
Special maintenance Remove dead flowerheads, specially if container is viewed from close quarters.
Other kinds to try 'White Carpet', white, double, a good background for red and yellow tulips such as 'Colour Cardinal'; 'Pink Carpet', pink, double, a nice carpet for ruby-purple lily-flowered tulip 'Captain Fryatt' and 'White Triumphator'; 'Pomponette', a miniature at 10cm (4in) high, with numerous button-like flowers in red, pink, white or mixed colours.

BERBERIS × STENOPHYLLA 'CORALLINA COMPACTA'

30cm (12in); evergreen dwarf shrub; **Zone 5**

Characteristics A neat hump with spiny stems with tiny shiny green lance-shaped leaves. Bright orange flowers in mid to late spring.
Position Tolerant of most conditions including full sun to half shade, but in total shade will produce fewer flowers.
Uses This tough little shrub has sufficient spines to deter cats and dogs so plant to defend the corner of a trough. It does help protect small bulbs like *Iris reticulata*, crocus and snowdrops which stand out well against its dark green leaves. Later in spring its orange flowers look well with *Narcissus* 'Sweetness'.

Compost Tolerates most composts.
Special maintenance Only patience is needed, since it is slower growing than any other *Berberis*.
Other kinds to try B. × *stenophylla* 'Irwinii', about 90cm (36in), otherwise similar.

BERGENIA 'BALLAWLEY' (*Megasea* 'Ballawley')

60cm (24in); evergreen perennial; **Zone 7**

Characteristics Round-to-oval leaves up to 30cm (1ft) across and dark green but turn deep burgundy red in winter. The flowers are bright crimson-rose borne on red stems well above the foliage in early to mid spring.
Position Very tolerant of all conditions including full sun to deep shade provided drainage is reasonably good.
Uses The reddish purple leaves are an excellent background for the white flowers of snowdrops and *Helleborus niger*. Grape hyacinth (*Muscari*) flowers at the same time to give a blue contrast to the crimson-rose flowers.
Compost Most composts will suit.
Special maintenance Remove dead leaves to tidy the plant and give access to thrushes and blackbirds who will eat the snails that may be in hiding. Dead flowers can be removed too.
Other kinds to try 'Silberlicht' ('Silver Light'), flowers white with pink centre, 30cm (12in), leaves more rounded and green; *B. ciliata*, flowers white becoming pink with age, 30cm (12in), leaves purplish and hairy – these can be damaged by very hard frost but will grow again.

BETA VULGARIS CICLA SWISS CHARD (SILVER SEA KALE)

60cm (24in); biennial ornamental vegetable; **Zone 7**

Characteristics Unlike beetroot, to which it is related, this vegetable has no bulbous root; it is the large bright green puckered leaves that are eaten. Its attraction is in the broad white leaf stems and midribs which contrast so well with the leaf blades.
Position For a plant with large leaves it is surprisingly tolerant of quite windy places. It will grow in full sun or partial shade.
Uses The dramatic leaves make an excellent textural contrast with the ferny foliage of carrots. The leaves can be picked, cooked and eaten just like spinach.

Compost Very tolerant of a wide range of composts.
Special maintenance Remove any old outer leaves that become discoloured – that is if they haven't been eaten already!
Other kinds to try 'Lucullus' (rhubard chard), similar to Swiss chard but with glistening crimson-red leaf stems and veins, looks good with white-variegated hairy-leaved *Mentha rotundifolia* 'Variegata' (apple mint); *Beta vulgaris*, this is the normal beetroot worth growing for its attractive 30cm (1ft) purplish leaves; *B. vulgaris* Hortensis, there are various forms of these ornamental beets, most have deep purple leaves but the small roots are not worth eating.

BETULA PENDULA 'TRISTIS' ELEGANT WEEPING BIRCH

3m (10ft); deciduous tree; **Zone 3**

Characteristics The trunk peels to show silver-white and the sub-lateral branches weep down so that the tree is slimmer than common birch. The diamond-shaped leaves move in the slightest breeze like a mobile set with green pendants; in autumn they turn yellow.
Position Tolerant of wind; full sun or partial shade.
Uses A slim and elegant tree for a container in a narrow space. It brings not only height and movement into the area but also birds, for it is a good perching tree (occasionally used for nesting) and the finches eat the seeds.
Compost It is happy in most composts.
Special maintenance If the stem gets grubby then gently scrub with a soft brush and water. Should the tree get a little too big, prune at the earliest opportunity because finger-sized branch wounds heal quicker than bigger wounds which are more easily attacked by fungi.

Other kinds to try *B. pendula* 'Purpurea', similar but purple leaves. Much better than purple beech or plum in a small space since its small leaves allow more sun to plants below; *B. pendula* 'Dalecarlica' (*B.* 'Laciniata') (Swedish birch), deeply cut leaves, casts only the minimum of shade. In front of a window its effect is like that of a lace curtain.

 deciduous

 semi-evergreen

 evergreen

 flowering period

 foliage/fruiting plant

 full sun

 ¼ shade-¾ sun

 ½ shade-½ sun

 ¼ sun-¾ shade

 full shade

 needs winter protection

127

BIDENS FERULIFOLIA

60cm (24in); trailing annual; **Zone 9**

BOUGAINVILLEA GLABRA

2.1m (7ft); semi-evergreen woody scrambling climber; **Zone 9.5**

BRACHYCOME IBERIDIFOLIA
'TINKERBELL'
SWAN RIVER DAISY

45cm (18in); annual; **Zone 9**

BRASSICA OLERACEA
'VARIEGATA'
ORNAMENTAL CABBAGE

30cm (12in); biennial evergreen vegetable; **Zone 7**

BIDENS FERULIFOLIA

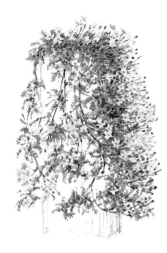

Characteristics Thin purplish stems trail and wind. The green leaves, divided into about 15 to 25 narrow leaflets, are arranged in well-spaced pairs. Yellow fine-petalled flowers are borne in open clusters at the stem ends from mid summer to mid autumn.

Position It seems to tolerate wind despite its frail appearance. It flourishes in full sun or shade.

Uses Once rare, this plant has suddenly become very popular because of the growing fashion for container gardening. Ungainly on the flat, in an elevated container it can trail its delicate stems through other plants and shower down attractively. It furnishes the container without obscuring it completely.

Compost Tolerant of most composts.

Special maintenance No special requirements.

BOUGAINVILLEA GLABRA

Characteristics Strong woody stems with a few spines scramble through shrubs or can be trained where you will. Elliptical green leaves about 5cm (2in) long. During summer and early autumn small white flowers appear, backed by clusters of purple-violet bracts, often turning the plant into a wave of colour.

Position Best against a sunny west- or south-facing wall but can be trained as a small standard weeping tree. Choose a sheltered spot out of the wind when first put out.

Uses This brilliant plant, although occasionally grown outside in protected places where winters are very mild, is normally overwintered in the house, glasshouse or shed. In late spring it can be put out against a wall on the patio.

Compost Happy in most composts but as a strong grower it will require extra feeding.

Special maintenance Before the hardest frosts start, thin out the main leaders removing older shoots that have lost vigour and any very thin growth. All side growths should then be pruned back to form a spur and by then the plant will fit easily into its winter home where it can be dried off until spring.

Other kinds to try 'Snow White', white bracts; 'Miss Manila', cerise pink bracts; 'Variegata', purple-violet bracts, creamy white-edged leaves; _B. × buttiana_ 'Mrs Butt' ('Clara Butt'), crimson-magenta bracts.

BRACHYCOME IBERIDIFOLIA

Characteristics Fine stems form a rounded open-textured bush with very thin divided leaves like green gauze. In summer it becomes covered with blue daisy flowers.

Position Full sun to light shade.

Uses They are an ideal companion for pelargoniums, with their rather heavy dense bush of rounded leaves; the light hazy quality of dainty blue Swan River daisies balances pelargoniums perfectly in texture and also provides a contrast colour not in their range.

Compost Tolerant of most composts given free drainage.

Special maintenance None.

Other kinds to try Mixtures provide both blue- and pink-flowered plants. They look good with white pelargoniums. 'Purple Splendour' has purplish-blue flowers.

BRASSICA OLERACEA 'VARIEGATA'

Characteristics The rosette of wavy edged bluish green leaves, so familiar of cabbages, have centres and veins of white or purplish pink.

Position Tolerant of wind and salt spray, full sun and light shade.

Uses In a container they look well backed by fennel or edged with parsley. In both cases they bring together bright colour and fine textural contrast. These most colourful leaves can be cooked and eaten too.

Compost Whatever compost is used good drainage and added lime will help deter club-root disease.

Special maintenance In containers with relatively few plants it is not difficult to pick off any caterpillars by hand, thus avoiding the use of chemicals. Put the caterpillars on the bird table. Remove any discoloured leaves and spray with soapy water against aphids and whitefly.

Other kinds to try _B. oleracea bullata gemmifera_ (Brussels sprouts), the type known as 'Rubine' has red-purple leaves; _B. caulorapa_ (kohlrabi), the stem is short and swollen like a turnip, easy to grow and matures in about ten weeks; _B. chinensis_ (pak choi or Chinese cabbage), similar to Swiss chard, grown like lettuce, and the leaves picked and boiled.

BROWALLIA SPECIOSA
BUSH VIOLET

30cm (12in); bushy perennial grown as an annual; **Zone 10**

Characteristics Forms a rounded bush with oval pointed green leaves. It becomes smothered in 4cm (1½in) violet-blue petunia-like flowers with white centres in mid summer to autumn if sown in spring.
Position Best in sun, but will tolerate quarter shade.
Uses A good blue filler around more upright plants in the red-purple colour range, such as *Lobelia cardinalis* and purple-leaved cannas.
Compost Tolerates most composts.

Special maintenance For continuity of flower do not let the compost dry out.
Other kinds to try 'Blue Troll', brighter blue flowers, 20cm (8in); 'White Troll', white flowers, 20cm (8in).

BUDDLEIA DAVIDII NANHOENSIS
BLUE NANHO BUDDLEIA

1.5m (5ft); deciduous shrub; **Zone 5**

Characteristics This is smaller and slower in growth than the familiar common buddleia. The leaves are more elegant at about 1.5cm (½in) wide and they tend to be a greyer green. The spikes of soft violet-blue flowers are about 12cm (5in) long and are prolific from mid summer to mid autumn.
Position Tolerates wind, full sun and partial shade.
Uses This compact buddleia is ideal for container culture because with its slimmer foliage it has lost the coarse effect of the more common kinds yet it has more flowers to attract hundreds of butterflies. It is best as the tallest plant in a group and looks well with pink flowers and silver foliage.
Compost Happy in any compost.
Special maintenance Unlike the common buddleia, this does not require hard pruning, merely thin out very old wood when it is about five years old and clip off the brown flowers if desired, although many people find them attractive.
Other kinds to try 'Petite Plum', plum purple; 'Alba', white flowers, a good background for dark butterflies; 'Dartmoor', the mauve-purple flowers branch – a new kind with more flowers than any other; *B. crispa*, light lilac flowers and broader silver grey leaves; *B. colvilei* 'Kewensis', crimson, stronger growing so train as a standard to show off drooping grape-like flower clusters to advantage, Zone 8; *B. asiatica*, slim white cowslip-scented flowers in mid spring makes an elegant weeping evergreen tree in warmer places.

BUXUS SEMPERVIRENS
'SUFFRUTICOSA'
DWARF BOX

30cm (12in); evergreen shrub; **Zone 6**

Characteristics A dense rounded shrublet with oval to round slightly cupped bright green leaves, 1cm (½in) across. The flowers are insignificant.
Position Tolerant of wind, full sun and light shade but not dense shade.
Uses A good clipped evergreen for edging. Particularly useful as a permanent green frame for an ever-changing pattern within, such as a group of vegetables to be removed in succession for the table.
Compost Tolerant of most composts provided drainage is adequate.
Special maintenance Clip to shape twice a year; this means only the minimum amount of material is removed – less shock to the plant than an annual clip – and a better appearance. Make absolutely sure that there are no weeds in among the plants or in the compost before planting. With the dense foliage weeds are difficult to remove later.

Buxus sempervirens

Other kinds to try *B. sempervirens*, the common box, 1.5m (5ft) with faster growth to clip balls, pyramids or what you will; *B. sempervirens* 'Elegantissima' ('Variegata'), similar but narrower, creamy white-edged leaves and grows more slowly. Looks nice either clipped or growing free.

CALCEOLARIA
'SUNSHINE'
SLIPPER FLOWER

25cm (10in); tender perennial grown as an annual; **Zone 10**

Characteristics Oval mid green leaves have a matt surface. The flowers, which appear in late spring to mid autumn, are clusters of inflated pouches, rounded and bright yellow.
Position Full sun to half shade.
Uses With their even height, dense growth and good flower cover they make good filling or carpeting plants between others of more erect habit and trailing edging plants. In a dull corner the bright yellow flowers bring warmth and light.
Compost Tolerant of most composts.
Special maintenance Remove dead flower clusters to encourage more flowers.
Other kinds to try *C. integrifolia*, 60cm (24in), evergreen upright sub-shrub with yellow flowers in summer, elliptic leaves give a lighter texture. The plant has a better chance of surviving the winter, Zone 8; *C.* 'Kentish Hero', similar but rusty red blooms; *C. herbechybrida*, 30cm (12in), mixed colours, usually grown as a pot plant.

Calceolaria integrifolia

---

deciduous

semi-evergreen

evergreen

flowering period

foliage/fruiting plant

full sun

¼ shade-¾ sun

½ shade-½ sun

¼ sun-¾ shade

full shade

needs winter protection

129

CALENDULA OFFICINALIS
'FIESTA GITANA'
POT MARIGOLD

30cm (12in); bushy annual;
Zone 7.5

Characteristics Neat dwarf plants with oval to lance-shaped light to mid-green leaves. They are also strongly aromatic. The double flowers are a tight rosette of many petals in a colour range from cream to orange. The Latin name *Calendula* means "throughout the months" and it is long flowering from late spring to late autumn.

Position Tolerant of most conditions, but best in sun; full sun to half shade.
Uses The neat habit and long flowering season make it a good container plant. It is used in the treatment of ulcers, for dyes and in salads, where the petals give colour and the leaves impart flavour.
Compost Tolerates any compost.
Special maintenance Since the dead flower petals fall naturally there is no need to deadhead except to prevent self-sown seedlings.
Other kinds to try 'Art Shades Mixed', 60cm (24in), this taller kind is useful for cutting and flower arrangements, flowers double apricot, orange and cream; 'Geisha Girl', 60cm (2ft), 'double deep orange flowers.

CALLICARPA BODINIERI GIRALDII
BEAUTY FRUIT

1.5m (5ft); deciduous shrub;
Zone 7.5

Characteristics Upright bushy shrub with relatively thin branches. Elliptic leaves of soft mid green. The summer flowers are lilac but tiny and not of much consequence compared with the dense clusters of round violet fruits in autumn, winter and even persisting until early spring.
Position A windy site should be avoided if pollination and maximum fruiting is to be achieved. It enjoys a sunny spot.
Uses When the leaves have fallen and the fruit can be seen against the silver grey leaves of *Santolina neapolitana* or *Senecio* 'Sunshine', it looks like tiny amethysts set in a silver bed. The enjoyment is prolonged because the birds leave these berries until last.
Compost Tolerant of most composts.

Special maintenance Do not overfeed or foliage will grow at the expense of fruit production. Hard pruning will also deter fruiting.
Other kinds to try *C. japonica* 'Leucocarpa', white fruits which look nice in combination with the violet fruits of *C. bodinieri giraldii*.

CALLISTEMON RIGIDUS
BOTTLEBRUSH

1.5m (5ft); evergreen shrub; **Zone 8**

Characteristics Upright branches come down at the tips and since the deep green leaves are narrow and pointed it gives the effect of a light-textured shrub willow. The flowers completely surround the stem with a tuft of leaves at the top. When they open early in summer they reveal masses of scarlet stamens. A unique flower like a brush for cleaning out bottles, hence the common name. In addition, after flowering the woody fruits, which last for about a year, are also attractive.
Position Best against a south- or west-facing wall.
Uses Ideal for fanning out against a wall since it is interesting in foliage and fruit even when not in flower.
Compost Tolerant of most composts.
Special maintenance After about five years some thinning may be required.
Other kinds to try *C. pallidus*, similar to above but foliage is pink-tinged in spring and the flowers are creamy yellow; *C. citrinus*, lemon-scented leaves, red flowers.

Callistemon citrinus

CALLISTEPHUS CHINENSIS
'MILADY BLUE'
CHINESE ASTER

30cm (12in); annual; **Zone 10**

Characteristics Erect bushy growth with oval toothed green leaves giving a pleasant somewhat fluffy effect. The flowers are fully double packed with numerous narrow petals. They are purplish blue and are effective from mid summer to early autumn.
Position Needs a sunny site or flowering is affected and shelter from too much wind.
Uses An excellent main bedding or carpeting plant.
Compost Tolerant of most composts.
Special maintenance Removal of dead flowerheads helps to prolong the flowering period.
Other kinds to try 'Milady Pink', the same as above except in colour; Milady Series is also available in mixed colours; 'Pepite Mixed', 30cm (12in), single flowers in mixed colours, very weather resistant; 'Teisa Stars Mixed', 25cm (10in), double quill-petalled flowers; 'Powder Puff Mixed', 60cm (24in), fully double flowers, plants resistant to wilt disease; 'Andrella Mixed' 60cm (2ft), these more open plants will rise up above lower carpeting kinds, star-like single flowers in crimson, pink, white, blue and lavender; 'Duchess Yellow' 45cm (18in), unusual for its yellow, fully double incurving blooms.

CALLUNA VULGARIS
'ROBERT CHAPMAN'
SCOTCH HEATHER

45cm (18in); evergreen shrublet; **Zone 5**

Characteristics Dense spreading branchlets are clothed with minute leaves giving a feathery appearance. In this particular kind they are golden bronze and in winter, on the sunny side of the plant, they become tinted with red. The summer flowers are individually small but densely clustered on the upper stems to create spikes of purply pink.

Position Extremely tough in the face of cold and wind, but sun is required to get good foliage colour.
Uses Effective throughout the year as a ground cover between upright plants with larger flowers such as *Camellia × williamsii* 'St Ewe'.
Compost Acid (lime-free) compost is essential.
Special maintenance After flowering the brown spikes can be cut off with shears; this helps to create denser and therefore more colourful foliage next year. However, some people like the brown spikes and will leave clipping until the spring.
Other kinds to try 'Golden Carpet', 5cm (2in), yellowish gold foliage, spreading habit, light purple flowers, slow growing; 'Sister Anne', 10cm (4in), silvery foliage and an abundance of pinky mauve flowers form a good low carpet.

CAMELLIA RETICULATA
'BUTTERFLY WINGS'
('Houye Diechi')

1.2m (4ft); evergreen shrub; **Zone 9**

Characteristics Slender stems have oval pointed leaves about 8cm (3in) long. The effect is lighter than with *C. japonica* hybrids, as the branching is less dense. The green leaves are net veined which give a matt texture. Flowers open in spring to reveal huge yet delicate wavy edged petals rose-pink in colour. 'Butterfly Wings' is semi-double and has yellow stamens in the middle of its gigantic flowers which can be up to 10cm (4in) across.
Position The ideal spot is a south-west-facing corner between walls (north-east facing in the southern hemisphere) in dappled shade. It is such an outstanding plant that it is worth overwintering in a greenhouse or by a window in a shed or garage.
Uses In a sheltered spot it is excellent for clothing a wall with its evergreen foliage. The flowers are a showstopper.
Compost This should be acid and contain plenty of organic matter.
Special maintenance Remove the dead flowers if they do not fall off naturally.
Other kinds to try *C. reticulata* 'Zaotaohung' ('Early Crimson'), double crimson; *C. × williamsii* 'St Ewe' (Zone 7), a much hardier yet equally elegant shrub with a long succession of single rose-coloured flowers with golden stamens opening late winter to early summer; *C. × williamsii* 'Donation', as above but double pink; *C. japonica* 'Margaret Davis', white flowers pink-edged, dense shiny foliage; *C. × 'Inspiration'*, double pink, net veined leaves, upright.

Camellia reticulata 'Zaotaohung'

CAMPANULA ISOPHYLLA
BELLFLOWER

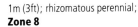

10cm (4in); perennial trailer, can grow as an annual; **Zone 8**

Characteristics Heart-shaped soft green leaves, 1cm (½in) across, are held on spreading and trailing stems. Open star-shaped bellflowers in sky blue are 2.5cm (1in) across and cover the plant. The attractive flowers open mid summer to early autumn.
Position Full sun to half shade; avoid a windy corner or the trailing stems will be blown off.
Uses An outstanding hanging basket or windowbox plant because of its trailing stems and the cooling effect of its blue flowers in a hot summer.
Compost Tolerant of most composts.
Special maintenance Remove any trails if they do get broken or turn yellow.
Other kinds to try *C. isophylla* var. *alba*, white flowers mix well with the blue; *C. muralis* (*C. portenschlagiana*), hardy evergreen alpine, 15cm (6in), dense cover of violet bells in summer, Zone 7; *C. carpatica*, hardy alpine, 8cm (3in), spreading plant with tiny leaves and star-shaped flowers in sky blue or white in summer, Zone 6; *C. medium* (Canterbury bell), erect biennial up to 1m (36in). The familiar cup-and-saucer flowers all the way up the spike can be blue, lilac, pink or white, ideal for cottage garden effect in late spring to early summer, Zone 7.

CANNA × GENERALIS
INDIAN SHOT

1m (3ft); rhizomatous perennial; **Zone 8**

Characteristics From the underground rhizome sturdy shoots arise with upright lance-shaped leaves, about 15cm (6in) wide and 45cm (18in) long. Held well above the leaves in mid to late summer is a spike of flowers each with three large petals and a lower lip. The plants can be bought when they are dormant from bulb firms and in larger garden centres. They are mostly mixed, occasionally separate kinds. The leaves range from deep purple to copper and green, and the flowers from crimson to orange and yellow.
Position Happy in most places except very windy sites where the leaves might get torn; full sun to partial shade.
Uses The broad bold leaves look well spurting from amongst fine-cut foliage and light-coloured flowers such as those of *Argyranthemum*, *Bidens* and *Verbena*. Alternatively, create a tropical effect with other bright-coloured foliage plants.
Compost Tolerates most composts but adequate organic matter can hold the reserve of water needed for quick growth in late spring.

Special maintenance In winter dig up the rhizomes and store in a frost free shed in boxes of sandy compost or peat. This should be slightly moist to keep them from shrinking. In Zone 8 or above a 5cm (2in) mulch of pulverized bark or similar material will protect plants left outside.

 deciduous

 semi-evergreen

 evergreen

 flowering period

 foliage/fruiting plant

 full sun

 ¼ shade-¾ sun

 ½ shade-½ sun

 ¼ sun-¾ shade

 full shade

 needs winter protection

131

CAPSICUM ANNUUM
'REDSKIN'
RED PEPPER (CHILLI PEPPER)

35cm (14in); annual branching fruit; **Zone 10**

Characteristics Branching green stems have shiny mid green oval pointed leaves. In the leaf axil small white flowers appear throughout summer, and from these develop the fruits. The fruits are green at first but turn yellow, then orange and finally deep red.

Position A sheltered warm area is needed in full sun to light shade.

Uses Primarily as an ingredient for salads it is also very attractive as a container plant on the patio.

Compost Most composts are suitable provided they are enriched.

Special maintenance Ensure the plants are well watered.

Other kinds to try 'Yellow Lantern', four-lobed fruit, golden yellow; 'Midnight Beauty', fairly round fruit, deep purple-red; 'Apache', many slim red fruits.

CAREX OSHIMENSIS
'EVERGOLD'
(*C. morrowii* 'Evergold')

20cm (8in); evergreen perennial sedge; **Zone 7**

Characteristics A tight tuft with delicate drooping thin leaves, green striped yellow. Upright triangular stems carry uninteresting brown flowers in summer.

Position Very wind tolerant; full sun to partial shade.

Uses An excellent hardy fine-textured edging for a trough, sink or windowbox; looks good with *Bergenia* 'Ballawley' and heathers.

Compost Grows in most composts provided they have adequate organic matter and are not allowed to dry out.

Special maintenance No special treatement apart from pulling out any noticeable dead leaves.

Other kinds to try *C. elata* 'Aurea' (*C. stricta* 'Aurea'), 40cm (16in) high golden leaves that make a good background for the dark brown flower spikes. An excellent golden tuft for brightening up dull winter spots; *C. buchananii*, 45cm (18in), coppery red leaves, looks good alongside *Euonymus fortunei* 'Emerald 'n' Gold'.

CASSIA CORYMBOSA

1.5m (5ft); evergreen shrub; **Zone 8**

Characteristics Smooth green stems have leaves with four to six bright green oval leaflets. In summer and spasmodically at other times of the year to late autumn sprays of rich yellow round-petalled flowers appear.

Position Best trained against a south- or west-facing wall which will give protection.

Uses A brilliant background shrub for training against a warm wall, looks superb with the sky blue *Plumbago capensis*.

Compost Tolerates most composts.

Special maintenance A mulch of straw or bracken 15cm (6in) thick pinned around the base with three to five short bamboo canes will ensure the plant's survival even in hard winters. Even if it dies back it will regrow from the protected branches. Remove the mulch in spring.

Other kinds to try *C. corymbosa plurijuga*, larger clusters of flowers but not quite so hardy as the species, Zone 9.

CASSIOPE
× 'EDINBURGH'

20cm (8in); dwarf evergreen shrub; **Zone 3**

Characteristics Upright stems have minute leaves pressed to them so that the plant appears like a mass of vertical dark green stems. In spring numerous small white bell-shaped flowers emerge from the upper parts of the stems. Flowering continues to mid summer.

Position At the front where its dainty beauty can be appreciated, whether it be in a windowbox or trough; sun to partial shade.

Uses Associates well with its relations the heathers. It provides a succession, flowering as it does after *Erica carnea* and before *Calluna vulgaris*.

Compost Must have acid (lime-free) compost.

Special maintenance Keep compost moist in summer drought.

Other kinds to try 'Muirhead', similar to above but the tiny sepals are reddish and contrast with the white bells.

CEANOTHUS THYRSIFLORUS VAR. REPENS
CALIFORNIAN LILAC

60cm (24in); low evergreen shrub; **Zone 7.5**

Characteristics The spreading green stems are covered with shiny 1–2cm (½in) oval green leaves. Tight racemes of light to mid blue powder-puff flowers cover the plant in late spring.
Position Flowers best in sun, but tolerates some shade.
Uses An excellent ground cover plant, its green carpet looks good throughout the year. It will trail over the edge of a container if allowed and with help can be trained up a wall. It provides an excellent background for white *Argyranthemum*.

Compost Any compost provided drainage is good.
Special maintenance Will look after itself unless trained up a wall when a little tying is needed.
Other kinds to try *C.* 'Puget Blue', 1.5m (5ft), more upright shrub, tiny deep-veined leaves are attractive, bright dark blue flowers, Zone 8; *C.* 'Autumnal Blue', 2m (7ft), upright shrub, leaves 3cm (2in) long. Light blue flowers from late spring to mid autumn give a continuous succession of flowers, although not a complete cover. It can be grown as a small container tree, Zone 7.5; *C.* 'Trewithen Blue', 3m (10ft), really a tree, 5cm (2in) leaves, flowers from early to late spring. The only spring-flowering evergreen tree, Zone 8.

CELOSIA PLUMOSA 'CENTURY MIXED'
PRINCE OF WALES FEATHERS

40cm (16in); tender perennial grown as an annual; **Zone 10**

Characteristics An upright bush with oval pointed green leaves. Conical feathery plume-like flowers emerge from the top and leaf axils in summer and autumn. They are bright yellow and fiery red in this mixture.
Position Flower plumes may be sparse in shade so choose a position in full sun.

Uses It is most useful as a fiery plume licking up amongst lower carpeting plants. It is also good as a replacement when early summer flowers tail off; a few plants of *Celosia* will bring back brightness.
Compost Tolerates most composts.
Special maintenance When plumes eventually discolour they can be removed, which encourages further lateral flowers to develop.
Other kinds to try 'Apricot Brandy', 40cm (16in), apricot orange plumes, good if you do not want mixed colours; 'Red Glitters', 15cm (6in), compact rounded growth, intense red plumes make it better for windowboxes; 'Fairy Fountains', 25cm (10in), mixed colours.

CHAMAECYPARIS OBTUSA 'CRIPPSII'
GOLDEN HINOKI CYPRESS

1m (3¼ft); evergreen conifer; **Zone 6**

Characteristics The overall shape is widely conical but with open flattened undulating sprays of tiny golden scale-like leaves.
Position Very tolerant; full sun to partial shade.
Uses A bright background for winter in association with winter-flowering heathers. A young specimen will easily make a bonsai with a little pruning and training. In a suitable container it will then give an oriental effect.
Compost Tolerant of most composts.
Special maintenance Remove thin lower branches when the foliage browns. Train as required.

Other kinds to try *C. obtusa*, the dark green equivalent, slightly stronger growing; *C. obtusa* 'Tetragona Aurea', bright light yellow foliage, slower growing; *C. obtusa* 'Nana Aurea', 90cm (36in), golden leaves; *C. lawsoniana* 'Ellwood's Gold', erect growth grey-green suffused with gold, medium spread, 1.5m (5ft); *C. lawsoniana* 'Ellwoodii', similar to 'Ellwood's Gold' but light grey-green; *C. lawsoniana* 'Green Pillar', erect growth, bright green foliage, 2.1m (7ft); *C. pisifera* 'Boulevard', silver-blue foliage, horizontal side branches give an irregular feathery outline; *C. pisifera* 'Aurea Nana', green, globular, slow growing to 25cm (10in).

CHAMAEROPS HUMILIS
DWARF FAN PALM

1.2m (4ft); evergreen palm; **Zone 9**

Characteristics Fan-shaped leaves 60cm (24in) across on the end of 60cm (24in) long leaf stems. The summer flowers are yellow and tiny, and not a main feature of the plant. This is a very variable plant; some have several trunks which make them shorter and wider, others have one trunk.
Position A sunny patio is ideal, although this palm will tolerate some shade and wind.
Uses A most useful plant for achieving a tropical or Mediterranean effect. In cooler zones it is probably best to have one palm in a container perhaps with a small trailer like *Tradescantia fluminensis* 'Albovittata' around its base. This attractive combination is then worthy for taking into the house during the winter.
Compost Tolerant of most composts.
Special maintenance Remove any old dead leaves with secateurs. Bring plant into the house, or a garage or shed with a window, during winter. Alternatively a 20cm (8in) mulch of straw or bracken placed around the base in early winter will save the crown if a hard winter kills back the top of a permanently planted specimen.
Other kinds to try 'Silver Sheen', uncommon but may become available, the silver hairs over the leaves give the plant a very light effect.

 deciduous

 semi-evergreen

 evergreen

 flowering period

 foliage/fruiting plant

 full sun

 ¼ shade-¾ sun

 ½ shade-½ sun

 ¼ sun-¾ shade

 full shade

 needs winter protection

133

CHEIRANTHUS CHEIRI
'ORANGE BEDDER'
WALLFLOWER

30cm (12in); perennial grown as a biennial; **Zone 7**

Characteristics A bushy plant with evergreen narrow bright green leaves. In spring the plant is covered with flowers, each one having four broad petals of a soft orange-bronze. The scent is delicious and attracts any early butterflies that may be around.

Position They are wind tolerant; and enjoy full sun or light shade.

Uses Wallflowers are the major filler or carpeting plant for mid spring and yellow tulips, with their big rounded flowers on straight stems, look well emerging from orange wallflowers. Two different kinds of tulip will give either more colour or provide a succession of flowers. An attractive alternative would be to mix wallflower 'Carmine King' with blue forget-me-nots with white tulip 'Alabaster' growing through.

Compost Tolerant of most composts but adequate lime is needed to deter club-root fungus.

Special maintenance Check the plants after very windy wet weather as they may need firming in.

Other kinds to try For container planting those of modest height have the best proportions. These are known as the Bedder Series; colours available are 'Golden', 'Orange', 'Scarlet', 'Primrose' and 'Mixed', all 30cm (12in) high. Other kinds are 'Ivory White', creamy white, 'Ruby Gem', ruby-purple; 'Carmine King', carmine pink – all 38cm (15in); C. 'Bowles Mauve' (*Erysimum* 'Bowles Mauve), a woody perennial, Zone 8, 60cm (24in) high with grey-green leaves. Although it flowers from mid spring to mid summer and more it is a shrub rather than a bedding plant.

CHLOROPHYTUM COMOSUM
'VITTATUM'
SPIDER PLANT

30cm (12in); evergreen tufted perennial; **Zone 10**

Characteristics this looks like a tufted grass with leaves up to 25cm (1in) wide. These are bright green and in this kind the centre has a broad cream stripe sometimes with a few green stripes running through it. Slim yellow stalks spray out from the centre of the plant terminating in small white star-shaped flowers, often followed by little plantlets whose weight cause the stalks to bend down like shooting stars.

Position Strong drying winds should be avoided, but they are very tolerant of different light conditions – from full sun to full shade.

Uses These plants, although common, can make an unusual edging to a trough or windowbox. They will shower over the edge of a windowbox as they mature in a way no other plant can.

Compost Happy in most composts.

Special maintenance Remove any leaves that turn brown.

Other kinds to try 'Variegatum' although sometimes confused with the above, is quite distinct. It has cream edges to the leaves and will also grow taller, 45cm (18in).

CHOISYA TERNATA
MEXICAN ORANGE BLOSSOM

1.5m (5ft); evergreen rounded shrub; **Zone 7.5**

Characteristics Smooth green stems are well furnished with shiny green aromatic leaves, each one divided into three oval leaflets. Clusters of scented white fine-petalled flowers appear in late spring and these often continue on and off until autumn.

Position Freezing strong winds, specially in spring when young leaves are soft, can singe foliage. Otherwise very easy going and tolerant of full sun and full shade.

Uses A good background for all plants and it can be pruned to various shapes. Since it has scent similar to orange blossom it is appropriate to plant it as an individual subject in a container.

Compost Tolerant of most composts.

Special maintenance Prune to whatever shape is required and remove any brown leaves or shoots.

Other kinds to try 'Sundance', yellow leaves create a warm light background in a dreary and shady place.

CHRYSANTHEMUM RUBELLUM
'CLARA CURTIS'

60cm (24in); hardy perennial; **Zone 7.5**

Characteristics This is the toughest of the common chrysanthemums. It has vertical stems and the lobed leaves are similar to those of an oak. In late summer and autumn yellow-centred pink daisy-like flowers give a succession of colour, each one being about 5cm (2in) across.

Position Those listed have individual flowers of moderate size, so this together with their lower height makes them resistant to all but the most violent winds. Since flower buds will have been initiated before planting out in late summer, they will flower in all sites – full sun to full shade.

Uses When summer flowers are over these tough chrysanthemums are the colour backbone for autumn, bringing brightness to upright conifers and green ivies that edge and trail down over containers.

Compost Happy in most composts.

Special maintenance Remove any dead flowers.

Other kinds to try This is a range of the shortest, toughest and most floriferous chrysanthemums: 'Wendy Baker', creamy white, single, 45cm (18in); 'Lemon Blanket', yellow, double, cushion shape, 30cm (12in); 'Moonlight', soft yellow, double, very weather resistant, 60cm (24in); 'Sheila', bronze, single, spoon-petalled, very late flowers, 45cm (18in); 'Brightness', bright red, semi-double, very compact, 30cm (12in); 'Moira', chestnut-red, single, 45cm (18in); 'Brown Eyes', two-tone brown, pompon, 45cm (18in); 'Irene', soft pink, single, spoon-petalled, 45cm (18in); 'Grandchild', lilac-mauve, double, very compact, 30cm (12in); 'Ruby Mound', ruby-purple, double, 45cm (18in); 'Pink Progression', 90cm (36in), single pale pink flowers; 'Innocence', 90cm (36in), single, white-edged pink; 'Anastasia', 70cm (28in), double, light purple; 'Emperor of China', 120cm (4ft), late silvery rose-pink flowers backed with crimson-tinted autumn foliage, ideal for troughs and urns.

CISTUS × AGUILARI 'MACULATUS'
SUN ROSE

90cm (36in); evergreen shrub; **Zone 7.5**

Characteristics Upright bushy habit densely covered with narrow lance-shaped mid green sticky leaves. The 4cm (1½in) wide flowers, rather poppy-like in the way they unfold, are produced throughout the summer. They are brilliant white with a conspicuous purple crimson blotch on each petal and a central boss of golden yellow stamens.

Position Avoid freezing winter gales; best in full sun.
Uses An excellent background evergreen for a sunny spot. The large white flowers are a perfect foil for fine hazy-textured verbenas in a trough or raised bed. Good as a single plant in a tub.
Compost Tolerates most composts but good drainage is essential.
Special maintenance If necessary shape and prune growth when shoots are still small after flowering.
Other kinds to try C. ladanifer, similar to above with leaves darker green and very sticky, growth a little more open, Zone 7.5; C. laurifolius, 1.5m (5ft), dark green broadly oval leaves, 6cm (2¼in), similar to those of laurel. White flowers with golden blotch, the hardiest kind, Zone 7; C. 'Peggy Sammons', 90cm (36in), grey-green leaves, flowers pale pink, Zone 8; C. 'Silver Pink', 60cm (24in), clear pink flowers with yellow stamens, Zone 8.

CITRUS LIMON
LEMON

1.2m (4ft); evergreen bushy shrub; **Zone 9.5**

Characteristics Upright rounded bush of irregular outline covered in oval glossy bright green leaves with a few thorns on the stems. White flowers of modest size but wonderfully scented and appearing on and off throughout the year. Some of these will be pollinated and the typical lemon fruit will result. These will remain on the plant for many months and are a major attraction.
Position Growth is best in a warm sunny spot, although it can tolerate shade.
Uses As an individual plant in a tub it is ideal for the patio. Cut lemon slices straight from the tree for a cocktail! The scent epitomizes the feeling of holidays spent in warm sunny climates.
Compost Will tolerate most composts, but extra feeding will encourage fruit production.

Special maintenance A regular spray of clear or soapy water will deter red spider mite. The plant will stand some frost so can be taken into a garage or shed with a window for the winter.
Other kinds to try
× Citrofortunella mitis, the calamodin, is related but is more decorative with lots of tiny tangerine fruits.

CLEMATIS ARMANDII

3m (10ft); strong evergreen climbing shrub; **Zone 7.5**

Characteristics The evergreen leaves have three lance-shaped leaflets each about 10cm (4in) long; they are a glossy mid to dark green but when young are an attractive coppery colour. The leaf stem twists around nearby objects and by this means the plant climbs. The flowers are 6cm (2¼in) wide clusters of white-petalled florets with cream centres in spring.
Position Avoid exposure to strong wind. Very light tolerant; from full sun to full shade.
Uses Excellent for training on a trellis or wall behind a trough or raised bed.
Compost Tolerant of most composts including those containing lime.
Special maintenance This is mainly training and involves tying in the flexible stems.
Other kinds to try C. montana, an even stronger-growing deciduous climber for covering a very large fence or building, white flowers in profusion late spring; C. cirrhosa var. balearica, 2.1m (7ft), evergreen with delightful divided ferny foliage. Bell-like flowers are cream with purple spots produced prolifically in mid winter to mid spring. Superb for an arch between two containers; C. alpina, 1.2m (4ft), small deciduous climber, delicate blue bells in mid to late spring; C. 'Jackmanii × Superba', 3 m (10ft), violet purple in midsummer to autumn.

deciduous

semi-evergreen

evergreen

flowering period

foliage/fruiting plant

full sun

¼ shade-¾ sun

½ shade-½ sun

¼ sun-¾ shade

full shade

needs winter protection

CLIANTHUS PUNICEUS
LOBSTER CLAW

2.1m (7ft); evergreen scrambling climber; **Zone 8**

Characteristics Green scrambling stems covered with green leaves about 10cm (4in) long which have about 15 bright green elliptical leaflets. In late spring to mid summer short stems hang down and on these are suspended clusters of soft red-crimson flowers, each one about 9cm (3½in) long and looking like a lobster claw.

Position A sheltered position against a south or west wall in full sun or partial shade.

Uses A good background evergreen for training against a wall. Dramatic flowers quite unlike any others. This outstandingly beautiful plant will be a talking point in any garden.

Compost Tolerant of most composts, occasional feeds of nitrogen, such as dried blood, will maintain healthy growth.

Special maintenance Train as required, remove old stems as they die back. In early winter mulch round stem of plant to a depth of 10cm (4in) with straw or similar material to protect stem base from severe frosts.

Other kinds to try *C.p. albus*, white, looks good intertwined with red; 'White Heron', slightly larger white flowers; 'Red Cardinal', scarlet-crimson'; 'Flamingo', soft pink.

COLEUS BLUMEI
'BRIGHTNESS'

45cm (18in); tender bushy perennial grown as an annual; **Zone 10**

Characteristics Upright to rounded bush with dense foliage, the leaves are 6cm (2½in) long, oval with pointed tips. The short spikes of blue flowers are of little importance compared with the brilliant coloured leaves. Most seed types come as a mixture of brilliant colours; for a specific colour scheme it may be best to grow the plants from cuttings. The plant illustrated has rusty red leaves with a lime green serrated pattern around the edge.

Position Avoid very windy places or the leaves will be damaged. They thrive in full sun or partial shade.

Uses For brilliant foliage colour few plants can outdo coleus, but in a container try to balance them with, for example, an edging of white alyssum or a few silver-leaved plants such as *Helichrysum petiolare* springing from the centre.

Compost Grows well in most composts provided there is adequate organic matter so the plants do not dry out completely.

Special maintenance Pick off the flower spikes when they first appear so the vigour goes into leaf production.

Other kinds to try 'Rainbow Mixed', 45cm (18in), wide range of colours; 'Fashion Parade', 30cm (12in), wide range of colours; 'Milky Way', 15cm (6in), wide range of colours, deeply cut foliage gives a fine-textured dwarf carpet; 'Scarlet Poncho', 25cm (10in), rich red with gold edge similar to 'Brightness' but with cascading stems. Ideal for hanging baskets.

CONVALLARIA MAJALIS
LILY OF THE VALLEY

15cm (6in); spreading herbaceous perennial; **Zone 3**

Characteristics Dark green oval pointed leaves about 10cm (4in) long. The plant spreads slowly to form a green summer carpet. In spring wine red stems with a curved tip arise bearing very fragrant pendulous white bell-like flowers.

Position This plant is amazingly shade tolerant and will grow at the base of shrubs.

Uses The oustanding scent makes this a worthy plant. It is easily accommodated in a trough or barrel since plants for summer effect can be planted nearby as shade is not a problem.

Compost Happy in most composts provided there is adequate organic matter.

Special maintenance The plants are best left undisturbed so that in a good position, around the base of shrubby subjects, even the dying leaves need not be removed.

Other kinds to try 'Flore Pleno', double flowers; 'Fortin's Giant', 45cm (18in), flowers a little earlier than the species.

CONVOLVULUS MAURITANICUS
(C. sabatius)

15cm (6in); trailing perennial; **Zone 8**

Characteristics Slender stems trail along the ground or over the edge of a container. The oval leaves are soft green and about 1cm (½in) long. In summer and early autumn circular trumpet-shaped flowers unfold almost like an umbrella. They are about 2cm (1in) across and a beautiful mid violet-blue.

Position A sunny spot normally results in plants with shorter joints and more flowers.

Uses A superb trailer for a hanging basket or windowbox and planted with pink verbenas and silver-leaved helichrysum, a most delicate yet colourful effect can be achieved.

Compost Provided there is adequate drainage it will grow in most composts.

Special maintenance Protect the crowns of permanent plants with an extra 2cm (1in) layer of compost applied in early winter.

Other kinds to try *C. althaeoides*, pink trumpet-shaped flowers. The leaves vary even on the same plant and they can be very deeply lobed, otherwise very similar to the above; *C. cneorum*, 50cm (20in), rounded dense evergreen shrub with narrow silver leaves of silky texture. Pink-tinged buds unfurl to white circular trumpet-like flowers. A superb shrub for a sunny spot.

COPROSMA × KIRKII 'VARIEGATA'

30cm (12in); evergreen prostrate shrub; **Zone 8.5**

Characteristics Branching prostrate growth bears 2cm (³⁄₄in) long narrow leaves with rounded tips which are green with a white edge. The flowers are insignificant but if plants of both sexes are grown, tiny white fruits can appear on the females in autumn.

Position Tolerant of salty winds and a wide range of light conditions from full sun to full shade.

Uses A useful shade tolerant ground cover plant providing a good carpet with a fringe spilling over the edge of the pot. Plant around the base of lemon bushes, daturas and bougainvilleas, all of which are taken inside for the winter. In mild areas it will form a good permanent ground cover for troughs.

Compost Tolerant of most composts.

Special maintenance In cooler areas a mulch of pulverized bark will give winter protection.

Other kinds to try C. repens 'Picturata', 1.2m (4ft), upright shrub, bright green rounded leaves with brilliant yellow centres. Good for training against a wall, Zone 9.

CORDYLINE AUSTRALIS
NEW ZEALAND LILY PALM, TORBAY PALM

1.8m (6ft); evergreen upright tree; **Zone 8.5**

Characteristics It looks like a green shooting star when young. As it matures the slim hairy trunk topped by a cluster of dark green, smooth, narrow leaves 30–90cm (12–36in) long, resembles a palm tree. After ten years or more it may produce a 90cm (36in) diameter cloud of tiny white scented flowers in summer and autumn.

Position Tolerant of strong winds and salt spray.

Uses In an urn with trailing plants it forms a good structural high point and forms a striking silhouette against the sky. When it reaches 1.8m (6ft) high the trunk becomes bare and the plant will give a tropical island effect to a patio or poolside and even provide a small area of shade.

Compost Tolerates most composts, but a loam-based type gives weight to the container that will reduce the chances of it being blown over.

Special maintenance Dead leaves can be cut off to give a tidy trunk. In Zone 8 or less it is wise to wrap around the trunk before winter sets in to prevent hard frosts causing trunk rupture. Plastic foam pipe lagging is a neat way to do this.

Other kinds to try C. australis purpurea, leaves coppery purple, good contrast with grey Eucalyptus; C. australis 'Albertii' white-edged, pink-veined leaves effective anywhere; C. australis 'Variegata', white-edged leaves make a good contrast with dark background; C. banksii 'Purpurea', very shiny, dark violet-purple leaves.

CORONILLA GLAUCA

75cm (30in); evergreen shrub; **Zone 7.5**

Characteristics A loosely rounded shrub with soft smooth grey-green evergreen leaves which are subdivided into five or so oval to round leaflets, each one being about 12mm (½in) long. As the botanical name suggests there is a coronet of brilliant yellow pea-like flowers. The scent is strong; indeed too heavy for some noses. The main flowering season is mid spring to mid summer, but hardly a month goes by without a few blooms.

Position Tolerates wind but needs full sun to flower well.

Uses Pleasant to look at all through the year, this adaptable plant can be trained up a wall, kept to a rounded bush or allowed to trail down over the edge of a large trough or windowbox. It is a good partner for Rosmarinus officinalis 'Severn Sea', which flowers throughout the year too, and contrasts with its blue flowers and finer dark green foliage.

Compost Tolerant of most composts provided drainage is good.

Special maintenance None, apart from a little pruning to form a particular shape.

Other kinds to try 'Variegata', as above but each leaflet is thinner and edged with creamy white which gives a daintier effect. Watch for all-green shoots and remove these or the plant will revert back to plain C. glauca.

CORTADERIA SELLOANA 'PUMILA'
DWARF PAMPAS GRASS

1.2m (4ft); evergreen clump-forming perennial grass; **Zone 7**

Characteristics The dense tufts of pampas grass are well known; this one is of more modest proportions that permit its use in a tub. The leaves are about 1m (3¼ft) long and no more than 12mm (½in) wide. The slim pyramidal silvery plumes wave impressively above. This is the most floriferous pampas grass of all and flowers from late summer into late winter.

Position Extremely wind tolerant and tough, it grows in full sun or light shade.

Uses A pair of these plants in tubs will provide a grand entrance to a patio or main approach to a house, even if the area is entirely paved.

Compost Does well in most composts provided drainage is good.

Special maintenance It is best to cut down the plant by hand in early spring to remove dead material before new growth starts. If this is done annually it will not be a difficult job. The old growth can be burnt off but the result does not look good and the container can be damaged.

Other kinds to try 'Gold Band', eventually reaches 1.5m (5ft), but slower growing than the species since its leaves are broadly margined gold and so has less chlorophyll to manufacture food. A lovely warm foliage effect topped with plenty of white plumes.

deciduous

semi-evergreen

evergreen

flowering period

foliage/ fruiting plant

full sun

¼ shade-¾ sun

½ shade-½ sun

¼ sun-¾ shade

full shade

needs winter protection

137

CORYLUS AVELLANA 'CONTORTA' TWiSTED HAZEL

1.5m (5ft); deciduous slow-growing shrub; **Zone 4**

Characteristics Curiously twisting brown stems look like corkscrews. In late winter they drip with pale yellow catkins, dangling in the breeze. Light green oval toothed leaves follow in spring and summer.

Position Tolerant of wind, full sun or shade, but less catkins in deep shade.

Uses An outstanding shrub for winter interest it associates well with *Erica carnea* and pink camellias. It will also give a patio an oriental feel, specially if it is planted alongside a tub of bamboo which provides a good background.

Compost Tolerant of most composts.

Special maintenance No real problems, just prune to any special shape as required.

COTONEASTER CONSPICUUS

1m (3ft); evergreen shrub; **Zone 5**

Characteristics Fairly stiff stems form a rounded shrub with an irregular outline. The twigs are covered with tiny leaves about 5mm (¼in) long, mid to dark green and oval. In late spring masses of tiny white flowers are humming with bees who pollinate them and ensure an outstanding crop of brilliant scarlet fruits. The fruits are not attractive to birds and often last from mid autumn to mid spring.

Position Wind and light tolerant but less fruit in shady places.

Uses In a trough or large windowbox the brilliant red fruits contrast superbly with a white-flowering winter heather or blue *Iris unguicularis*.

Compost Tolerant of most composts.

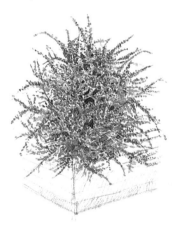

Special maintenance No special treatement apart from a little pruning to whatever shape is needed.

Other kinds to try *C. dammeri*, 30cm (1ft), white flowers, red fruit; *C. horizontalis* 'Variegatus', with white margined leaves; *C. microphyllus thymifolius*, 60cm (24in), prostrate shrub with an minute dark green leaves, 2.5cm (1in) white flowers followed by long-lasting plum-crimson fruit; *C.* 'Hybridus Pendulus', evergreen prostrate shrub, oval leaves, clusters of red fruit, normally trained with a 2.1m (7ft) stem to produce a weeping standard tree.

CROCUS CHRYSANTHUS 'BLUE PEARL'

6cm (2½in); hardy corm; **Zone 6**

Characteristics Very narrow dark green upright leaves have a white central line. Before these develop fully the scented flowers emerge in early spring. These are funnel-shaped at first opening out to reveal yellow centres and lavender blue and bluish white petals. The flowering period is longer than the Dutch crocuses, from late winter to mid spring, as many more flowers develop from each corm.

Position Being short, wind seldom troubles them, but heavy rain spoils the flowers although new ones will soon follow. For permanent planting a sunny site is best with cool conditions.

Uses It is easy to plant crocuses in among low-growing shrubs in a windowbox or trough, and for winter effect heathers such as an *Erica carnea* with purple flowers, look specially good.

Compost Tolerant of most composts.

Special maintenance Mice do like to eat the corms; should they be a trouble, pin down fine-mesh chicken wire over the corms the following year – the flowers will grow through it.

Other kinds to try 'Cream Beauty', cream flowers, good edging for scarlet early tulips; 'Ladykiller', petals alternating white and purple; 'Snowbunting', white, superb with *Erica carnea* 'Springwood Pink'; *C. tommasinianus* 'Ruby Giant', brilliant purple, superb with *Erica carnea* 'Springwood White', more shade tolerant than *C. chrysanthus*; *C. vernus* 'Vanguard', a profusion of large soft mauve flowers.

CRYPTOMERIA JAPONICA 'ELEGANS COMPACTA' DWARF JAPANESE CEDAR

1m (3¼ft); evergreen conifer; **Zone 7**

Characteristics Rounded to irregular outlined shrub. Its dark green foliage is very fluffy in texture and becomes purplish bronze in winter. (Small shrubs resemble a fluffy toy animal!)

Position Avoid a place where snow might pile up and tear its branches. It is reasonably wind tolerant; from full sun to half shade.

Uses The Japanese cedar contrasts well with dark green pyramid-shaped dwarf conifers, the grey rounded leaves of *Senecio compactus* or the trails of *Hedera helix* 'Glacier'.

Compost Tolerant of most composts.

Special maintenance When it snows gently shake the branches so they are not weighed down.

Other kinds to try *C.j.* 'Spiralis' 1m (3¼ft), a small tree, bright light green foliage tightly spirals round the weeping branches which look almost like pieces of green rope; *C.j.* 'Vilmoriniana', 60cm (24in), globular mound of yellowish green foliage turns bronze-russet in late autumn.

CUCURBITA PEPO
'GOLD RUSH'
GOLDEN ZUCCHINI

50cm (20in); tender spreading annual; **Zone 10**

Characteristics Green fleshy yet rough stems sprawl and trail and give rise to rough-textured rounded leaves about 20cm (8in) across supported by stems about 15cm (6in) long. The large yellowish flowers of summer are fairly short-lived if pollinated and will develop into golden yellow sausage-shaped fruits up to 60cm (2ft) or more.

Position They grow best in full sun.

Uses Pick fruit when no more than 10cm (4in) long and they will be tender after cooking. These plants make a good summer cover. For example, growing in a trough it will become a green mound of foliage with attractive yellow fruit.

Compost Tolerant of most enriched composts. An extra feed at monthly intervals will sustain fruit production.

Special maintenance Keep picking, because leaving zucchinis to grow large will deter succession of new fruits. Keep well watered as this helps to deter mildew disease.

Other kinds to try 'Blackjack Zucchini', deep green fruits; 'Golden Butter Zucchini', bright golden cylindrical fruits; 'Gourmet's Selection', mixture of golden, dark green and white types; C. maxima (pumpkin), exciting for those with plenty of space and big containers; C. maxima 'Turbaniformis' (Turk's cap gourd), of unusual shape and various colours used mainly as ornamental fruit for decoration.

CUPRESSUS CASHMERIANA
KASHMIR CYPRESS

2m (7ft); evergreen coniferous tree; **Zone 9**

Characteristics The main stem is upright with branches slightly ascending or vertical. From these the sub-laterals or side branches weep down like green lace curtains. This effect is caused by the very fine strands of tiny blue-grey-green leaves.

Position Avoid freezing cold winds, but thrives in full sun or shade.

Uses A beautiful tree to behold and the slightest breeze causes a delightful shimmering movement. Allow it to arch over a path and the flexible trails act like a bead curtain across a doorway. If grown in a tub it can be moved around so the branches catch the breeze.

Compost Very tolerant of most composts.

Special maintenance It can be trained to produce a flatter shape if space is lacking by stopping the leading shoot at the required height. Remove any lower foliage which goes brown when the tree matures.

Other kinds to try C. sempervirens 'Stricta' (Italian cypress), dark green foliage tightly packed on a vertical main stem. It forms a dark green column and contrasts well with spreading and weeping containerized trees. A matching pair in large terracotta pots will give a feeling of southern Spain or Italy to a patio; 'Swane's Golden', slender golden form ideal for container growing.

CYCLAMEN NEAPOLITANUM
(C. hederifolium)

10cm (4in); hardy herbaceous tuberous plant; **Zone 6**

Characteristics This neat plant has very attractive dark green leaves, the blades of which are about 5cm (2in) long, somewhat ivy-like in shape and beautifully marbled with silver. They are at their best in autumn and winter. The pink flowers appear in autumn before the leaves fully expand.

Position Very shade tolerant.

Uses Being shade tolerant they are invaluable for planting at the foot of a deciduous shrub such as hydrangea or rose. When the leaves of the shrub begin to thin, the cyclamen brings the container to life again.

Compost Very tolerant of most composts.

Other kinds to try C. neapolitanum var. album, white flowers look brilliant in deep shade; C. coum, similar with lilac-rose flowers in winter and round marbled leaves; C. persicum, familiar florists' cyclamen, 30cm (12in), not so hardy (Zone 9) but otherwise similar to above. Plants in bud can be purchased at any time of the year, therefore a useful gap filler for windowboxes in late summer and autumn; Pannevis Concerto series, compact growth, early large flowers in wide range of colours.

CYPERUS ALTERNIFOLIUS
(C. involucratus)
UMBRELLA PLANT

60cm (24in); evergreen perennial sedge; **Zone 9**

Characteristics Vertical cylindrical green stems are bare of foliage except at the top where a whorl of narrow green grass-like bracts radiates out like the framework of an umbrella. The flowers also radiate out from the top in summer, but they are small and brown.

Position Very light tolerant – full sun to full shade – provided the roots are kept wet. Avoid windy sites.

Uses The distinct form and texture of this plant is a good contrast to spreading bushy subjects. A half-barrel pond with dwarf white waterlilies, blue water forget-me-nots spreading over the edge, and the cyperus giving a dainty vertical contrast, is very effective.

Compost Very tolerant but must be kept moist to saturated.

Special maintenance Remove any stems that go brown. In cold winters keep root submerged or take in and put on windowsill.

Other kinds to try 'Variegata', leaves and stems are striped with white. An even more dramatic plant but it requires partial shade or leaves will scorch; C. papyrus, 2.1m (7ft), giant species with larger "umbrellas" of more numerous but thinner bracts, extremely beautiful in a terracotta or glazed urn by a swimming pool. Sit permanently in a saucer of water.

deciduous

semi-evergreen

evergreen

flowering period

foliage/fruiting plant

full sun

¼ shade-¾ sun

½ shade-½ sun

¼ sun-¾ shade

full shade

needs winter protection

CYTISUS × KEWENSIS
SMALL BROOM

30cm (12in); deciduous spreading shrub; **Zone 7**

Characteristics The arching mass of dense, spreading green stems bears leaves composed of three small leaflets. In mid to late spring creamy-yellow pea-like flowers are borne prolifically.

Position Flowers best in full sun but does well in half shade; very wind tolerant.

Uses In a large trough or windowbox it contrasts well with evergreen shrubs like *Nandina domestica* 'Firepower' with broad reddish leaves. The bright green stems are good winter textural contrast to *Hedera colchica* 'Sulphur Heart' with broad lime-green- to yellow-centred leaves.

Compost Tolerant of all composts.

Special maintenance None.

Other kinds to try *C. × beanii*, similar to above but bright golden yellow flowers; *C. demissus*, 7.5cm (3in), prostrate shrub, bright yellow flowers. Very low growing so excellent in windowbox for bulbs of medium height to grow through, e.g. *Narcissus*, and for filling in around dwarf conifers; *C. purpureus* (purple broom), 45cm (18in), semi-upright green stems massed with soft purple flowers in early summer.

DAPHNE ODORA
'AUREOMARGINATA'

60cm (24in); evergreen shrub; **Zone 7.5**

Characteristics Rounded bush with irregular outline. Light green glossy elliptical leaves with a thin cream margin. A pleasant shrub at all times of the year. Rounded clusters of white flowers flushed purplish pink dot the bush and give off a delightful perfume in the cold and dreary days of winter and early spring.

Position Tolerant of full sun or shade.

Uses Worth a place in a windowbox or trough for the winter scent alone. Gives height and background to small winter-flowering bulbs, such as crocus – especially *C. chrysanthus* 'Blue Pearl', irises and snowdrops.

Compost Happy in most composts provided drainage is good.

Special maintenance Only a little shaping if the site demands.

Other kinds to try *D. × burkwoodii* 'Somerset', 60cm (24in), semi-evergreen, with smaller lance-shaped leaves and more branching habit than above. Delightfully scented, light pink flowers in late spring. It looks good with lily-flowered tulips, such as ruby-purple 'Captain Fryatt', Zone 7.5; *D. mezereum*, deciduous upright shrub, 45cm (18in), purple flowers in late winter to early spring. Looks good in a windowbox or trough springing from a drift of *Crocus chrysanthus* 'Snowbunting' with ivy trailing over the edge, Zone 5.

DATURA
'GRAND MARNIER'
(*Brugmansia* 'Grand Marnier')

2.1m (7ft); tender evergreen tree; **Zone 10**

Characteristics Stout vertical stems have soft green oval pointed leaves about 20cm (8in) long. Huge trumpet-like flowers hang from the top shoots in late spring through till mid autumn. They are about 20cm (8in) long and 18cm (7in) across, a most delicate peach colour for all the world like a lady's silk swirling dress. The scent is marvellous and is even greater in the evenings.

Position A site sheltered from wind is best but it is tolerant of a wide range of light conditions.

Uses One plant in a tub or large urn is a sensation worthy of a sheltered patio or poolside.

Compost Tolerant of most composts but additional feeding will keep growth and flower production going through the summer.

Special maintenance Spray over regularly with water or soapy water to help deter red spider mite. This pest is less troublesome on plants growing outside. In winter bring the plant in; a garage with a window would be suitable if the tub and plant stem are wrapped in bubble plastic.

Other kinds to try *D. suaveolens*, similar but with white flowers; *D. cornigera* (*D. arborea*), white double flowers; *D. sanguinea*, slimmer yellow tube with scarlet-orange trumpet, slightly tougher, Zone 9.

DAUCUS CAROTA
'FAVOURITE'
CARROT

30cm (12in); vegetable; **Zone 5**

Characteristics The foliage of carrots is so familiar that its beauty is normally overlooked. The upright but slightly spreading leaf stems carry hundreds of leaflets, as fine as any fern and a most pleasant green. The root develops gradually, swelling and becoming orange-red, but this is not visible above ground. In this kind the roots are short so that it can be grown in containers with a depth of only 15cm (6in).

Position Carrots are wind resistant, but prefer a light place in full sun or dappled shade.

Uses Pick fresh for salads or for cooking. As a growing plant the foliage is a fine edging for the broad colourful leaves of Swiss chard, or indeed many other vegetables.

Compost Tolerant of most composts.

Special maintenance None.

Other kinds to try 'Nantes', similar to above, stump-rooted about 15cm (6in) long; 'Parmex', globe-shaped and about 7.5cm (3in) long, ideal for shallow containers.

DIANTHUS NANUS GIGANTEUS
(*D. chinensis*)
'SNOW FIRE'

DIASCIA CORDATA

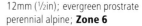

DIONYSIA TAPETODES

20cm (8in); annual; **Zone 7**

15cm (6in); prostrate perennial; **Zone 8**

12mm (½in); evergreen prostrate perennial alpine; **Zone 6**

Characteristics This plant has virtually replaced the true sweet William because, although very similar, it is an annual and fits into the container planting programme well. Slender blue-green stems give rise to pairs of narrow grass-like blue-green leaves. Overall it has an open light effect. The flowers are borne at the top of the shoots in open clusters in summer. Each one is about 2.5cm (1in) wide, with serrated petals; 'Snow Fire' is white with a brilliant scarlet eye.

Position Flowers best in sun; it is wind tolerant.

Uses For achieving a cottage garden effect this plant is a must. It looks like the old-fashioned sweet William and, as a fine-leaved rounded plant, it contrasts perfectly with the towering hollyhock (*Althaea rosea*). Add to these blue love-in-a mist (*Nigella*) and silver-leaved helichrysum flowing over the edge of a wooden half barrel for perfection.

Compost Tolerant of most composts except very acid.

Special maintenance Pick off dead flowers if time permits.

Other kinds to try 'Strawberry Parfait', 15cm (6in), pink flowers with a strawberry eye; 'Raspberry Parfait', 15cm (6in), white stripes on deep crimson; 'Princess Purple', 20cm (8in), violet-purple. The Princess Strain is also available in crimson, scarlet, salmon, white and mixed; *D. barbatus* 'Giant Auricula Eyed', 45cm (18in), the true and very scented biennial sweet William, scarlet, crimson and pink forms all with white-eyed or white-edged flowers; *D. alpinus*, a perennial, 20cm (8in), low tufted blue-green grassy foliage supports slim stems each topped with a few light pink or rose-coloured flowers. Old-fashioned pinks are compact, grey-leaved perennials: 'Brympton Red', single, bright crimson with good scent; 'Dad's Favourite', semi-double white with chocolate lacing, heavily scented. Modern pinks are longer flowering: 'Denis', double magenta flowers; 'Doris', pale pink with a red base.

Characteristics Horizontal stems clothed with tiny pale green heart-shaped leaves form a basal carpet from which vertical stems arise. These bear spike-like clusters of five-lobed flowers from mid summer to early autumn. The flowers are unique; pink, with a big lip, a yellow dusting inside and a spur at the back.

Position As it is low growing it tolerates wind. Grows well in full sun to half shade.

Uses Perfect for a windowbox or urn because the carpet of dainty foliage will trail over the edge and the striking flowers are best seen close up. It contrasts well with *Osteospermum*.

Compost Tolerates most composts.

Special maintenance Dead flower spikes can be removed, although they are not unsightly.

Other kinds to try *D. vigilis*, 30cm (12in), pale green rounded toothed leaves, upright branches with loose spikes of pale pink flowers; *D*. 'Ruby Field', 8cm (3in), wiry stems with pale green heart-shaped leaves, wide-lipped salmon-pink flowers on short spikes.

Characteristics A tight mat of tiny green leaf rosettes. In early spring cup-shaped flowers, each with five petals, gild the green cushion with gold.

Position Full sun is needed for good flowering.

Uses A windowbox or sink where it can be seen properly is best to display the beauty of this minuscule plant. It should be associated with other alpines and low-growing plants that will not overpower it. *Sempervivum tectorum* (houseleek) with its succulent rusty red rosettes is a good companion.

Compost A gritty well-drained compost is needed.

Special maintenance Never let other plants overpower or shade this tiny alpine.

Other kinds to try *D. aretioides*, 7.5cm (3in), similar to above but greyish green leaves and scented flowers.

	deciduous
	semi-evergreen
	evergreen
	flowering period
	foliage/ fruiting plant
	full sun
	¼ shade-¾ sun
	½ shade-½ sun
	¼ sun-¾ shade
	full shade
	needs winter protection

E

ECCREMOCARPUS SCABER
CHILEAN GLORY FLOWER

2.1m (7ft); evergreen climber grown as an annual; **Zone 8**

Characteristics Thin vine-like stems clamber over shrubs or fences by means of fine twisting tendrils. The green leaf is formed of several small oval leaflets. At the ends of stems many spikes of tubular flowers hang down from mid summer to late autumn. They are orange-red and yellow within.

Position Very light tolerant, growing well in full sun or shade.

Uses A lightweight climber because of its small leaves, it is therefore very useful for training over a small tree such as a cherry that has spring flowers but benefits from "colouring up" in summer. It is also very good for covering a trellis, fence or wall.

Compost Tolerant of most composts.

Special maintenance Remove the dead flowers or leave them to allow the attractive pods to develop. The plant can be left outside during winter as it usually regrows from the base if cut back by frost. As a safety precaution save a few seeds since it is very easy to grow.

Other kinds to try *E. scaber aurantiacus*, pure yellow flowers; *E. scaber roseus*, rose-red flowers with yellow inside. Allow a plant of each of the above to intertwine and create an extremely attractive background curtain.

ECHEVERIA GIBBIFLORA 'ROSEA'
ROSE ECHEVERIA

50cm (20in); woody succulent with an erect rosette; **Zone 9.5**

Characteristics Sturdy upright stems, generally unbranched, are topped with a close rosette of many rounded leaves each about 5cm (2in) across. They are smooth, waxy and a beautiful mauve-pink. The autumn flowers are of secondary importance, carried on stems which arise from the rosette. They are red, cup-shaped and yellow inside.

Position Wind tolerant but sun loving.

Uses For a Mexican or Spanish effect this plant is superb in a stone or terracotta pot or trough with cacti such as *Cereus peruvianus* or the hardier opuntias. The pink rosettes contrast well with the other shapes and colours.

Compost Most kinds suit but good drainage is essential.

Special maintenance A container filled with these plants looks good at all times, so take it in and enjoy it in the house for the winter, placed near a window.

Other kinds to try There are numerous hybrids with rosettes of blue, grey and purple, some with frilled edges and others with rough-textured leaves: *E. secunda*, 4cm (1½in), blue-grey rosette, leaf tips often tinged purple-red, good for making a carpet at the base of other succulents or yuccas, Zone 9.

ERANTHIS HYEMALIS
(E. cilicicus)
WINTER ACONITE

7.5cm (3in); tuberous herbaceous plant; **Zone 7**

Characteristics Bright green shiny leaves, deeply lobed into radiating strips, are attractive in themselves. At the top of the tiny stems a whorl of leafy bracts is topped by the smooth golden cup of oval overlapping petals. Inside this is a "gold dust" of yellow stamens. It flowers in late winter.

Position Very light tolerant; from full sun to full shade.

Uses In a windowbox the brilliant green and gold bring warmth and brightness to winter days. They look well backed by *Cotoneaster conspicuus* with its brilliant scarlet round fruits and common ivy trailing over the edge of the container.

Compost Very tolerant of most composts but likes organic matter.

Special maintenance None; but mark where they are planted, so as not to dig them up by accident.

Other kinds to try *E.* × *tubergenii* 'Guinea Gold', similar, 10cm (4in) high, leafy bract beneath the flower is bronzy green.

ERICA CARNEA
'SPRINGWOOD PINK'
(E. herbacea)
ALPINE HEATH

15cm (6in); spreading woody evergreen; **Zone 5**

Characteristics Spreading wiry stems have small lateral branches with needle-like leaves. In winter the short vertical shoots have narrow buds which open in late winter to mid spring. The individual flowers are long, narrow and mauvy pink with chocolate brown stamens emerging from the ends. The flowers tend to hang down to one side of the flower stem like a fringe.

Position Very wind tolerant but prefers a sunny place.

Uses Forms a fine carpet with warm pink flowers which looks well around the base of the silver trunk of a birch tree in a tub. This erica will trail over the edge too. Other good contrasts are made with white-flowered camellias or *Corylus avellana* 'Contorta'.

Compost It will tolerate most composts including alkaline ones even though most ericas prefer acid soils.

Special maintenance After flowering clip off the old flowerheads with shears to give a more compact plant.

Other kinds to try 'Springwood White', white flowers, looks good with pink camellias; 'Vivellii', wine-purple flowers and compact bronze foliage looks good with 'Springwood White'. There are numerous other variations; *E. canaliculata*, 1m (3¼ft), upright growth massed with pearl-like light pink flowers in early to mid spring, Zone 8.5; *E. australis* 'Riverslea', 75cm (30in), massed with purple-pink flowers in mid to late spring; *E. pageana*, 60cm (24in), rich yellow flower spikes, Zone 8.5; *E. gracilis* (Cape heath) 40cm (16in), pink-apricot, Zone 10.

ERIGERON MUCRONATUS
(*E. karvinskianus*)

10cm (4in); lax spreading perennial; **Zone 7.5**

Characteristics A spider's web of fine trailing stems gives rise to tiny lance-shaped green leaves. In summer these are dotted with exquisitely delicate daisies that open white and change to pink and cerise.
Position Wind tolerant; prefers a sunny place.
Uses The delicate trails are superb for windowboxes, raised urns, and even hanging baskets, where they bring a light texture to stocky plants like dahlias, *Tagetes* and pelargoniums.

Compost Tolerant of most composts but needs good drainage.
Special maintenance The plants are slow to establish so be patient and do not replace them with something else.

EUCALYPTUS PERRINIANA
SPINNING GUM

4.8m (16ft); evergreen tree; **Zone 7**

Characteristics Fast-growing tree. The stem is blue-green at first but darkens with age and then peels to a bluish white. The leaves on the immature shoots are most unusual for they are perfectly circular with the stem piercing through the centre. They are an attractive blue-grey. As the plant matures the leaf shape and arrangement gradually changes through opposite round leaves to alterate oval leaves and finally lance-shaped leaves. Numerous small white tassel-like flowers occur in summer, when the plant is several years old.
Position Wind tolerant; full sun to half shade.
Uses This is the answer for a very fast-growing evergreen tree to take the eye away from an ugly feature. It needs a large container or tub.
Compost Tolerant of any compost.
Special maintenance When the tree is nearing the required height prune it to 90cm (36in) below what is required. Annual thinning and pruning in the early spring will keep the tree the same height.

Other kinds to try *E. cinerea*, leaves stay silvery blue, slower growing, Zone 8; *E. nicholii*, very narrow delicate grey-green leaves, Zone 8.5; *E. nitens*, huge scimitar-shaped grey-green leaves, 25cm (10in) long, Zone 7.5; *E. urnigera* 'Glauca', grey-green leaves, moderate growing, Zone 7.5; *E. citrodora*, lemon scented, Zone 9.

EUONYMUS FORTUNEI
'EMERALD 'N' GOLD'

50cm (20in); evergreen shrub; **Zone 6**

Characteristics This bushy shrub has glossy oval leaves, green broadly margined with bright golden yellow, sometimes tinged pink in winter.
Position Tolerant of sand and wind, full sun to full shade.
Uses Good for growing at the foot of taller shrubs or trees such as *Pyracantha atalantioides*, cotoneasters and skimmias – its golden leaves look well with their scarlet fruits. Add to these *Hedera helix* 'Goldheart' with trails of dark green, yellow-centred leaves for the perfect trio in a tub that will look good throughout the year.
Compost Tolerant of most composts.

Special maintenance None, unless any special training is required.
Other kinds to try 'Silver Queen', similar but with broad white-edged leaves. Occasionally seen trained vertically to enliven a dull wall; 'Sunspot', each leaf has a golden yellow centre; *E. japonicus* 'Macrophyllus Albus', 1.8m (6ft), upright shrub with bigger leaves, 5 cm (2in) long, broadly margined with white. A larger background shrub for purple *Iris reticulata* and violet-fruited *Callicarpa*.

EUPHORBIA MYRSINITES

5cm (2in); evergreen prostrate perennial; **Zone 7.5**

Characteristics Thick trailing light green stems have fleshy oval pointed grey-green leaves. Since these radiate out all around the horizontal stems it looks a little like a crawling reptile, a crocodile perhaps! In spring the tips produce a welcoming cluster of bright yellow-green flowers backed by similar coloured bracts.

Position Wind tolerant; full sun to half shade.
Uses The geometrical form and succulent leaves associate well with rosette plants such as a group of *Sempervivum tectorum* with reddish purple leaves. Add to this *Iris pallida* 'Variegata' with vertical white-edged leaves for a well-matched group for a shallow trough or bowl.
Compost Tolerant of most composts provided drainage is good.
Special maintenance Best left alone; its milky sap irritates skin.
Other kinds to try *E. polychroma* (*E. epithymoides*), 50cm (20in), herbaceous perennial. Mid green leaves come early in spring and give rise to yellow to lime bracts that back up the tiny yellow flowers. They look good with scarlet tulips, Zone 7; *E. pulcherrima* (poinsettia), 1.7m (5½ft), upright fairly evergreen shrub, oval leaves about 10cm (4in) long, pointed and sparsely toothed. In autumn the big red bracts start to appear, backing tiny flowers. Normally grown as a dwarfed house-plant, but keep it growing and it will make a tall plant to give a summer patio a touch of the West Indies.

---

deciduous

semi-evergreen

evergreen

flowering period

foliage/ fruiting plant

full sun

¼ shade-¾ sun

½ shade-½ sun

¼ sun-¾ shade

full shade

needs winter protection

143

F

EURYOPS PECTINATUS

75cm (30in); evergreen upright shrub; **Zone 8.5**

Characteristics Deeply cut leaves have a fern-like quality except in their grey-green colour. In late spring bright yellow daisies commence flowering and continue in variable quantity for most of the year.

Position Wind tolerant; full sun to half shade.

Uses The fine-textured leaves and daisy flowers look well in a tub with plants of coarser texture: for example the large crimson leaves of cannas, the tight-packed flowerheads of scarlet pelargoniums and the big trumpets of petunias to trail over the edge. A standard lantana or streptosolen would give extra height and orange colour.

Compost Tolerant of most composts.

Special maintenance If required the plant can be broadened out by pinching out leading shoots. In colder areas the plants can be lifted or cuttings taken for the following year.

Other kinds to try *E. chrysanthemoides*, similar but with bright green lobed leaves which are less dainty; *E. virgineus* 1.2m (4ft), upright shrub with thread-like green leaves, very dainty foliage but not so prolific flower production; *E. acraeus* (*E. evansii*), 30cm (12in), dome-shaped shrublet, densely covered in narrow-toothed silvery blue leaves, yellow daisy flowers late spring.

× FATSHEDERA LIZEI 'LEMON AND LIME'
(× *Fatshedera lizei* 'Annamikels')

1.2m (4ft); evergreen shrub; **Zone 8**

Characteristics Loose branching shrub that can be trained easily in various shapes. Large-lobed ivy-like leaves about 15cm (6in) across are glossy deep green generously and irregularly blotched lime green in the centre with lemon veins. In autumn spherical sprays of white flowers are formed which contrast with the leaves.

Position Very light tolerant, from full sun to full shade.

Uses It is a worthy plant on its own and grows well in the darkest corner in a large pot. It teams up well with other tropical-looking plants which are equally hardy such as *Cordyline australis* with its narrow leaves and the fiery foliage of *Nandina domestica*.

Compost Tolerant of most composts.

Special maintenance Train to shape as desired; stake with cane if for upright growth, pin down for ground cover effect.

Other kinds to try 'Variegata', dark green leaves with a creamy white edge.

FATSIA JAPONICA 'VARIEGATA'
JAPANESE ARALIA

1.5m (5ft); evergreen shrub; **Zone 7.5**

Characteristics Stout shoots with few branches bear long-stemmed rounded 45cm (18in) wide leaves. These are leathery, glossy and deeply divided into about nine lobes. Being so large and dark green with an irregular creamy white margin they look very tropical. Dense clusters of white flowers appear in mid autumn followed by black fruits.

Position A sheltered position in shade is best as very strong winds can tear the leaves and full sun will scorch their edges.

Uses The beautiful leaves are of a size to balance those of banana (*Musa ensete*) with huge vertical paddle-like leaves and *Eucalyptus nitens* with hanging scimitar-shaped leaves, 25cm (10in) long. These three bring the jungle to a patio and can all be grown in tubs.

Compost Tolerant of most composts but enjoys extra organic matter.

Special maintenance None, other than to remove dead leaves and train up to form a tree if required.

Other kinds to try *F. japonica*, the plain green species, is equally useful, less prone to leaf edge scorch because of the absence of white.

FEIJOA SELLOWIANA
(*Acca sellowiana*)
PINEAPPLE GUAVA, FRUIT SALAD BUSH

1m (3¼ft); evergreen shrub; **Zone 8**

Characteristics Twiggy bush of irregular outline with mid green slightly greyish oval leaves that are grey beneath. In mid summer soft crimson flowers with white reverse and edges, 2.5cm (1in) across, occur. These are followed by green fruits with a reddish flush.

Position Better flower and fruit production on a sunny site. Shelter from wind encourages more bees and better pollination.

Uses A pleasant background shrub with unusual flowers that are partly obscured by the foliage. The petals of the flowers are edible and have a mild sweet taste like fruit salad. The fruit is ripe when it starts to fall; it is tart rather than sweet and myrtle-like in flavour. Good for making jellies.

Compost Happy in most composts.

Special maintenance None, unless training to a special shape is required.

Other kinds to try 'Variegata', rare but beautiful because the white-edged leaves show up the flowers. 'Apollo' and *F.* 'Coolidge' produce larger fruits.

FELICIA AMELLOIDES
'SANTA ANITA'
(*Agathaea coelestis* 'Santa Anita')

30cm (12in); evergreen shrublet; **Zone 9**

Characteristics Neat spreading to rounded plant, clothed in lance-shaped to oval mid green leaves. Sky blue daisy flowers about 4cm (1½in) across with yellow centres give a delightful light effect from late spring until the first frosts.
Position Wind tolerant; full sun to partial shade.
Uses Of value in any container because its neat foliage will fill in between other plants and the light texture of the sky blue daisies can partner any other coloured flowers or foliage.
Compost Tolerant of most composts.
Special maintenance None; but take autumn cuttings in case a hard winter kills the plants.
Other kinds to try *F. amelloides*, the species, is similar but shorter, 15cm (6in) and with smaller but more numerous blue daisy flowers. It forms low ground cover so is particularly valuable for around the base of taller plants such as impatiens and mimulus which have a wide range of colours and glossy foliage; *F. amelloides* 'Variegata', similar to above but with white-edged leaves, an excellent backing for its own flowers, also slower growing; *F. papper* (*Aster pappei*), similar to *F. amelloides* but lighter and brighter green, very narrow leaves that make the bush a green haze; *F. bergeriana*, similar to above but an annual with smaller darker flowers; *F. petiolata*, a climber that throws fine trails of tiny oval leaves and pale pink daisies over and between its neighbours.

FICUS CARICA
FIG

2.1m (7ft); deciduous large shrub; **Zone 7.5**

Characteristics Robust twigs support 15cm (6in) palm-shaped leaves with three to five deep lobes. The tops of the shoots can bear a few flowers in each leaf axil. No petals are visible and they look like tiny green figs. In warm climates there can be three crops a year but in cool climates the fruits do not start to turn a pinkish grey until autumn when their softness indicates picking time.
Position A sunny wall is the best site to ripen fruit, but if fruit is not important a shady spot will do.
Uses The large leaves are quite attractive but the production of fresh fruit is the delight of the connoisseur.
Compost Very well drained and not too rich, consequently they do very well in containers such as half barrels.

Special maintenance Thinning the shoots allows the sun to ripen the wood and fruit better, so train fanned out against a wall or as an open-centred bush.
Other kinds to try 'Brown Turkey', the hardiest kind, fruit brownish purple, red flesh; 'Black Ischia', hardy, smaller fruit, purplish black, orange-red flesh; 'White Marseilles', fairly hardy, medium pale green, white flesh.

FOENICULUM VULGARE
'PURPUREUM'
PURPLE FENNEL

1.2m (4ft); herbaceous perennial; **Zone 7**

Characteristics Erect smooth light green robust stems branch and give rise to thousands of extremely fine hair-like leaflets of a bronzy copper colour. When pinched or brushed they exude a scent reminiscent of aniseed. From the top of the stem in summer many tiny yellow flowers appear arranged in an open flat head.

Position Tolerant of salt winds. Does well in full sun or partial shade.
Uses Well known flavouring particularly suited to fish dishes. Grown in a pot on its own set by the kitchen door or in association with the broad-leaved *Beta vulgaris cicla*, rhubarb or Swiss chard, its dainty foliage is charming.
Compost Tolerant of all composts.
Special maintenance Remove the dead flowers and stems if desired, but they have great form and texture even when dead.
Other kinds to try *F. vulgare*, the green-leaved species, may fit better in some colour schemes in the garden and on the plate!; *F.v. dulce* 'Finnochio' (Florence fennel), similar except the leaf bases swell up to form a "bulb" with a taste between celery and aniseed.

FRAGARIA × ANANASSA
'VARIEGATA'
STRAWBERRY

12cm (5in); semi-evergreen herbaceous plant; **Zone 7**

Characteristics This is the variegated form of the familiar fruiting plant. Tufts of leaves each divided into three saw-edged leaflets give rise to long horizontal runners which produce tiny plantlets by which the plant spreads. White flowers in clusters in late spring are followed by the delicious conical red fruit. In this kind the leaves have broad white edges, an attractive background for the red fruit. It is slower growing than the green-leaved kinds, an advantage between other plants, but this also means fewer and smaller fruits.
Position Does well in full sun to full shade.
Uses An attractive foliage plant to trail down over the edge of windowboxes and hanging baskets.
Compost Tolerant of most composts provided they have adequate organic matter.
Special maintenance Young plantlets in excess can be cut off and rooted.

Other kinds to try 'Rabunda' perpetual, fruits from summer to mid autumn; *F. vesca* 'Semperflorens' (Alpine strawberry), 7cm (3in) high, this little trailing evergreen is a useful short ground cover and also bears its tiny 14mm (½in) fruits from mid summer to late autumn. Never a huge crop but nearly always of delicious flavour; *F.v.* 'Alexandria', a newer kind than 'Baron Solemacher'. Both have fruits about 2cm (¾in) long.

---

deciduous

semi-evergreen

evergreen

flowering period

foliage/ fruiting plant

full sun

¼ shade- ¾ sun

½ shade- ½ sun

¼ sun- ¾ shade

full shade

needs winter protection

145

G

FREMONTODENDRON
'CALIFORNIA GLORY'

2.4m (8ft); upright evergreen shrub;
Zone 7.5

Characteristics The fast-growing upright slightly furry stems bear rounded three- to five-lobed attractive leaves of dark to mid green. Bright yellow glistening golden chalices are borne from late spring to mid autumn. These flowers have five rounded petals each with a short point; from the centre arises a stem from which the fine golden stamens radiate like a little candelabrum.
Position Fairly wind tolerant if well secured, but needs sun to flower well.
Uses A lovely evergreen at any time of year but the unique golden flowers over a long season make it a valuable main plant for a large container on the patio, where it will associate well with *Ceanothus* 'Puget Blue'.
Compost Happy in most composts provided drainage is good.
Special maintenance Reduce side-shoots to about half, or in accord with space available, in late autumn, to reduce winter wind rock and keep the plant within bounds.
Other kinds to try *F. mexicanum*, leaves a slightly darker green and more deeply lobed than above. Flowers golden yellow flushed orange, Zone 8.5.

FUCHSIA
'DOLLAR PRINCESS'

75cm (30in); half-hardy shrub;
Zone 9

Characteristics Upright shrub with 7.5cm (3in) oval pointed toothed leaves. The flowers, which appear from mid summer to mid autumn, are rose-cerise with horizontal sepals and fully reveal the billowing very double violet-purple petals from which the long red stamens hang.
Position Avoid very windy spots, but happy in full sun to full shade.
Uses Good as a centrepiece for a large pot or urn specially where blue trailing lobelia and/or silver *Helichrysum petiolare* can furnish the base and tumble over the edge.
Compost Tolerant of most composts.

Special maintenance Train as required. House the plants in winter.
Other kinds to try 'Princessita', white tube and slim sepals, dainty rose bell, looks good in a basket in a dark place; 'Checkerboard', red tube and bell, white sepals, grows well as a standard with white daisies beneath; 'Swingtime', rose-pink tube and sepals, billowing double white petals from which hang the rose-coloured stamens. Very good in a hanging basket; 'Chang', a rose-red flower with green-tipped unfurling sepals reminiscent of a Chinese pagoda roof; 'Thalia', upright plant with green leaves flushed red-purple and clusters of long slim pendant orange-rose flowers; 'Tom West', white-edged leaves with a pink flush, rose-crimson flowers with a violet-purple bell; 'Golden Marinka', similar to above but with lime green leaves broadly margined gold.

FUCHSIA MAGELLANICA
GRACILIS 'VARIEGATA'
HARDY FUCHSIA

60cm (24in); hardy deciduous shrub;
Zone 7.5

Characteristics Fairly slender stems shoot up from the compost with feathery side branches and 5cm (2in) lance-shaped toothed leaves. Since these are edged white they are an attraction in themselves but also provide a fine background for their dainty pendant rose-red flowers with their violet bell beneath. These open from mid summer to mid autumn.
Position Give shelter from strong drying winds during periods of drought. It does well in full sun to full shade.
Uses In a hanging basket, windowbox or elevated urn they look superb since their pendant flowers are seen to full advantage. *Lobelia erinus* 'Blue Cascade' or 'Blue Fountain', each with trails of light blue flowers, associate very well.
Compost Tolerant of most composts.
Special maintenance In extremely cold winters they may become herbaceous; pack straw or bracken around the base to prevent stem dieback.
Other kinds to try *F. magellanica* 'Versicolor', similar but leaves irregularly tinted pink, looks good with the blue daisies of *Felicia amelloides*; *F.* 'Tom Thumb', 30cm (12in), bush with upright branches, red with violet-purple bell. Very dwarf therefore suitable for a windowbox; *F.* 'Mrs Popple', 1m (3¼ft), similar to 'Tom Thumb' but bigger in growth and flower therefore much better for spraying out of an urn or large hanging basket; *F.* 'Phyllis', 1.2m (4ft), even larger with plumper rose-pink flowers; *F.* 'Alice Hoffman', 60cm (24in), compact habit, red with a white bell.

GALANTHUS
'ATKINSII'
SNOWDROP

15cm (6in); hardy bulb; **Zone 6**

Characteristics Strap-shaped grey-green leaves vertical then arching emerge from the soil to create a very pleasant foliage tuft. The typical snowdrop flowers on slender stems open in winter. They are composed of three snow white outer petals flared at a fairly wide angle to reveal the three minor petals, each of which is tipped with a bright green spot.

Position Grows well in full sun or full shade.
Uses These welcome flowers of winter show up well backed by a dark green fine-textured conifer such as *Chamaecyparis obtusa* 'Nana', or copper-coloured *Thuja occidentalis* 'Rheingold', and an ivy such as *Hedera helix* 'Goldheart' will give contrasting leaf shape and add a green carpet splashed with gold.
Compost Tolerant of most composts.
Special maintenance If possible allow the leaves and flowers to die back naturally; the plants will then increase in number.
Other kinds to try *G. nivalis* (common snowdrop), 10cm (4in), similar to the above but smaller therefore more difficult to mix with other plants that will not compete with it. Associates well with the alpine strawberry (*Fragaria vesca* 'Semperflorens') and mosses; *G.n.* 'Flore Pleno' (double common snowdrop), has many inner petals forming a white rosette tipped with green, the flowers last longer than those of the species; *G.* 'Magnet', the outer petals are near horizontal and the flower stem arching so that the flower sways in the breeze.

GAZANIA 'DAYBREAK BRONZE'

20cm (8in); tender perennial grown as an annual; **Zone 9**

Characteristics A plant of spreading habit which gradually forms a carpet of lance-shaped dark green glossy leaves. The daisy-like flowerheads are about 5cm (2in) across and of a bronzy russet colour. They will flower from late spring until the cold weather slows growth but do not open well in the shade.
Position Wind tolerant but choose a very sunny spot.
Uses Excellent carpeting plant for a windowbox, trough or tub in an open sunny situation. The taller scarlet pelargoniums and common African marigolds look well growing above them with fine silver-leaved *Lotus berthelotii* tumbling over the edge.

Compost Tolerant of most composts provided drainage is good.
Special maintenance None, unless cuttings are taken or the plants are potted up in late autumn to save them over winter.
Other kinds to try 'Daybreak Sun', golden orange with a lighter gold edge and dark disc; 'Daybreak Orange', brilliant orange with a dark disc, silvery leaves; 'Daybreak Yellow', clear yellow with a dark brown disc; 'Daybreak Mixed', a mixture of all above; 'Mini Star Yellow', 23cm (9in), silvery leaves, bright yellow flowers; 'Mini Star White', as above with creamy white flowers; 'Mini Star Tangerine', as above with light orange flowers; *G. uniflora*, 23cm (9in), narrow glossy green foliage with a grey reverse and orange or yellow flowers; *G. splendens* 'Variegata', green leaves with a cream margin and orange flowers; *G.* 'Silver Beauty', silver grey foliage and golden flowers.

GENISTA AETNENSIS MOUNT ETNA BROOM

2.1m (7ft); small effectively evergreen tree; **Zone 7**

Characteristics Strong slim green vertical stems have fine lateral branches which as they mature weep at the ends to give a willow-like outline. The minute leaves do not last long but the numerous rush-like branches give the effect of a green lace curtain throughout the year. In early summer the branches are showered with lemon-yellow pea-like flowers.
Position Wind tolerant; it prefers sun.
Uses The perfect plant softly to screen an ugly view but give the minimum shade throughout the year. Ideal in a tub on the patio since its leaves and flowers, although numerous, are small so it creates the minimum of litter.
Compost Tolerant of most composts given adequate drainage.
Special maintenance Best bought as a 1m (3¼ft) container plant and trained up a bamboo cane to give a single stem and create a semi-transparent umbrella shape.
Other kinds to try *G. hispanica* (Spanish gorse), 75cm (30in), dense spreading spiny shrub with yellow flowers in late spring to early summer. Similar in flower and its green stems to the above, but the low dense spring growth can be a useful defence in a trough or tub against animals!; *G. lydia*, 45cm (18in), spreading hummocky shrub with yellow flowers in late spring. The spineless green stems can trail over the edge of a trough, tub or widowbox without harm to anyone.

GENTIANA SINO-ORNATA GENTIAN

5cm (2in); evergreen spreading perennial alpine; **Zone 6**

Characteristics Slim sword-shaped bright green leaves radiate from the tiny vertical stems. Rich blue trumpet-shaped flowers with a creamy green throat bloom in autumn.
Position Full sun is needed for best flowering.
Uses Outstanding in a windowbox where the detailed markings of these wonderful blue flowers can be seen. Associates well with *Polygonum vacciniifolium* whose stems of tiny oval leaves will trail over the edge of the container while the slim spikes of small pink flowers contrast so well with the gentian's bold trumpets.
Compost Lime-free compost with adequate organic matter.
Special maintenance About every three years divide and replant in spring in order to maintain strong growing and flowering plants. Keep moist at all times.

Other kinds to try *G. acaulis*, 5cm (2in), as above but darker blue trumpets with green spotted throats in spring and often again in autumn; *G. verna*, as above but rosettes of oval leaves and bright blue white-throated flowers in spring; *G. septemfida*, 15cm (6in) high with oval leaves and mid blue flowers in summer and autumn; *G. asclepiadea*, 60cm (24in), deciduous, arching stems of long pointed oval leaves topped with clusters of mid blue flowers in late summer and autumn, shade tolerant.

GERANIUM ENDRESSII

30cm (12in); semi-evergreen herbaceous plant; **Zone 6**

Characteristics Rounded plant with soft green lobed leaves forms a dense ground cover and an excellent background for the rose-pink cupped and petalled flowers. Although the flowers are modest in size they occur throughout the summer.
Position Very tolerant of different light conditions but expect less flowers in deep shade than in full sun.

Uses An excellent labour-free ground cover for around the base of a small tree or large shrub growing in a trough or large tub. Bulbs, such as medium to large daffodils, will grow through its carpet to give spring colour.
Compost Tolerant of most composts.
Special maintenance Remove the brown leaves if they look untidy.
Other kinds to try *G. renardii*, 30cm (12in), similar to the above but with sage green leaves and white flowers in summer delicately veined with purple; *G. cinereum subcaulescens*, 10cm (4in) high, with magenta-purple flowers in summer; *G. wallichianum* 'Buxton's Blue', 30cm (12in), blue flowers with a white centre from mid summer to mid autumn; *G.* 'Johnson's Blue', 30cm (12in), deeply lobed leaves and deep lavender blue flowers from mid summer to mid autumn.

deciduous

semi-evergreen

evergreen

flowering period

foliage/ fruiting plant

full sun

¼ shade-¾ sun

½ shade-½ sun

¼ sun-¾ shade

full shade

needs winter protection

147

GLECHOMA HEDERACEA 'VARIEGATA'
VARIEGATED GROUND IVY

10cm (4in); trailing semi-evergreen herbaceous plant; **Zone 7**

Characteristics Long thin stems bear rounded to heart-shaped leaves about 12mm (½in) across. Each one has prettily rounded teeth and an attractive irregular white margin. The tiny blue summer flowers are somewhat hidden but it is the foliage that is the main attraction.
Position Scorching winds can brown the foliage but given adequate moisture it will grow well in full sun to full shade.
Uses Long trails of this delicate foliage look almost like droplets of water about to splash. In the slightest breeze they will gently sway bringing delicacy and movement to a hanging basket, wall pot or windowbox in a lofty position.
Compost Tolerant of most composts.
Special maintenance None, save to ensure that it does not dry out.

GREVILLEA JUNIPERINA SULPHUREA
SULPHUR SPIDER FLOWER

75cm (30in); evergreen shrub; **Zone 7.5**

Characteristics Rounded and spreading in shape, this shrub has needle-like leaves dark green above and greyish beneath. The whole plant does resemble a juniper, hence its botanical name; however, it has clusters of pale yellow flowers with long spidery stamens. These are very unusual and attractive over a long period – from late spring to late summer.
Position Wind tolerant, it thrives in full sun to half shade.

Uses Grow in a trough where it associates well with heathers; its flowers give contrast of colour and form.
Compost Prefers an acid (lime-free) compost.
Special maintenance None, unless it needs to be pruned back to keep in shape.
Other kinds to try G. 'Robyn Gordon', a spreading evergreen shrub with deeply and finely divided leaves, racemes of crimson flowers with long curving filaments issuing from their centres occur from early spring to late summer, Zone 10; G. robusta, fast-growing evergreen tree often grown as an annual, fern-like dark green leaves wide-spaced on a slim vertical stem make this a common foliage plant for giving height, but minimal shade, for the centre of an urn or at each end of a windowbox, Zone 10.

GUNNERA MANICATA

1.8m (6ft); huge herbaceous perennial; **Zone 7.5**

Characteristics A stout prickly leaf stem shoots up from ground level and as it does so the leaf blade gradually opens. Mid green rounded with coarsely toothed lobes, just one leaf can be 1.8m (6ft) high and 1.5m (5ft) across. The veins are inset giving a very interesting pattern and texture. Early in summer the flower appears: a conical light green spike, smaller than the leaves.
Position Strong winds will tear the leaves, so keep it in a sheltered place. It is tolerant of different light conditions, from full sun to shade.
Uses No need for a garden umbrella with this plant! Furthermore if it is grown in a large tub it can be moved to give shade and privacy where required. Water forget-me-not and other marginal aquatics that share its love for wet conditions can be grown at the edge of the tub.
Compost Not fussy about compost provided it is kept moist and well fed.

Special maintenance Keep it well supplied with water at all times.
Other kinds to try G. tinctoria, similar but 1.5m (5ft) high – more suitable for a modest-sized patio; G. magellanica, 2.5cm (1in), this is the other amusing extreme, and can be grown in the same container as the giant G. manicata!

GYPSOPHILA PANICULATA 'BRISTOL FAIRY'
BABIES' BREATH

60cm (24in); herbaceous perennial; **Zone 7**

Characteristics A wiry branching system of stems is daintily hung with small narrow greyish green leaves. In summer even finer branches arise above the foliage to carry the tiny double white flowers. The overall effect is lighter than falling snowflakes!

Position Reasonably wind tolerant; full sun to half shade.
Uses A perfect balance for plants which are dark, vertical or heavy in texture. For example, grow in a tub with towering pink hollyhocks and Geranium 'Johnson's Blue' with its dense foliage and blue flowers.
Compost Tolerant of most composts, but prefers lime to acidity.
Special maintenance In a very windy spot it may need support from a few hazel twigs.
Other kinds to try 'Flamingo', similar to above but double pale pink flowers; G. repens, 10cm (4in), similar to above but much shorter and more spreading, single white or pale pink flowers which look very good trailing over the edge of a windowbox.

HEBE ALBICANS 'RED EDGE'

30cm (12in); evergreen shrub; **Zone 6**

Characteristics A fairly dense spreading mound of irregular outline. The stemless leaves are very neat being perfectly oval and arranged in four ranks. They are smooth and a blue-grey green but with a thin red edge which gives great contrast. In mid summer racemes of flowers appear from the upper leaf axils; they are white with the slightest hint of mauve.

Position Tolerant of exposed situations, full sun and shade.

Uses The neat foliage makes this an excellent choice for a windowbox in winter.

Compost Very tolerant of a wide range of composts.

Special maintenance None.

Other kinds to try *H. pimeleoides* 'Quicksilver', very small leaves 5mm (¼in) long, oval and tapered both ends, silver-blue-grey, well-spaced on dark wiry stems, pale bluish mauve flowers in mid summer, as dainty as raindrops on grass, Zone 6; *H. × franciscana* 'Blue Gem', 60cm (24in), mid green 4cm (1½in) leaves and dense spikes of violet-blue flowers mid summer to late autumn, Zone 7.5; *H. × franciscana* 'Variegata', as above but with creamy white leaf edges; *H.* 'Spender's Seedling', 70cm (30in), greyish narrow willow-like leaves 5cm (2in) long, white flower spikes from mid summer to mid autumn, Zone 7.5; *H.* 'Midsummer Beauty', similar to above but 1.2m (4ft) and mauve flowers in 10cm (4in) spikes mid summer to late autumn, very scented, Zone 8; *H.* 'Andersonii Variegata', as above but leaves with broad white margin, Zone 9.

HEDERA COLCHICA 'DENTATA VARIEGATA' VARIEGATED ELEPHANT'S EAR IVY

2.1m (7ft); evergreen self-clinging climber; **Zone 7**

Characteristics The clinging stems have large 10cm (4in) oval leaves with a pointed tip. These hang down and are reminiscent of an elephant's ear. In 'Dentata Variegata' they have a dark green centre surrounded by an irregular band of mid green and a broad margin of creamy white. The autumn flowers are small and greenish yellow but not produced for several years.

Position Tolerant of wind and different levels of light, from full sun to full shade.

Uses Most useful to lighten a dull dark corner or to form a screen, either growing against a wall or trained on a fence or trellis; also excellent for ground cover.

Compost Tolerant of all composts.

Special maintenance None, except where training is necessary.

Other kinds to try *H. colchica* 'Sulphur Heart', similar to above but leaves have a sulphur yellow centre surrounded by an irregular lime green zone, remainder of leaf is green; *H. canariensis* 'Gloire de Marengo', similar to above but thinner leaves

with a dark green centre, grey-green middle zone and white edge. In very cold winters it will defoliate, Zone 8; *H. helix* 'Pedata' (common ivy), leaves about 4cm (1½in) long with three very narrow lobes, fine textured, very dainty, good for trailing from a basket or windowbox, Zone 6; *H. helix* 'Glacier', similar to above but lobes wider and leaf greyish green with a white margin; *H. helix* 'Anna Marie', as above but broader leaves; *H. helix* 'Goldheart', dark green 4cm (1½in) leaves with a gold centre; *H. helix* 'Buttercup', leaves golden to lime green depending on light, slow growing; *H. helix* 'Angularis Aurea', light green leaves with irregular light yellow variegation; *H. helix* 'Atropurpurea', dark green leaves that turn purple in winter, an excellent trailing edge for a windowbox of snowdrops; *H. helix* 'Parsley Crested' ('Cristata') bright green leaves with ruffled edges.

HEDYCHIUM GARDNERIANUM GINGER LILY

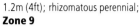

1.2m (4ft); rhizomatous perennial; **Zone 9**

Characteristics Strong shoots grow vertically from the base and bear glossy oval to lance-shaped flexible leaves about 40cm (16in) long. From the top of the shoots 30cm (12in) spikes appear densely packed with narrow-petalled, lemon yellow flowers whose red stamens and styles provide a dramatic contrast. The flowers are deliciously scented and open from late summer to early autumn.

Position Best in a sheltered place as extreme wind can damage the foliage but full sun or shaded conditions will do.

Uses This plant associates well with bananas, lemons and blue-flowered plumbago to give a tropical effect. It looks well in a terracotta pot or urn on the patio or by the poolside.

Compost Happy in most composts.

Special maintenance Remove dead leaves and flowers. In colder areas apply a mulch to form a protective winter blanket or take the container into a shed or garage for the winter.

Other kinds to try *H. densiflorum*, similar but with slightly broader soft orange-yellow flowers.

 deciduous

 semi-evergreen

 evergreen

 flowering period

 foliage/fruiting plant

 full sun

 ¼ shade-¾ sun

 ½ shade-½ sun

 ¼ sun-¾ shade

 full shade

 needs winter protection

149

HELIANTHEMUM 'WISLEY PINK'
ROCK ROSE

15cm (6in); small spreading evergreen shrub; **Zone 6**

Characteristics Thin lax spreading branches bear attractive 2cm (³⁄₄in) lance-shaped grey-green leaves. In summer the tips of the branches provide a succession of 2cm (³⁄₄in) wide round five-petalled flowers, pink with a yellow centre, not unlike those of a dog rose but of a more definite pink.
Position Very wind tolerant, but needs sun for good flowering.
Uses They are valuable edging plants, for a windowbox, tub or trough; the grey foliage trails over the edge and in summer the pink flowers are a delight. Associates well with a permanent planting of lavender, *Ceanothus* and *Convolvulus cneorum*.

Compost Given good drainage it is tolerant of most composts.
Special maintenance None, save pruning back any unwanted trails after flowering.
Other kinds to try 'Wisley Primrose', similar with yellow flowers; 'Wisley White', similar with white petals and yellow centres; 'Raspberry Ripple', similar but with petals irregularly mottled white and deep rose, leaves green; 'Jubilee', double lemon yellow flowers which tend to last longer than the single-flowered forms, leaves green.

HELIANTHUS TUBEROSUS 'DWARF SUNRAY'
JERUSALEM ARTICHOKE

1.5m (5ft); deciduous tuberous vegetable; **Zone 7**

Characteristics Strong vertical stems bear oval mid green leaves, 15cm (6in) long, with a rough surface. Flowerheads measure about 7.5cm (3in) in diameter with a brownish centre surrounded by yellow rays; just like small sunflowers. They open in late summer. Rounded irregular shaped tubers are formed beneath the ground. In this kind they are less knobbly than others on the market.
Position Shade tolerant but does best in full sun.
Uses The fast-growing leafy stems make an excellent screen during the summer which, when planted in tubs, can be moved to give privacy where required – perhaps for sunbathing. The yellow flowers are modestly attractive and in late autumn and winter the roots will yield the potato-like tubers which when cooked have a distinct and rich flavour.
Compost Grows in any compost but better tubers are produced if it is enriched with extra organic matter.
Special maintenance After the tubers are harvested in late autumn, put some by to replant in early spring for both next year's crop and a summer screen.

HELICHRYSUM PETIOLARE
(*H. petiolatum*)

30cm (12in); trailing or semi-climbing evergreen shrub; **Zone 8.5**

Characteristics The long grey stems will trail down or, when growing among shrubs or small trees, will clamber up in the centre of their branches with good effect and doing little harm. The round to heart-shaped 2cm (³⁄₄in) leaves are beautifully felted white, which gives a silvery sheen. In late summer papery cream flowers appear but the main beauty of the plant is in its foliage.
Position Wind tolerant, it grows well in full sun to full shade.
Uses One of the very best plants for silvery trails. It can be used with great effect in hanging baskets, urns and windowboxes to "pour silver" from amongst other colourful flowers.
Compost Tolerates most composts provided drainage is good.
Special maintenance Train and prune as necessary. In colder regions cuttings are easily struck so that small plants can grace a windowsill over winter to be planted the following year.
Other kinds to try 'Variegatum', as above but leaves edged cream. Useful where a less vigorous plant is required but with the same effect; 'Limelight', leaves all creamy silver. An interesting colour variation but it is prone to leaf scorch; *H. microphyllum* (*Plecostachys serpyllifolia*), a small version of *H. petiolare* as it is only 10cm (4in) high with leaves 1cm (³⁄₈in) diameter. Daintier for small containers; *H. italicum* (*H. angustifolium*) (curry plant), 60cm (24in), upright shoots but gradually spreading, thin grey-green leaves are aromatic, yellow papery flowers in summer, Zone 8.

HELIOTROPIUM PERUVIANUM
(*H. arborescens*)
MARINE CHERRY PIE

60cm (24in); evergreen bushy shrub, grown as an annual; **Zone 10**

Characteristics The oval pointed leaves are quite attractive. They are dark green with a slight purplish tinge, glossy and with fine net veining. From this pleasant foliage spreading clusters of numerous purple-mauve flowers arise late spring to late autumn. They have a delicious scent said to be like cherry pie.
Position Reasonably wind tolerant, it will grow in full sun and light shade.
Uses Just one plant in a container will give a wonderful scent. It looks well with silver grey foliage such as that of *Helichrysum petiolare* or *Calocephalus brownii*, either of which will fill in below and trail down.
Compost Tolerant of most composts.

Special maintenance Remove dead flower sprays. Train it up to a standard if desired. Take cuttings in late summer and over winter under cover, or grow new ones from seed in early spring.
Other kinds to try 'Chatsworth', similar not quite so dark, more vigorous, so better for training as a standard.

HEUCHERA MICRANTHA
'PALACE PURPLE'
PURPLE ALUM ROOT

30cm (12in); evergreen clump-forming herbaceous plant; **Zone 7.5**

Characteristics The rounded to heart-shaped leaves with palm-shaped vein system are the main attraction. It is the soft mauve-purple colour of the foliage which is maintained throughout the year that makes the plant unique. From this 15cm (6in) carpet, thin purple stems arise which produce open conical sprays of tiny white flowers during summer.
Position Avoid extremely windy places; grows well in full sun or full shade.

Uses It is a good ground cover subject for carpeting a container and an excellent foil for white or silver flowers and foliage. Combine with *Narcissus* 'Thalia', with its many-headed white flowers, for spring effect or, in a permanent arrangement beneath, a young *Eucalyptus cordata* or *E. gunnii* with *Hedera helix* 'Glacier' trailing over the edge.
Compost Tolerant of most composts.
Special maintenance Remove dead flowerheads and leaves if required.
Other kinds to try *H.* 'Red Spangles', similar to above, the green leaves are a good foil for the crimson-scarlet flowers.

HOSTA
'THOMAS HOGG'
(*H. undulata* 'Albomarginata')

60cm (24in); clump-forming herbaceous perennial; **Zone 5**

Characteristics The oval to lance-shaped leaves have a heart-shaped base and their vertical green stems arise from the ground. Each leaf is about 30cm (12in) long and has an attractive undulating edge, broadly and irregularly margined with white. In mid summer numerous trumpet-shaped pale violet flowers are held above the dense tuft of leaves on vertical flower stems.
Position Keep away from hot drying winds, otherwise this does well in full sun to full shade.
Uses Ideal for brightening a dark corner, it contrasts well with the fine foliage of astilbes, the purple foliage of *Heuchera micrantha* 'Palace Purple' or the trails of *Lysimachia nummularia* which will hang down over the edge of the tub or trough.
Compost It will tolerate most composts if given extra organic matter to ensure a reserve of moisture.
Special maintenance Snails and slugs will enjoy the young foliage. These can be picked off by hand in the evening or, since they love beer, bait them with an almost empty beer can.

Other kinds to try *H. fortunei* 'Albopicta', light green leaves with cream-yellow centre; *H. sieboldiana elegans*, 75cm (30in), deeply ribbed oval leaves of a wonderful blue-grey.

HYACINTHUS ORIENTALIS
'PINK PEARL'
HYACINTH

15cm (6in); hardy bulb; **Zone 7**

Characteristics Green vertical strap-shaped leaves, which curve back at the top when mature, surround the thick hollow flower stem. The numerous tubular florets with their six flared-back petals are densely packed at the top of the stem in spring. They are extremely fragrant and in this kind are a good mid pink.
Position Very tolerant of different light conditions; from full sun to full shade.
Uses Few flowers can compete with hyacinths for early spring scent. A windowbox with these hyacinths underplanted with a carpet of *Viola* 'Universal True Blue' brightens the dullest day.
Compost Very tolerant of most composts.
Special maintenance Flower spikes from large bulbs – 17cm (6½in) or more in circumference – will be heavy and may need staking with a split cane; smaller bulbs, 14–16cm (5½–6½in) in circumference, still have good flower spikes but seldom need support.
Other kinds to try 'Anne Marie', soft salmony pink; 'Delft Blue', mid blue with a hint of turquoise; 'Myosotis', light blue; 'L'Innocence', white.

HYDRANGEA SERRATA
'BLUEBIRD'
HYDRANGEA

75cm (30in); deciduous shrub; **Zone 6**

Characteristics A rounded shrub with oval to lance-shaped green leaves. In summer stems like the spokes of an umbrella support the flat open flowerheads of mauvy blue. The inner florets are small and bluer whilst the outer florets have wider petals and are more mauve.
Position Tolerant of wind and light; from full sun to full shade.

Uses Effective in an urn or tub, in particular a white-painted Versailles tub with *Hedera helix* 'Glacier'.
Compost Tolerant of most composts but regular feeding is necessary with peat-based compost. If the compost is acid (lime-free) the flowers will be blue; if alkaline they will bloom pink. Aluminium sulphate is a convenient way of increasing acidity to promote blue flowers.
Special maintenance Even when brown the flowers are attractive in texture and their removal can be delayed until early spring.
Other kinds to try *H. serrata* 'Grayswood', similar but tends to be pinker; *H. macrophylla* 'Altona', globular flowers which, in acid compost, are the best sky blue with a hint of turquoise; *H. macrophylla* 'Ami Pasquier', in alkaline compost each flowerhead is a good rose-crimson 10cm (4in) globe of large florets; *H. macrophylla* 'Madame E. Mouillère', many globes of white florets which eventually become flushed with pink; *H. macrophylla* 'Blue Wave', blue or lilac; *H. petiolaris* (*H. anomala petiolaris*), when mature a climber with white lace-cap flowers that will flourish against a north wall.

deciduous

semi-evergreen

evergreen

flowering period

foliage/fruiting plant

full sun

¼ shade-¾ sun

½ shade-½ sun

¼ sun-¾ shade

full shade

needs winter protection

151

IBERIS SEMPERVIRENS
EVERGREEN CANDYTUFT

10cm (4in); spreading evergreen shrub; **Zone 5**

Characteristics Wiry stems are covered with tiny dark green narrow lance-shaped leaves. Against this background the disc-shaped heads of pure white flowers create great contrast in spring.
Position Wind tolerant, but for a permanent planting choose a spot with reasonable light to ensure flower buds are initiated.

Uses An excellent evergreen carpet for around the base of golden *Narcissus* 'Sweetness' or ruby 'Captain Fryatt', a lily-flowered tulip. They look well in a windowbox with a small *Cordyline australis* at each end to give height.
Compost Tolerant of most composts if reasonable drainage is given.
Special maintenance Clip over with shears after flowering to remove dead flowerheads and any straggly shoots.
Other kinds to try *I.s.* 'Little Gem' ('Weisser Zwerg'), shorter and more compact for the smaller container.

ILEX AQUIFOLIUM
'PERRY'S WEEPING'
PERRY'S WEEPING HOLLY

1.5m (5ft); weeping evergreen tree; **Zone 7**

Characteristics The leaves are typical of a holly, dark green, wavy and spiny edged, but in this case they are broadly and irregularly margined with white. They are a marvellous background for the bright red fruits that last from autumn until the birds take them. Remember that this is a female variety and will require a male plant for pollination.
Position Very wind and light tolerant; from full sun to full shade.
Uses A wooden half barrel is a suitable container and a link with Christmas good cheer. Clothe the base with ivy and have snowdrops, *Galanthus* 'Atkinsii', growing through for a perfect winter composition.
Compost Tolerates any compost.
Special maintenance None, save training as required.
Other kinds to try 'Ferox Argentea', leaves with spines all over the blade and a creamy white margin, much slower growing and defensive, suitable for the ends of a windowbox — it will keep the cats off; 'Handsworth New Silver', upright with purple branchlets, leaves with a broad creamy white margin, red fruit; 'Myrtifolia Aureo-maculata', smaller golden-centred leaves for windowboxes; 'J. C. van Tol', dark green leaves are less spiny than above, pyramid habit, masses of red fruit as it is self-fertile; 'Bacciflava' with yellow fruits; *I. cornuta*, 1m (3¼ft), rounded shrub, square leaves with spines in the corners.

IMPATIENS
'NOVETTE RED STAR'
BUSY LIZZIE

15cm (6in); evergreen bushy perennial grown as an annual; **Zone 10**

Characteristics Green spreading rather succulent stems have oval pointed shallow-toothed leaves of a fresh green colour. A long succession of flowers produced from late spring to late autumn. Each rounded petal is rose-crimson with a white central line so together they make a star pattern.

Position Reasonably wind tolerant and grows well in full sun to full shade.
Uses An extremely good carpeting plant because of its continuous flowering. A tub, windowbox or trough planted with this busy Lizzie, a few plants of sky blue *Plumbago capensis* to give height and an edging of light blue *Lobelia erinus* 'Blue Cascade' will give a very fine effect.
Compost Tolerant of most composts.
Special maintenance None.
Other kinds to try 'Super Elfin' range, similar in a wide range of colours: 'Fuchsia', rich purple; 'Red Velvet', deep red; 'Rose', cherry rose; 'Orange'; 'Salmon Blush', salmon with deeper eye; 'White'; 'Blue Pearl', bluish white; 'Accent' range similar to above but with even denser flowers. The range includes 18 separate colours and three different mixtures; 'Tango', 25cm (10in), this was raised from one of the New Guinea hybrids. It has dark bronze foliage and large deep orange flowers.

IPOMOEA RUBROCAERULEA
'HEAVENLY BLUE'

3m (10ft); fast-growing annual climber; **Zone 9**

Characteristics Twining stems rapidly grow up to bear heart-shaped mid green leaves and 6.5cm (2½in) diameter funnel-shaped flowers, like so many swirling sky blue silk dresses. This lovely display starts in mid summer and continues to mid autumn.
Position Flowers best in sun.
Uses Even on days with grey skies a trellis covered with these sky blue flowers gives the feeling of sunshine. It contrasts well with the formal shape and dark green leaves of a palm-like plant, such as *Cordyline australis*, in a pot nearby.
Compost Although tolerant of most composts it is highly sensitive to magnesium deficiency. A weak solution of Epsom salts (a pinch in a can of water) applied every two weeks will overcome this problem.
Special maintenance A little tying will train the plant as required.

IRIS DANFORDIAE

7.5cm (3in); bulb; **Zone 7**

Characteristics Narrow leaves push up through the soil in early spring; they are more or less quandrangular in cross section. In late winter before the leaves have achieved their full length, the flowers open. These are bright yellow with green spots on the falls (the three lowest petals). After flowering the leaves grow to their full length.
Position Its short stature is not affected by wind; from full sun to half shade.
Uses It brings brilliant colour to late winter and associates well with snowdrops, bringing warmth to their white flowers. As both are short they suit a windowbox and do not obscure the view.
Compost Tolerant of most composts provided drainage is good.
Special maintenance None.
Other kinds to try *I. reticulata* 'Cantab', 10cm (4in), similar to above but mid blue flowers with a yellow mark on each fall; *I. reticulata* 'Joyce', sky blue with an orange ridge on the falls; *I. reticulata* 'Pauline', deep purple with an orange mark on the falls.

IRIS UNGUICULARIS
(*I. stylosa*)
ALGERIAN IRIS

20cm (8in); evergreen rhizomatous herbaceous plant; **Zone 6**

Characteristics Flat mid-green leaves, 20cm (8in) long, spray out to form a dense clump. In winter the flowers give a long succession of blooms until mid spring. They are mid to deep sky blue with white and gold feathering on the falls.
Position Flowers best in a sunny place against a wall, but also tolerates half shade.

Uses Permanently planted in an urn or trough this iris is a most effective plant during the winter. The yellow winter jasmine flowers at the same time and would make an excellent background.
Compost A well-drained compost is best, not too rich, with added grit.
Special maintenance Old brown leaves can be cut off or pulled out.
Other kinds to try 'Walter Butt', light sky blue with white and golden feathering; 'Mary Barnard', dark blue with white and golden feathering; 'Alba', white with gold feathering; *I. pallida* 'Variegata', broad 45cm (18in) spear-like grey-green leaves edged white, sky blue flowers in early summer. A wonderful soft effect; *I. foetidissima*, 30cm (12in), tuft of dark green leaves, a very good background for the open pods of bright scarlet seeds in winter, flowers dull yellow or blue in summer; *I. pseudacorus* 'Variegata', 60cm (24in), vertical bright green leaves striped creamy yellow in spring, golden yellow flowers in mid summer. For the pool edge; *I. laevigata* 'Variegata', 45cm (18in), leaves variegated white, royal blue and white flowers in mid summer; *I. japonica* 'Variegata', bright green leaves edged white, Zone 8.5.

JASMINUM POLYANTHUM
JASMINE

2.1m (7ft); evergreen climbing shrub; **Zone 9**

Characteristics The green stems are clothed with attractive leaves composed of five or seven oval pointed leaflets. In late spring the main flush of flowers appears but spasmodic flowering often occurs later in the year. The deliciously scented flowers are in many clusters along the ends of the branches. The pink flower buds open to reveal white petals which show up clearly against the dark green leaves.
Position A south-west-facing corner is best, in full sun or full shade.
Uses As the plant is marginally hardy it can be kept permanently in a very sheltered spot or brought in for the worst of the winter. It is best planted in its own pot or urn.
Compost Tolerant of most composts, but an enriched peat-based type is best with added organic matter.
Special maintenance No special requirements except training to the required shape.

Other kinds to try *J. officinale* 'Argenteovariegatum', similar to the above but the very fragrant white flowers appear in mid summer to mid autumn, semi-evergreen leaflets are edged with creamy white – so the plant is slower growing, Zone 8; *J. nudiflorum*, deciduous with small oval leaves. In winter the weeping green stems are showered with yellow flowers from early winter to mid spring, Zone 6; *J. parkeri*, evergreen, yellow summer flowers.

JUNIPERUS SABINA
'TAMARISCIFOLIA'
JUNIPER

60cm (24in); evergreen spreading conifer; **Zone 2**

Characteristics It has an irregular outline of somewhat tiered horizontal feathery branches covered with tiny mid green needles.
Position Very wind tolerant; from full sun to partial shade.
Uses In a windowbox, tub or trough it both softens the edge and provides a good dark background for light-coloured winter pansies and flowering bulbs.
Compost Tolerant of most composts.
Special maintenance None, save pruning out the occasional branch should it get in the way.

Other kinds to try *J. × media* 'Pfitzeriana Aurea', 1m (3¼ft), spreading flat-topped shrub with golden green needles. For a taller background plant, *J. communis* 'Hibernica', 1m (3¼ft), columnar small tree, tiny mid green needles. It has the effect of exclamation marks to punctuate a windowbox or trough and contrast with horizontal plants; *J. communis* 'Hornibrookii', a prostrate mid green mat, 15cm (6in) high, Zone 4; *J. horizontalis* 'Wiltonii' (*J. horizontalis* 'Blue Rug'), 20cm (8in) high, spreading blue-grey rug of fine foliage, Zone 3; *J. squamata* 'Blue Star', 45cm (18in), dense rounded bush of glaucous blue spiky foliage, Zone 5; *J. scopulorum* 'Skyrocket', 2m (6ft), slim blue-green pillar-shaped tree.

deciduous

semi-evergreen

evergreen

flowering period

foliage/ fruiting plant

full sun

¼ shade- ¾ sun

½ shade- ½ sun

¼ sun- ¾ shade

full shade

needs winter protection

L

LACTUCA SATIVA
'SALAD BOWL'
LETTUCE

20cm (8in); rosette-leaf annual vegetable; **Zone 7**

Characteristics The loose rosette of light green leaves is very attractive and quite different from round types of lettuce. Each leaf is separate and has a curled edge.

Position Reasonable light is needed for success, so choose a place in full sun or light shade.

Uses 'Salad Bowl' contrasts well with the vertical leaf tufts of onions and chives, in particular when the latter have their purple pompon flowers. Red fruit of any kind, such as peppers or tomatoes, look good with these lettuces. They are useful for the table because leaves can be picked over a long period for use in salads, yet the plant will continue to grow.

Compost Most enriched composts are suitable as they retain water. Good drainage is essential.

Special maintenance Grow with onions as they seem to help each other's development. Beer in saucers will attract and drown slugs and snails, the worst pests of lettuces.

Other kinds to try 'Lollo Rossa', as above but russet red leaves; 'All the Year Round', a cabbage lettuce with a tight heart and crisp green leaves; 'Little Gem', 12cm (5in) high, crisp, sweet and green. The latter is most useful in containers because of its compact upright habit – more plants will fit into a small space. The leaves are straighter than normal so are easier to wash, offer less corners for slugs to hide in and provide fewer enclosed places that favour disease. It is also resistant to root aphid.

LANTANA CAMARA
'SPREADING SUNSET'

75cm (30in); fairly tender evergreen shrub; **Zone 9.5**

Characteristics The stiff rather rough green stems are long and in combination with the well-spaced leaves form an open shrub. The leaves are mid to deep green, oval and covered with fine wrinkles. Towards the ends of the shoots rounded clusters of flowers appear in mid spring to late autumn. Individually the florets are tubular with flared petals of orangy pink.

Position It is fairly wind tolerant and will thrive in full sun or partial shade.

Uses A good plant for a tub, underplanted with a carpet of yellow African marigolds. Lantana is easy to train up as a standard.

Compost Well-drained but enriched compost with extra organic material for continuous growth.

Special maintenance Stop side-shoots when young if a bushy plant is needed, or train up for a standard.

Other kinds to try Most varieties available from garden centres are bought under colour: red, pink, orange and yellow; *L. montevidensis* (*L. sellowiana*), a shorter plant at 45cm (18in), mauve-purple flowers.

LATHYRUS ODORATUS
'PATIO MIXED'
DWARF SWEET PEA

30cm (12in); hardy annual; **Zone 7**

Characteristics Green shoots with short joints result in a bushy plant. Strong green flower stems above this normally bear about four large pea-like flowers, that is with a standard – circular petals held upright at the back – and a keel of two petals pointing forwards. They emit that familiar light fragrance of sweet peas and bloom from mid summer to early autumn.

Position More resistant to wind than the tall types of sweet pea; from full sun to half shade.

Uses The introduction of dwarf sweet peas was a great breakthrough for container gardeners. With the wide range of colours this mixture will bush out over the edge of a tub or windowbox and only requires a green contrast, perhaps *Asparagus sprengeri*, to trail down and *Grevillea robusta* to spring up above.

Compost Tolerates most composts.

Special maintenance Remove dead flower stems.

Other kinds to try 'Bijou Mixed', similar to above but 45cm (18in); 'Supersnoop Mixed', no tendrils so the plants are tangle free, if unsupported they grow up to about 1m (3¼ft) but also trail down over a container; *L. latifolius* (everlasting sweet pea), an herbaceous climber that will come up every year, about 2.1m (7ft) high, self-clinging, pink-mauve flowers, *Zone 7*; *L. latifolius* 'Albus', white form of above, useful because it does not clash with any other colours.

LAURUS NOBILIS
BAY

1.5m (5ft); evergreen shrub or tree; **Zone 7.5**

Characteristics Bay has a somewhat upright growth form with stiff branches. The leaves are oval and pointed, about 10cm (4in) long, dark green and aromatic. The pale yellow flowers of spring are not a major feature and are few and far between on clipped plants.

Position Strong freezing winds will brown the leaf edges, so choose a fairly sheltered position in full sun to partial shade.

Uses A pair of bays in tubs or urns will give an air of grandeur to an entrance or doorway. Bays may be trained to many different shapes: a ball-topped standard, a cone or column. Their solemn importance contrasts well with containers of *Argyranthemum frutescens* or *A. gracile* 'Chelsea Girl', whose dainty daisies and delicate foliage bring lightness of colour and texture.

Compost Tolerates any compost provided drainage is good.

Special maintenance Train to the required shape.

Other kinds to try *L. nobilis angustifolia*, narrower leaves, an advantage for a smaller clipped bush.

LAVANDULA ANGUSTIFOLIA 'MUNSTEAD' LAVENDER

60cm (24in); evergreen shrub; **Zone 7**

Characteristics In an open situation this is a rounded shrub with aromatic narrow grey-green leaves. The soft mauve-blue flowers form tight cylindrical heads at the top of long stems in summer.

Position Wind tolerant, but sun is needed to encourage flower production.

Uses For the perfect cottage garden effect plant this lavender in a half barrel with a dark-leaved white-flowered myrtle and a prostrate blue rosemary to trail over the edge. Lavender has many uses: for dried flower arrangements, lavender bags to scent cupboards and deter insects and for medicinal purposes.

Compost Tolerates all composts provided drainage is good.

Special maintenance Clip over the plant after flowering to encourage a shapely bush.

Other kinds to try 'Hidcote', similar but a rich purple-blue; *L.* 'Nana Alba', 45cm (18in), with white flowers, a good contrast with the above; *L. stoechas* (French lavender), 60cm (24in), like 'Hidcote' but denser greyer foliage and flowers topped with longer wing-like bracts, Zone 8; *L. stoechas pedunculata*, as above but with reddish purple flowers; *L. dentata*, similar to above in flower but with toothed leaves which are deliciously scented, Zone 8.5.

LEWISIA COTYLEDON HYBRIDS

30cm (12in); evergreen rosette-forming alpine; **Zone 6**

Characteristics Toothed spoon-shaped leaves form a rosette from which, in late spring to late summer, leafless erect stems give rise to sprays of salmon-pink, or purplish flowers.

Position This plant can grow happily with no direct sunlight so it is suitable for a windowbox against a north-facing wall.

Uses Since in nature it is found in rock crevices, where the rosettes can grow in a vertical position, it does well in the "pouches" of herb pots or in windowboxes wedged between rocks.

Compost Well-drained, ericaceous (lime-free) compost is needed.

Special maintenance Added grit around the rosette every year ensures good drainage.

Other kinds to try *L. tweedyi*, 15cm (6in), white to pale pink flowers.

LILIUM SPECIOSUM RUBRUM LILY

1m (3¼ft); bulb with stem roots; **Zone 7**

Characteristics The stout and vertical stem, clothed with lance-shaped leaves, branches at the top. In summer these branches carry up to twelve six-petalled flowers, each petal up to 10cm (4in) long. In some forms of *speciosum* the superbly scented flowers are white and in others, as shown here, they are pink. Whatever their colour they are spotted with crimson and have a crimson line along the midrib. The petals curl back to display the long stamens.

Position Place in a sheltered position away from strong wind; from full sun to half shade.

Uses Create a very distinctive and fragrant feature by planting these lilies in an urn or barrel.

Compost Good drainage is important and an enriched compost with extra organic matter is best, although most neutral to acid composts will be satisfactory.

Special maintenance It is worth tying each flower stem to a slim cane.

Other kinds to try *L. auratum*, ten fragrant bowl-shaped white flowers, each petal 15cm (6in) long with a central yellow band and red or yellow spots, needs semi-shade and acid soil; 'Enchantment', a hybrid with upward-pointing orange-red cups with black-spotted throats; 'Golden Melody', similar but yellow and spotted with red-brown; 'Sterling Star', white with red-brown spots; *L. longiflorum*, white outward-facing trumpets.

LINUM ARBOREUM SHRUBBY FLAX

30cm (12in); evergreen compact shrub; **Zone 7.5**

Characteristics An irregular mound of dense bluish-green oval leaves. In summer a succession of short stems are topped with clusters of five-petalled, funnel-shaped, bright yellow flowers.

Position Flowers best in full sun.

Uses Good for a windowbox or trough of alpines as it extends the mainly spring season of colour. It looks well with the finer leaves and round flower clusters of *Armeria maritima*.

Compost Organic well-drained compost is best.

Special maintenance After flowering the flower stalks can be clipped off with shears.

Other kinds to try *L. suffruticosum salsoloides*, 15cm (6in), fine greyish-green leaves and pearl white flowers.

deciduous

semi-evergreen

evergreen

flowering period

foliage/fruiting plant

full sun

¼ shade-¾ sun

½ shade-½ sun

¼ sun-¾ shade

full shade

needs winter protection

155

LOBELIA
'QUEEN VICTORIA'

60cm (24in); herbaceous perennial; **Zone 8**

Characteristics Purple vertical stems have lance-shaped leaves which are broader near the ground and narrower near the top. They are smooth, glistening and purplish, and very attractive in their own right. In summer the spikes of brilliant crimson-scarlet flowers appear. Each floret has three basal lobes like an apron and two smaller upright lobes.

Position Quite light tolerant; from full sun to partial shade.
Uses The purple foliage contrasts well with grey, particularly with the broad bluish leaves of *Hosta sieboldiana elegans*; they are an excellent foil for the scarlet flowers.
Compost Prefers moist conditions, so it is important to add extra organic matter such as leafmould.
Special maintenance Where there are only a few plants it is worth supporting each flower stem with a thin bamboo cane and a few ties. In winter, mulch over the top of the plant to protect it from severe frost. In the coldest areas lift the plants, pot or box them up and put in a cool shed or similar place.
Other kinds to try 'Cherry Ripe', cerise-scarlet flowers, leaves mainly green; *L.* 'Vedrariensis', purple flowers, dark green leaves; *L. syphilitica*, blue flowers, green leaves.

LOBELIA ERINUS
'BLUE CASCADE'

10cm (4in); half-hardy perennial grown as an annual; **Zone 10**

Characteristics A creeping carpet of trailing stems which are clothed with tiny lance-shaped leaves. The flowers are like a three-lobed apron hanging down with smaller petals at the top. They are a beautiful sky blue and open from mid summer to mid autumn.
Position Avoid very exposed places and drying winds, but it is very light tolerant and will flower well in full sun or full shade.
Uses These plants are invaluable wherever an annual plant is required to form a trailing carpet of blue. The cool blue flowers look well spilling over the edges of hanging baskets, urns and windowboxes. Fuchsias, in particular, with their reds, whites and purples, make good partners.
Compost Tolerant of most composts.
Special maintenance Ensure the plants are kept well watered.
Other kinds to try 'Red Cascade', purple-red with a white eye; 'Sapphire', deep blue with a white eye; 'Cascade Mixed', mixed colours; 'Lilac Fountain', lilac flowers; 'White Fountain', white to palest blue flowers; 'Cambridge Blue', sky blue flowers, non-trailing for carpeting; 'Crystal Palace', deep blue flowers and bronzy leaves; 'Rosamund', carmine-red with a white eye; 'White Lady', white to palest blue flowers.

LONICERA JAPONICA
'AUREO-RETICULATA'
VARIEGATED JAPANESE HONEYSUCKLE

2.1m (7ft); evergreen climber; **Zone 6**

Characteristics A twining climber whose oval pointed bright green leaves have very distinctive bright yellow veins which form a most delicate net-like pattern. In summer little clusters of delightfully scented cream flowers appear. These become yellow with age.
Position Very light tolerant; from full sun to full shade.
Uses This plant looks good at all times of the year. It will trail down the sides of an urn or windowbox and in winter it makes a pleasant change from ivy which fulfils a similar function. It associates well with *Nandina domestica* whose leaves are orangy red in winter.
Compost Tolerant of most composts.
Special maintenance Train as required or leave alone.
Other kinds to try *L.j.* 'Halliana', similar but with green leaves, a more vigorous plant ideal for a quick-growing scented screen against a fence, wall or tree; *L.* × *brownii*, deciduous with blue-green leaves and orange-red flowers. *L periclymenum* (common honeysuckle), 4m (15ft), apricot, scented, summer flowers.

LONICERA NITIDA
'BAGGESEN'S GOLD'
SHRUBBY HONEYSUCKLE

1m (3¼ft); evergreen shrub; **Zone 7**

Characteristics A rounded shrub with an attractive very feathery outline if left unclipped. The leaves are tiny about 5mm (¼in) across, oval and yellow to lime green. The small flowers open late in spring and are also yellowish green.
Position Tolerant of wind and most light conditions; from full sun to partial shade.
Uses It is useful as a background plant, particularly in winter and spring. It looks well behind scarlet tulips, red *Anemone coronaria* De Caen and the salmon-pink striped foliage of *Phormium tenax* 'Sundowner'.
Compost Tolerant of most composts.
Special maintenance No problems, just train it to any special shape required or leave alone to form its natural outline.

LOTUS BERTHELOTII

15cm (6in); trailing perennial grown as an annual; **Zone 9**

Characteristics Lax stems cover the container and trail down the sides. The stems and the fine needle-like leaves are a very silvery green. In summer the foliage is studded with rusty red pea-like flowers. Flowering is sometimes erratic.
Position Wind and light tolerant, it thrives in full sun to partial shade.
Uses This fine-textured silver trailer looks good in any hanging basket, windowbox or urn. It is the perfect foil to the heavier texture and upright growth of orange African marigolds and scarlet pelargoniums.
Compost Tolerant of all composts provided drainage is good.
Special maintenance None. The plant can be brought in over winter and treated as a half-hardy perennial.
Other kinds to try *L. maculatus*, similar to above but the yellow flowers with orange tips are more attractive and, because of their lighter colour, less likely to clash with other plants.

LYCOPERSICON ESCULENTUM 'PIXIE'
TOMATO

45cm (18in); annual bush; **Zone 10**

Characteristics Strong-stemmed bushy plant with soft green leaves divided into seven or more oval leaflets. The hanging clusters of small yellow flowers are followed by round fruits about 2.5cm (1in) diameter, green at first changing through yellow and orange to shining scarlet. Although tomatoes are well known to everyone their decorative effect is often forgotten.
Position Choose a sheltered place. Sun encourages flower and fruit development rather than leaf growth.
Uses Delicious fruit, mouthwatering when picked fresh during an alfresco meal on the patio. Grow in a tub and this plant will be a delightful decoration when in fruit.
Compost Most composts are suitable provided extra feed is given regularly after flowering has commenced.

Special maintenance A cane may be needed for support. Keep moist in periods of drought.
Other kinds to try 'Sweet 100', 1m (3¼ft), long trusses of numerous cherry-sized very sweet tomatoes. Attractive plant, needs more tying-in than above. 'Tumbler', 30cm (12in), ideal for a hanging basket, a short bush from which numerous sweet small red fruits hang down. Plant with *Lobelia erinus* 'Blue Cascade'. 'Dombello', individual fruits may weigh up to 1kg (2½lb), no central core so very meaty, very disease resistant.

LYSIMACHIA NUMMULARIA 'AUREA'
CREEPING JENNY

4cm (1½in); creeping evergreen perennial; **Zone 7.5**

Characteristics The creeping stems that root as they spread have pairs of round yellow-green leaves, 12mm (½in) in diameter. The bright yellow cupped flowers are also about 12mm (½in) across and open in summer.
Position Provided the soil does not dry out it is reasonably wind tolerant and very light tolerant. However it flowers less in shade than in sun.

Uses An excellent trailer for hanging baskets, windowboxes and urns. It looks particularly well with ferns since their fine foliage contrasts with the shiny circular leaves and they both enjoy moisture and shade.
Compost Tolerant of most composts provided the roots are kept moist.
Special maintenance None, unless any excess growth needs to be removed.
Other kinds to try *L. nummularia*, the common green-leaved form, is useful where the yellow foliage would be unsuitable, for example, as a ground cover for the golden *Narcissus* 'February Gold' and the later flowering *N.* 'Sweetness'. These and other bulbs will easily grow through the short carpet of leaves.

MAGNOLIA STELLATA
STAR MAGNOLIA

1.5m (5ft); deciduous shrub; **Zone 6**

Characteristics A rounded outline of sturdy somewhat twiggy grey stems. In early spring before the leaves appear, it looks very dramatic as it is covered with many-petalled star-shaped white flowers. Each flower is deliciously scented and measures about 7.5cm (3in) across with lance-shaped round-tipped petals. After flowering light green oval leaves clothe the bush.
Position Reasonably tolerant of wind and light. Sun in summer results in more flower buds forming than would do so in a shady place.
Uses In a tub or trough this plant has tremendous appeal in spring, particularly if it is grown with dark blue *Muscari armeniacum* around its base. Out of season it can be moved to provide a background for more colourful container plantings.
Compost Tolerant of most composts provided they are not very limy; an ericaceous compost is safest. Add extra organic matter to help growth.
Special maintenance None.
Other kinds to try 'Rubra', pink-flowered form.

 deciduous

 semi-evergreen

 evergreen

 flowering period

 foliage/ fruiting plant

 full sun

 ¼ shade-¾ sun

 ½ shade-½ sun

 ¼ sun-¾ shade

 full shade

 needs winter protection

MAHONIA JAPONICA

1.2m (4ft); evergreen shrub; **Zone 6**

Characteristics The irregular rounded outline of this shrub is due to the stiff branches. Long leaves composed of pairs of glossy spine-edged leaflets are 15cm (6in) long. They are dark green but often turn a bronzy colour with age. In winter long horizontally spreading sprays of soft yellow flowers appear, gradually opening in sequence over a long period. Although they are quite small, about 12mm (½in) in diameter, each flower emits a superb scent. The blue-black fruits which follow the flowers are also attractive.
Position Fairly tolerant of wind, this plant flourishes in full sun and full shade.

Uses For those with a nose for perfume and the space, plant this mahonia in a tub by a doorway. It will be a constant source of delight in winter. The lack of colour at other times can be remedied by planting the base with *Hedera colchica* 'Dentata Variegata' or *H. colchica* 'Sulphur Heart' and the everlasting sweet pea will give summer flowers.
Compost An enriched compost is best with added organic matter, such as leafmould, which will help retain water in a windy or sunny place.
Special maintenance None.
Other kinds to try *M.* × *media* 'Charity', similar but a little more vigorous and with narrower leaflets; *M. aquifolium* 'Atropurpurea', 60cm (24in), purplish green 10cm (4in) leaves with fine leaflets, flowers in short upright 7.5cm (3in) spikes, insignificant scent, Zone 5; *M.* × *wagneri* 'Moseri', similar to above but with pink-flushed leaves.

MALUS
'ELLISON'S ORANGE'
APPLE

2.1m (7ft) on an M9 or M27 rootstock; deciduous fruit tree; **Zone 6**
Characteristics This apple is self-fertile – even if it is the only plant in the neighbourhood it will still produce apples. It is a medium grower so can make a traditional tree shape to give shade but can be kept to a reasonable size with ease. Oval mid green leaves turn yellow with occasional orange tints in autumn. Pale pink flowers open in late spring. The fruit is yellowish green with a reddish flush and russeting, not unlike 'Cox's Orange Pippin' from which it was bred. This crisp and juicy apple with an aniseed flavour is best eaten in mid autumn. It crops well in alternate years with a lighter crop in between.
Position Choose a sheltered place to encourage bees to pollinate the flowers. Plenty of sun is needed to ripen the fruit.
Uses Enjoy the delicious fruit straight from the tree. It is nice to sit in the shade of its branches and observe the ripening apples!
Compost An enriched loam-based compost is best.
Special maintenance Prune in autumn by reducing side growths by about two-thirds if they are too long. Hang a pheromone trap in the tree to catch codling moths in late spring until mid summer.
Other kinds to try A family tree, grafted with several varieties so that they will pollinate each other, is a good idea but make sure one variety does not overgrow and force out the others. So keep watch and prune to maintain a balance. Ballerina apples are specially bred to grow like columns. No pruning except topping the leader where required. Plant at least two different trees to achieve fruit. It can be trimmed to many other shapes.

MALUS SARGENTII
SARGENT'S FLOWERING
CRAB APPLE

1.5m (5ft); deciduous tree or shrub; **Zone 5**

Characteristics One of the slowest growing of the flowering crab apples, it has an irregular outline of twiggy growth. In late spring it becomes covered completely with a profusion of 2.5cm (1in) white fine-petalled flowers. Each flower is prettily centred with a group of primrose yellow stamens. Oval 6.5cm (2½in) mid green leaves follow the flowers and turn yellow in autumn when the masses of fruit develop. These are about 12mm (½in) across, yellow at first gradually becoming red.
Position Choose a sheltered place to encourage insects to pollinate the flowers and so ensure a crop of fruit; full sun to half shade.
Uses Since this is a slow-growing very floriferous tree of great seasonal interest it is ideal for container culture. The birds seem to leave the fruit longer than other crab apples so extending the period of interest. Beauty all the year round can be achieved if this crab is grown in a tub underplanted with spring bulbs – yellow daffodils followed by scarlet tulips – and *Clematis alpina* to climb through the branches for a display of summer flowers.
Compost Tolerates most composts.
Special maintenance None, save training as required.
Other kinds to try 'Golden Hornet', white flowers, masses of golden fruit; 'Red Jade', pale pink flowers, crimson-red long-lasting fruits on weeping branches.

MANDEVILLA × AMABILIS
'ALICE DU PONT'

2.1m (7ft); evergreen climber; **Zone 9.5**

Characteristics Twining stems have 10cm (4in) oval leaves with the veins impressed which gives a pleasant texture to the shiny surface. In summer trumpet-shaped glowing pink flowers enliven the plant. Since they are each about 7.5cm (3in) across they make an impressive display.
Position Plant out of the wind in full sun or full shade.
Uses This magnificent South American plant is bound to impress. Plant in a large terracotta pot or urn on a sheltered patio to give a touch of the exotic.
Compost Best in an enriched peat-based compost with additional organic matter.
Special maintenance As the plant matures its growth gets very congested so spur-prune side branches. It is best to bring the plant in for the winter.

Other kinds to try *M. laxa* (*M. suaveolens*), semi-evergreen with fragrant white flowers, hardier than the above, can be left out in winter in warmer areas, Zone 8.

MATTEUCCIA STRUTHIOPTERIS
OSTRICH FERN

75cm (30in); deciduous fern; **Zone 5**

Characteristics The crown is covered with dark brown scales and it also produces stolons by which the plant can spread. The leaf-like fronds vary in length according to growing conditions. They are twice divided into over one thousand tiny lobes and held at an angle so that they look like a great green feathery shuttlecock.

Position Best sheltered from strong wind and shaded from the sun.

Uses They create a dramatic effect in a damp and sunless corner. An urn or half barrel with this upright circle of "feathers" at the rear, the shorter rounded outline of the delicate *Adiantum pedatum* in front and the undivided tongue-like leaves of Hart's-tongue fern (*Phyllitis scolopendrium*) to one side, make a superb composition of form and texture in green. Around the base *Saxifraga stolonifera* 'Tricolor' will add a cover of white and pink.

Compost Tolerates most composts provided extra organic matter is added for moisture-retention.

Special maintenance Remove old brown fronds in early spring.

MATTHIOLA INCANA
BROMPTON STOCK

45cm (18in); bushy biennial; **Zone 7**

Characteristics The erect bushy stems are well clothed in grey-green round-tipped lance-shaped leaves. In late spring the flower spikes lengthen and the highly scented flowers open. There are several types of this stock but the most widely grown is called "selectible" since the seedlings can be sorted by leaf colour and all the plants will then produce the double-rosette flower. The range of colours includes rose-pink, white, mauve and blue.

Position They are wind tolerant but require a place in good light.

Uses It is one of the old cottage garden flowers and looks well in a half barrel edged with pansies and perhaps mixed with dianthus.

Compost Most composts are suitable, but some addded lime will help to deter club-root disease.

Special maintenance Remove dead leaves and flowers.

Other kinds to try *M.* 'East Lothian Mixed', 30cm (12in), these can be grown to flower in mid to late summer. *M. bicornis* (night-scented stock), 15cm (6in), sweetly fragrant.

MELIANTHUS MAJOR
LARGE HONEY FLOWER

1.8m (6ft); evergreen shrub; **Zone 8**

Characteristics The stems are few and they tend to spread out at first and then curve up to a more vertical position. The impressive blue-grey leaves are 30cm (12in) or more long, oval with interesting serrated edges. They provide an excellent background for the terminal 30cm (12in) spikes of deep crimson tubular flowers in late spring to mid summer.

Position Choose a sheltered place in sun or shade as the large leaves may become tattered in the wind.

Uses It can be left as a bush or trained to a trellis or wall which affords the plant more protection. It forms an excellent background for dark-coloured flowers such as *Fuchsia* 'Mrs Popple' with its red sepals and violet-purple bell. Purple-red foliage such as *Canna* × *generalis* and *Lobelia cardinalis* 'Queen Victoria' also looks good with melianthus. Planted together in a tub, these three would create a very tropical effect.

Compost Tolerant of most composts.

Special maintenance In spring remove any shabby looking stems as new ones will spring from the base. Train as required.

MENTHA ROTUNDIFOLIA 'VARIEGATA'
(*M. suaveolens* 'Variegata')
VARIEGATED APPLE MINT

30cm (12in); herbaceous perennial herb; **Zone 6**

Characteristics Vertical shoots with square stems are clothed in rounded to oval leaves. These are slightly hairy with rounded teeth and an irregular white edge. It is called apple mint because the leaves smell like mint but a little like apples too. Flowers are seldom produced.

Position Very tolerant of wind and light conditions, from full sun to full shade.

Uses This is very useful for filling in between other plants. Its variegation creates a nice contrast with the smooth green foliage and purple pompons of chives or the dark green broad leaves of bay; therefore plant them together in a half barrel or raised bed. Although it is visually superior, it can be used for cooking in the same way as common spearmint.

Compost Tolerant of all composts.

Special maintenance Remove any old dead stems.

Other kinds to try *M. spicata* (common spearmint), useful in the kitchen, prefers a moister compost. Best in its own container as it spreads fast. *M. aquatica* (water mint), prefers wet soil, good for the pond-side, leaves smooth and purplish green; *M.* × *gentilis* 'Variegata' (variegated ginger mint), leaves dark green with yellow veins and spots.

deciduous

semi-evergreen

evergreen

flowering period

foliage/fruiting plant

full sun

¼ shade-¾ sun

½ shade-½ sun

¼ sun-¾ shade

full shade

needs winter protection

MICROBIOTA DECUSSATA
SIBERIAN CYPRESS

30cm (12in); spreading coniferous shrub; **Zone 2**

Characteristics Low spreading evergreen conifer with flat sprays of tiny scale-like leaves, these are yellowish green in summer and turn to a distinct bronzy copper in winter.

Position Very wind tolerant and will thrive in full sun to partial shade.
Uses An excellent and extremely tough ground cover plant for a raised bed, large trough or tub. It looks well with the upright *Taxus baccata* 'Aurea' with its yellow foliage and the more rounded shape and green foliage of *Chamaecyparis obtusa*. It is also a good background for evergreen broadleaved subjects such as *Ilex cornuta*.
Compost Tolerant of most composts.
Special maintenance None.

MIMULUS AURANTIACUS
(Diplacus glutinosus)
SHRUBBY MONKEY FLOWER

45cm (18in); evergreen trailing shrub; **Zone 8**

Characteristics Somewhat sinuous spreading stems give rise to opposite lance-shaped glossy green leaves. Throughout the summer soft apricot-orange trumpet-shaped flowers appear in succession. The petals have an attractively wavy edge.
Position Wind tolerant, but prefers a position in good light.
Uses The flowers look well with the scarlet velvet-textured flowers of *Salvia fulgens* and the dainty white daisies of *Argyranthemum frutescens*, both of which have an upright habit. All three will grow well together in an urn or tub as they like similar conditions.
Compost Tolerant of most composts provided drainage is good.
Special maintenance The plant can be trained up a wall or trellis if required. In very cold areas the whole container can be taken inside.

Other kinds to try *M. puniceus*, similar to above but with reddish brown flowers; *M.* Malibu Series: 'Malibu Yellow', 15cm (6in), half-hardy perennial grown as an annual, oval mid green glossy leaves form a dense carpet, summer flowers are flared, yellow with a red-spotted throat; 'Malibu Ivory', pale cream with red-spotted throat; 'Malibu Orange', glowing orange; 'Malibu Red', rich red; 'Malibu Mixed', a mixture of the above.

MISCANTHUS SINENSIS 'ZEBRINUS'
ZEBRA GRASS

1.2m (4ft); herbaceous perennial grass; **Zone 6**

Characteristics A thick clump of slim vertical stems which unfurl at the top to display flattened narrow green leaves which curl back. Distinctive yellow bars go across the leaf to give a most tropical effect. The whitish flower spikes of autumn are a secondary feature.
Position It is wind tolerant and will grow in full sun to partial shade.
Uses It makes a suitable companion for *Fatsia japonica*, with its luxuriant palm-shaped leaves, and hostas. Since they all enjoy moisture they do well together both culturally and visually. Grow them in a half barrel or large urn.

Compost Tolerates most composts provided they do not dry out, so add some organic matter in the form of leafmould or garden compost.
Special maintenance In extremely windy places support might be needed, otherwise cut down dead growth in the early spring when it may get untidy.
Other kinds to try *M.s.* 'Variegatus', white-striped leaves, good in an urn or trough to bring a lighter texture to dense carpeting bedding plants such as busy Lizzies and pelargoniums; *M.s.* 'Gracillimus', greyish green leaves much thinner than above and about 1m (3¼ft) high. For the smaller container. *M. sacchariflorus*, mid green leaves, a giant at 3m (10ft), looks good with *Gunnera manicata* in an enormous container such as an old bath.

MUSA ENSETE
(Ensete ventricosum)
ABYSSINIAN BANANA

3m (10ft); enormous evergreen herbaceous plant; **Zone 9.5**

Characteristics Huge paddle-like leaves arise from a thick stalk. The leaves are a fresh mid green with contrasting red main vein. The unusual reddish green flowers are not the main attraction and are unreliable.
Position Choose a sheltered place as the leaves get torn by wind. Very light tolerant; from full sun to full shade.
Uses This plant could be the answer for a tropical effect on a patio or by a pool. The leaves form a natural sun-shade. Grow in a half barrel, clothe the base with bright annuals and imagine you are in the Canary Isles or the West Indies!
Compost Tolerates most composts provided some organic matter is added in the form of leafmould or garden compost to hold the moisture, and additional feed is give once a month.
Special maintenance Spray with soft soap and water against red spider mite. In winter cut off outer leaves, tie in the remainder and house in a building which will keep out the frost. Alternatively sow seeds in February under glass – they grow very quickly.
Other kinds to try *M. basjoo* (*M. japonica*), the hardiest banana, similar to above but slower growing and will stand several degrees of frost, Zone 9.

MUSCARI ARMENIACUM
GRAPE HYACINTH

15cm (6in); hardy bulb; **Zone 6**

Characteristics Long narrow smooth bright green leaves grow up from the bulb in a tuft. As the leaves are flexible they curve downwards. The flowerheads, carried at the top of bright green cylindrical stems, are tightly packed columns of globular florets. Each of these florets is deep blue with a small mouth which is paler blue round the lips. They open in spring.
Position It is short so wind is not a problem. Grow in full sun or full shade.
Uses Planted in groups it will form a blue carpet which looks superb beneath the leafless branches of white-flowered *Magnolia stellata* or pink-flowered *M. stellata* 'Rubra'. It will also give colour to a tub of roses which are just beginning to open their red-tinted leaves; as the rose foliage expands it will hide the dying leaves of *Muscari*.

Compost Tolerant of most composts.
Special maintenance None.
Other kinds to try *M. neglectum*, very similar but flowers have white-rimmed mouths; *M. botryoides* 'Album', white flowers, looks nice as a small drift alongside the blue-flowered kinds.

MYOSOTIS ALPESTRIS
'ROYAL BLUE'
FORGET-ME-NOT

30cm (12in); biennial; **Zone 6**

Characteristics This rounded plant has lance-shaped matt-surfaced mid green leaves covered with soft hairs. From delicate branching stems arise clusters of tiny-petalled blue flowers. Each one has a most dainty ring of white around its tiny mouth. The delicately poised flowers open in spring.
Position Wind tolerant and thrives in full sun or full shade.

Uses The haze of blue flowers is the perfect foil to the great gleaming globular cups of most tulips. Pink goblets of 'Clara Butt' and white cups of 'Alabaster' growing in a pot or urn of blue forget-me-nots look delightful.
Compost Tolerant of most composts.
Special maintenance Water the plants in a dry spring to help deter powdery mildew.
Other kinds to try 'Blue Ball', 15cm (6in), compact ball-shaped plant; 'Victoria Rose', 25cm (10in), rose-pink flowers; 'Victoria White', 25cm (10in), white flowers; try a mixture of 'Victoria Rose' and 'Blue Ball' – it looks mauve when seen from a distance. Similarly 'Blue Ball' and 'Victoria White' gives a light blue effect; *M. palustris* (*M. scorpioides*) (water forget-me-not), deciduous perennial waterside plant, creeping habit, lighter green than above, smooth leaves, blue flowers throughout the summer. Very good for the edge of a tub pond.

MYRTUS COMMUNIS
COMMON MYRTLE

2.1m (7ft); upright evergreen shrub; **Zone 8**

Characteristics Erect main branches have many side-shoots with tapered oval- to lance-shaped leaves. These are shiny, dark green and pleasantly aromatic. In spring and early summer white flowers with many white stamens open from pink buds. These fragrant flowers are followed by purple-black fruits.
Position Tolerant of wind, sun and partial shade.
Uses These are fine evergreens and traditionally were planted by the side of cottage doors. A myrtle will grow well in a half barrel with the climber *Eccremocarpus* to clamber over its branches and shower it with yellow-orange or red flowers in late summer.
Compost Tolerant of most composts provided drainage is good.
Special maintenance Clip to shape if required.

Other kinds to try *M. communis* 'Variegata', leaves with a white edge are a better background for the purple-black fruits, slower growing; *M. communis tarentina*, 60cm (24in), much slower growing and with smaller leaves.

NANDINA DOMESTICA
'FIREPOWER'
SACRED BAMBOO

1m (3¼ft); evergreen shrub; **Zone 7.5**

Characteristics An open branching upright shrub. The leaves are twice divided so that each one has many leaflets. The overall effect is very elegant. In spring the newly opened leaves are reddish, in autumn they turn purplish. Small white flowers occur some years in summer and in warm areas they may produce orange-red fruits, but neither of these is the major beauty of the plant.
Position This plant does best in a sheltered area out of the wind, but tolerates full sun or full shade.
Uses The reddish leaves of spring are an excellent background for yellow daffodils growing through a carpet of white-flowered *Iberis sempervirens*. This trio planted in an urn or tub would give a warm and light effect to a patio on cold spring days.
Compost Tolerant of most composts provided some extra organic matter is added in the form of leafmould or garden compost.
Special maintenance None.

 deciduous
 semi-evergreen
 evergreen
 flowering period
 foliage/fruiting plant
 full sun
 ¼ shade-¾ sun
 ½ shade-½ sun
 ¼ sun-¾ shade
 full shade
 needs winter protection

161

NARCISSUS
'FEBRUARY GOLD'
DAFFODIL

30cm (12in); hardy bulb; **Zone 6**

Characteristics This is a shorter and more robust plant than the common daffodil. The narrow strap-shaped leaves look neat as they tend to stay erect. In early spring the golden yellow flowers open, one per flower stem, held just above the height of the leaves. The trumpet is quite long with a frilled and fluted edge, and the petals bend slightly backwards.

Position Untroubled by wind, it grows well in full sun to full shade.
Uses Grow this brilliant harbinger of spring in a tub or trough with the scarlet-fruited *Cotoneaster conspicuus* as a background and trailing ivy beneath, or in a windowbox underplanted with pansy 'Universal True Blue'.
Compost Tolerates any compost.
Special maintenance No problems if healthy bulbs are purchased.
Other kinds to try 'Tête-à-Tête', similar to above but several flowers per stem; 'Sweetness', pure yellow, very fragrant, straight shorter cup than above; 'Ice Follies', 40cm (16in), milk white petals, primrose cup, coarser foliage; 'Soleil d'Or', 35cm (14in), golden petals, tangerine cup; 'Thalia', 30cm (12in), three milk white flowers per stem; 'Minnow', 18cm (7in), four or more flowers, creamy yellow petals; 'Cheerfulness', 35cm (14in), yellow or white, scented; *N. triandrus albus*, 10cm (4in), about three ivory white flowers per stem; *N.t.a.* 'Paper White', 35cm (14in), 10 white flowers on each stem.

NICOTIANA
'DOMINO LIME'
FLOWERING TOBACCO PLANT

30cm (12in); bushy annual; **Zone 10**

Characteristics The large oval pointed leaves are mid green with a soft matt texture. From the top of leafy shoots the trumpet-like flowers arise. The narrow tube is about 8cm (3in) long, sticky and covered with fine hairs and flares out widely to form round to oval lobes. In this kind they are a delicate lime green, an unusual colour for a flower. The flowers have a pleasant scent, specially at night, and last all summer and into autumn.
Position Plant in a sheltered spot away from very strong winds, in full sun or light shade.
Uses The scent and colour make this a valuable plant. Combine it in an urn or windowbox with blue verbena and an edging of *Lobelia erinus* 'Blue Cascade' and the overall colour will be a unique sea green to turquoise.
Compost Tolerant of most composts if drainage is good.

Special maintenance No special requirements.
Other kinds to try 'Domino White', creamy white flowers; 'Domino Crimson', crimson-red; 'Domino Pink White Eye', soft pink with white eye; 'Domino Mixed', crimson-red, pink, lime and white; 'Nicki Mixed', 45cm (18in), similar to above but taller; *N. alata* 'Lime Green', 60cm (24in), greenish yellow flowers; *N. langsdorfii*, 1m (3¼ft), pendant green bell-like flowers.

NYMPHAEA PYGMAEA
'RUBIS'
MINIATURE WATERLILY

Deciduous aquatic with floating leaves; **Zone 6**

Characteristics This has leaves about 4cm (1½in) across. They are round with a cleft in one side and sometimes have a purplish tinge. The flowers are wine red, slightly paler on the outer petals, and the centre has numerous orange-yellow stamens. They are about 4cm (1½in) across and appear on the water surface in the summer.
Position Since they are low growing they tolerate wind but they enjoy a place in the sun.
Uses A half barrel or an old bath, not more than 45cm (18in) deep, filled almost to the brim with these delightful circular floating leaves and bowl-like flowers floating on the water surface will give an air of tranquillity to a patio. A few *Iris laevigata* 'Variegata', with their vertical white-edged leaves and majestic blue flowers, and the hazy pale blue flowers of water forget-me-not planted at the edge, complete the scene and soften the rim of the container.
Compost A heavy loam-based compost is required.
Special maintenance Remove old leaves and flowers.
Other kinds to try *N.p.* 'Alba', as above but white flowers; 'Helvola', as above but canary yellow flowers and mottled purplish brown leaves.

OCIMUM BASILICUM
'PURPLE RUFFLES'
PURPLE BASIL

30cm (12in); branching annual herb, **Zone 9**

Characteristics Branching stems and shining oval leaves form a dense bush. The foliage is dark purple with a metallic sheen, corrugated and ruffled at the edge. Small spikes of purple flowers appear in summer; they are pleasant but not a major feature.

Position Fairly wind tolerant but prefers a light sunny place.
Uses As well as its useful culinary properties it looks superb in contrast with the long thin green leaves of chives and the bright green mossy leaves of parsley.
Compost Tolerant of most compost given good drainage.
Special maintenance None.
Other kinds to try 'Green Bouquet', green leaves with small flower spikes of lime green to gold.

OLEA EUROPAEA
OLIVE

1.2m (4ft); evergreen shrub; **Zone 9**

Characteristics Stiff grey-green stems become grey and gnarled with age. The branches bear dark grey-green glossy leaves about 2.5cm (1in) long and oval in shape. Since the leaves are small the tree casts only light shade as it matures. In late summer short sprays of tiny white flowers open; they are insignificant visually but their scent is very fragrant. In warmer climates they are followed by edible green fruits that become purplish as they ripen.
Position Wind tolerant, but plenty of sun is needed.

Uses Well known for its fruit, for many people the olive brings back memories of holidays in warmer climates. In a tub it brings a delicious scent to the patio and as it matures the branches will look dramatic if festooned with the winter-flowering *Clematis cirrhosa balearica* and an underplanting of *Rosmarinus* 'Severn Sea', with its blue flowers and fine green foliage. These three are good company since they all hail from the Mediterranean.
Compost Very good drainage, otherwise any enriched compost will do.
Special maintenance With good drainage and plenty of sun plants survive outside in Zone 8. In colder zones bring the plant, complete with container, in for the winter.

OPHIOPOGON PLANISCAPUS
'NIGRESCENS'

15cm (6in); evergreen herbaceous perennial; **Zone 7**

Characteristics The roots give rise to a tufted clump of curving leathery grass-like leaves. They are glossy and so dark in colour that they appear black rather than dark purple. In summer racemes of small lilac flowers are formed and these are followed by black fruits. However, it is the black leaves that are the main feature.

Position They will grow in most situations, from full sun to full shade, and tolerate wind.
Uses This dark glossy tuft is unique. It looks dramatic as a background to pure white snowdrops in winter or as an edging to the broad blue-grey leaves of *Hosta sieboldiana elegans* in summer. These combinations will give a startling effect in any windowbox or urn.
Compost Tolerant of most enriched composts with added organic matter in the form of garden compost or leafmould.
Special maintenance None.
Other kinds to try *O. jaburan*, 15cm (6in), dark green leaves, bell-shaped white flowers in summer give rise to deep blue berries; *O. jaburan* 'Variegatus', as above but with cream stripes to the leaves, also slower growing.

ORIGANUM VULGARE
'AUREUM'
GOLDEN MARJORAM

20cm (8in); woody-based herbaceous perennial; **Zone 6**

Characteristics A thick spreading rootstock throws up many vertical shoots with rounded to oval leaves, upcurled at the edge. They are aromatic and golden yellow in spring becoming lime green in summer. Occasionally tiny mauve flowers are produced in summer.
Position Tolerant of wind, sun and partial shade.
Uses Primarily a culinary herb, the plant is also a vigorous ground coverer that will smother invading weed seedlings. Therefore use it in a pot as a herb, or in an urn or tub around a strong-growing shrub that needs to be slowed down. It might be appropriate to plant it around the base of an established bay, for both are herbs and the golden marjoram will highlight the dark bay.
Compost Any will suit provided it is well drained.
Special maintenance Tidy up dead stems in winter or early spring.

Other kinds to try *O. vulgare*, the common green kind, which is taller 45cm (18in); *O. laevigatum*, 25cm (10in), dark green leaves, a mist of tiny tubular cerise pink flowers in summer; *O.* 'Kent Beauty', 15cm (6in), grey-green leaves, in summer short spikes of tubular pale pink flowers; *O. marjorana*, 45cm (18in) high, annual, leaves elliptic, insignificant greyish flowers. For flavouring meat.

OSTEOSPERMUM
'CANNINGTON ROY'
(*Dimorp-hotheca* 'Cannington Roy')

10cm (4in); evergreen spreading sub-shrub; **Zone 8**

Characteristics Mat-forming branches are covered with shining mid green somewhat spoon-shaped leaves with toothed edges. Elegant daisy flowers, 5cm (2in) in diameter, are produced from late spring until the first frosts. When they first open the flowers are glistening white with purple tips to the petals and a purple eye, but become mauve-pink all over as they mature; an interesting dual effect.
Position Wind tolerant, but they require a sunny situation.
Uses Osteospermums form an excellent carpet of weed-suppressing foliage covered with flowers. Plant them in an urn, tub or windowbox with taller subjects like phormiums or cannas.
Compost Tolerant of most composts given good drainage.
Special maintenance Trim back the occasional lanky shoot in winter or spring. In colder regions take cuttings for the following year. Keep them in a cold frame from autumn and plant out in late spring.
Other kinds to try 'Tresco Purple' ('Peggyi'), a parent of the above, rapidly spreading growth, purple flowers produced only occasionally, Zone 9; 'James Elliman', deep purple flowers in profusion, upright habit; 'Buttermilk', primrose flowers with white bases to the petals and a dark eye, upright habit; 'Bodegas Pink', pink flowers and creamy white-edged leaves, upright habit; 'Pink Whirls', petals pink and spoon-shaped, upright habit; *O. ecklonis* 'Blue Streak', white petals with blue reverse and blue eye, upright habit; *O. jucundum compactum*, deep pink flowers, clump-forming, Zone 7.5.

deciduous

semi-evergreen

evergreen

flowering period

foliage/fruiting plant

full sun

¼ shade-¾ sun

½ shade-½ sun

¼ sun-¾ shade

full shade

needs winter protection

163

P

PARAHEBE CATARRACTAE
WATERFALL VERONICA

20cm (8in); evergreen sub-shrub; **Zone 7.5**

Characteristics Slim wiry stems are both upright and spreading. The leaves are about 1cm (⅓in) long, mid green, oval and toothed. In summer thread-like erect stems bear loose sprays of open-cupped flowers which are light mauvy blue, veined purple and with a white central circle.
Position Since it is low growing it is quite wind tolerant and light tolerant too; from full sun to partial shade.

Uses A group of these plants forms an attractive green carpet of irregular outline, scattered with dainty flowers through much of the summer if the soil is kept moist. It looks well in a tub beneath the strong-textured shiny foliage of *Phormium cookianum* 'Tricolor'.
Compost Tolerant of most composts, preferably enriched and loam-based, provided they are kept moist.
Special maintenance After flowering clip over to tidy up and encourage good dense growth.
Other kinds to try *P.* 'Porlock', blue flowers with violet markings; *P. lyallii*, white flowers with pink veins.

PARTHENOCISSUS TRICUSPIDATA
(*Ampelopsis tricuspidata*)
BOSTON IVY, JAPANESE IVY

4.2m (14ft); vigorous deciduous climber; **Zone 5**

Characteristics Tendrils tipped with sucker-pads cling to a wall or tree trunk to support the fast-growing stems. The leaves are shiny mid green, about 8cm (3in) wide and with three pointed lobes, round toothed at the edges. In autumn the leaves turn scarlet and crimson.
Position Wind will soon blow away the autumn leaves so choose a sheltered spot in full sun to full shade.
Uses The overlapping foliage will completely cover an ugly wall without the chore of having to provide support, but because it is so vigorous it needs its own large container, a half barrel or big square Versailles tub. Boston ivy will provide an excellent background for the yellow berries of *Sorbus* 'Joseph Rock' or the white berries of *S. cashmiriana*.

Compost Tolerant of most composts.
Special maintenance Since it is vigorous it is wise to cut the stems back each winter or early spring to about 30cm (12in) away from windows, doors and gutters.
Other kinds to try *P. quinquefolia* (Virginia creeper), similar to above but not quite so vigorous and with five leaflets, Zone 4; *P. henryana*, less vigorous again, leaflets are a bronzy green in summer with white or pinkish veins, they turn a soft purple in autumn, Zone 7.5.

PASSIFLORA QUADRANGULARIS
GRANADILLA

2.4m (8ft); tender evergreen climber; **Zone 10**

Characteristics Winged green stems give rise to 10cm (4in) oval mid green leaves from the base of which grow curling tendrils. It is by means of these tendrils that the plant is able to climb. The fascinating flowers appear in summer. They measure 7.5cm (3in) across, are complicated in structure and white, pink, red and violet. If pollination is successful, egg-shaped yellow fruits are produced which vary in length from 5 to 10cm (2 to 4in).
Position A sheltered sunny place is best.
Uses The fruit contains a mass of purple sweet but acidic pulp with many seeds. The ideal way to grow this plant is in a very large pot and trained over a pergola to show off the dramatic pendant flowers to best advantage.
Compost It needs rich conditions so an enriched loam-based compost is best.
Special maintenance With the first frosts of autumn the growth can be pruned back to a 1.5m (5ft) vertical stem and the plant taken in to

a frost-free building. In late spring put out again and train as required.
Other kinds to try *P. caerulea* (blue passion flower), hardy semi-evergreen, leaves deeply five-lobed, flowers white with blue-tipped corona, fruit orange-yellow, Zone 7.5; *P. caerulea* 'Constance Elliott', as above but white flowers and more fruit; *P. × caeruleo racemosa*, purple flowers arranged in twos and threes, Zone 8.5; *P. amethystina*, lilac-mauve petals and a blue corona, Zone 8.5; 'Star of Bristol' has the lovely lilac-mauve petals and blue corona of *P. amethystina* and the hardiness of its other parent *P. caerulea*, Zone 7.5; *P. edulis* (common passion flower), greeny white flowers, purple fruit, Zone 10.

PELARGONIUM SENSATION 'CHERRY'
BEDDING GERANIUM

30cm (12in); tender perennial grown as an annual; **Zone 9**

Characteristics Sturdy green stems form a short compact bush with rounded to heart-shaped leaves marked with a darker zone. Throughout the summer a succession of light cherry red flowers in clusters top the plant.

Position Wind tolerant but prefers a sunny place.

foliage and very trailing growth suitable for hanging baskets, mixed reds and pinks; 'Amethyst', another ivy-leaved trailing type raised from cuttings, mauve; 'L' Elegante', ivy-shaped leaves edged white, pale pink flowers; 'Flower of Spring', upright growth, leaves green edged white, a good background for the scarlet flowers, grown from cuttings; *P. crispum* 'Variegatum', very upright growth, rounded parsley-like leaves each one edged white, flowers small, mauve and white; *P. tomentosum* (peppermint geranium), 60cm (24in), leaves give off a pungent aroma. *P.* 'Royal Oak', deeply lobed leaves with a central coppery-purple blotch and a spicy fragrance, flowers light mauve; *P. frutetorum* 'The Boar', lax growth for training up or trailing down, green leaves with a black central blotch, a good background for the dainty salmon-pink flowers.

Uses A superb main plant for filling any container, this looks well with *Lobelia erinus* 'Blue Cascade' or yellow *Bidens ferulifolia* trailing down and *Helichrysum petiolare* springing up in between.

Compost Tolerant of most composts given good drainage.

Special maintenance Remove dead flowerheads.

Other kinds to try Sensation Series includes: 'Lavender'; 'Rose'; 'Salmon'; 'Blush'; and mixed colours; Century Series is similar in characteristics and range but it also includes 'Cardinal', deep red; 'Orchid', lavender-rose; 'Apple Blossom', soft pink; and 'White'. Breakaway Series have more shoots from the base so that they cascade down the container, in 'Red' and 'Salmon'. 'Summer Showers', ivy-leaf

PENSTEMON PINIFOLIUS

15cm (6in); evergreen bushy spreading shrub; **Zone 7.5**

Characteristics A slowly spreading plant with narrow willow-like leaves of dark to mid green. In summer orange-scarlet tubular flowers are borne in loose spikes.

Position Wind tolerant; from full sun to half shade.

Uses In a windowbox the low evergreen foliage is very pleasant and the scarlet flowers look well with the creeping blue-flowered *Rosmarinus × lavandulaceus*.

Compost Tolerant of most composts.

Special maintenance Remove dead flowers.

Other kinds to try
P. heterophyllus 'True Blue', 20cm (8in), sky blue flowers; *P. newberryi*, 15cm (6in), oval dark green leaves, deep rose-pink flowers; *P.* 'Apple Blossom', 45cm (18in), tubular pink flowers with white throats. Very nice in an urn.

PETROSELINUM CRISPUM 'CURLINA'
PARSLEY

15cm (6in); biennial herb; **Zone 7**

Characteristics Green stems give rise to stalked leaves which have blades so intricately divided and curled they look like moss. The summer flowers are not of great beauty and, in any case, are normally removed.

Position Tolerates wind but does best in a sunny place.

Uses In the kitchen this herb has many culinary uses. Visually it forms an attractive edging to a trough or raised bed planted with vegetables. Grown alone the mossy green foliage is a lovely contrast to the browny red of a simple terracotta pot.

Compost A well-drained compost is important.

Simple maintenance Remove any flowering stems for the maximum display of green foliage.

Other kinds to try 'Moss Curled', the more common type, usually taller at about 23cm (9in); 'Plain Leaved', good flavour but the leaflets are flat, not curled; Hamburg parsley, flat leaflets, thick root like a parsnip, can be cooked in the same way, although the flavour is like parsley.

deciduous

semi-evergreen

evergreen

flowering period

foliage/fruiting plant

full sun

¼ shade-¾ sun

½ shade-½ sun

¼ sun-¾ shade

full shade

needs winter protection

PETUNIA × HYBRIDA MULTIFLORA
'RESISTO RED STAR'
PETUNIA

20cm (8in); bushy perennial grown as an annual; **Zone 10**

Characteristics Dense branches are clothed with oval pointed stemless leaves. Being slightly hairy and sticky they appear a soft greyish green. Throughout the summer and autumn a succession of trumpet-shaped flowers appear, 5cm (2in) in diameter. In this kind they are very prolific and red attractively marked with five contrasting white bands.
Position This kind is wind resistant; full sun or a little shade.
Uses These modern types have been specifically bred for windowboxes, urns and baskets.
Compost Tolerant of most composts.
Special maintenance None, save deadheading.

Other kinds to try Resisto Series includes 'Scarlet'; 'Rose'; 'White'; 'Blue'; 'Iced Blue', blue with white. Frenzy Series are similar but flowers 6.5cm (2½in) in diameter, range includes 'Orchid', cerise; 'Red'; 'Coral'; 'Rose'; 'Pink'; 'White'; 'Blue'. Daddy Series is similar. Delight Series, double flowers resembling carnations. Grandiflora petunias, bred for their very large flowers, 7.5–10cm (3–4in) wide, but spotted by rain. About 20cm (8in) high, the group includes Express Series with 'Ruby'; 'Plum'; 'Red'; 'Rose'; 'Pink'; 'Salmon'; 'Blue'; 'Sky Blue'; 'White'. All with five white bands: 'Crimson Star'; 'Red Star'; 'Rose Star'; 'Blue Star'. Ice Series have a white outer band: 'Blue Ice'; 'Rose Ice'; 'Scarlet Ice'. Cascade Series has trailing stems good for baskets, wide colour range. Pirouette Series, one example of the double Grandifloras.

PHASEOLUS COCCINEUS
'PAINTED LADY'
SCARLET RUNNER BEAN

2.1m (7ft) perennial herbaceous climber grown as an annual; **Zone 9**

Characteristics The stems twist around any support and bear well-shaped mid green leaves. From the axil of the leaf a shoot bears the cluster of pea-like flowers in mid to late summer. In this kind the keel (petals at the front) is white and contrasts dramatically with the scarlet standard (upright petals at the back). The well-known beans are bright green and are best picked when about 23cm (9in) long.
Position Fairly wind tolerant; crops best in sun.
Uses Delicious to eat, this plant is very pretty too. It will make an excellent screen or create an arch over a path. Easily accommodated in an urn or half barrel.
Compost Tolerant of most composts provided they are kept moist.
Special maintenance Give the twining stems support and keep the plants well watered when the beans are swelling.
Other kinds to try For a similar effect to the above, try mixing 'White Achievement', 'Desirée' (both have white flowers and slender tender beans) and 'Enorma' (heavy cropper) or 'Achievement' (for exhibition) – the last two have scarlet flowers; 'Gulliver', a dwarf plant at 40cm (15in), scarlet flowers, many 20cm (8in) beans. P. vulgaris (French or kidney bean), an annual, varieties include 'Masterpiece', white flowers, 60cm (24in) bush; 'Purple Podded', attractive purple pods, 1.5m (5ft) climber.

PHLOX DRUMMONDII
'TWINKLE MIXED'

15cm (6in); annual; **Zone 9**

Characteristics Erect growth has lance-shaped pale green leaves. A cluster of five-petalled flowers opens in summer at the top of somewhat leafy stems. The blooms are star-shaped in various bright colours, most of them have a white edge to the petals and in addition a star-shaped central marking.
Position Fairly wind tolerant but prefers a place in the sun.
Uses A bright carpeting plant for windowboxes and troughs. The star-like flowers give a unique floral effect which contrasts well with the solid carpet of colour of Lobelia erinus or Alyssum maritimum.
Compost Tolerant of most composts.

Special maintenance Remove old flowerheads.
Other kinds to try Beauty Series, 20cm (8in), in red, pink, blue, purple and white. Palona Series, 20cm (8in), weather-resistant flowers, larger so that they give dense heads of colour, in carmine, crimson, rose, salmon, light salmon and white, also bi-coloured: 'Light Blue', pale blue with mauve eye; 'White Eye', white with crimson eye; 'Rose Eye', rose with white eye. Dwarf Petticoat Series, 10cm (4in), dwarf plants with star-shaped flowers in a wide range of colours, can be used to edge a windowbox. P. douglasii 'Boothman's Variety', 5cm (2in), perennial matt of narrow grass-like leaves, lavender flowers with a violet eye in late spring; P. subulata 'Marjorie', 10cm (4in), similar, pink flowers with rose eye.

PHOENIX CANARIENSIS
CANARY ISLAND PALM

2.1m (7ft); evergreen upright palm; **Zone 9.5**

Characteristics The stem becomes a vertical trunk, stouter than most palms. The leaves on young plants are about 50cm (20in) long, on a five-year-old plant they measure 1–1.5m (3¼–5ft) and in very old plants of 15 years the leaves can be 3m (10ft) long. Each leaf is like a giant feather with a shaft from which there are many narrow lance-shaped leaflets. It takes some years before the yellowish flower stalks appear. These have yellow-brown flowers in summer followed by yellow-brown fruit, but neither of these are a major attraction.
Position A wind tolerant and sun-loving palm.
Uses Plant this hardy relative of the date palm in a large tub or urn. Grey-leaved plants like Helichrysum petiolare or Lotus berthelotii, or succulents such as echeverias, planted around the base also suggest a hot dry climate and give visual contrast.
Compost Tolerates a wide range of composts provided drainage is good.
Special maintenance Remove dead fronds and where colder than Zone 9.5, house in winter.

Other kinds to try P. roebelenii (miniature date palm), similar to above but 1m (3¼ft) high; P. dactylifera (common date palm), grows much bigger, easily raised from a date stone, Zone 10.

PHORMIUM COOKIANUM 'TRICOLOR' TRICOLOURED MOUNTAIN FLAX

1m (3¼ft); evergreen tufted perennial; **Zone 7.5**

Characteristics The rootstock sends up leaves about 2.5–4cm (1–1½in) wide. These are upright but since they are flexible the tops arch over in a most elegant way. In 'Tricolor' the leaves are a glistening bright green in the centre, white at the edge with a narrow rim of cherry red. In summer plants established for three or more years send up a stout blackish purple flower stem, 1–1.5m (3¼–5ft) high, atop of which are about five to ten narrow tubular yellowish beak-like flowers. Whilst these are neither colourful nor the main feature of the plant, they make an interesting silhouette.
Position Tolerant of wind and salt, but a sunny position is required.
Uses In a large tub, urn or raised bed these architectural plants will give a tropical effect throughout the year.
Compost Tolerates most composts if plenty of organic matter is added.

Special maintenance Remove dead leaves and unwanted stems.
Other kinds to try *P. tenax* 'Purpureum', similar but upright purple leaves, about 1.5–2.1m (5–7ft) at five years so two plants will form an arch of leaves; *P. t.* 'Sundowner', 1.5m (5ft), upright coppery leaves with a pink centre; *P.* 'Yellow Wave', 1m (3¼ft), arching green leaves with a yellow centre; *P.* 'Maori Maiden', 45cm (18in), arching coppery leaves with a pink centre; *P.* 'Dazzler', 45cm (18in), arching purple leaves with a red centre, Zone 8.5; *P.* 'Bronze Baby', 45cm (18in), upright coppery bronze leaves.

PHYGELIUS CAPENSIS 'COCCINEUS' CAPE FIGWORT

1m (3¼ft); semi-evergreen shrub or climber; **Zone 7.5**

Characteristics The shoots, upright in the main, bear oval mid green leaves which are from 2.5 to 7.5cm (1–3in) long and fairly widely spaced on the purplish stem. In summer and autumn the stems elongate and slender spires of tubular hanging flowers open scarlet-red with a yellow throat.

Position Very light tolerant; from full sun to full shade.
Uses In an urn or tub the slender spires look well growing through other denser foliage and flowers, for example African marigolds or *Argyranthemum frutescens* 'Penny'. Some trails of grey or green foliage will complete the group.
Compost Tolerant of all composts.
Special maintenance Support each major flower stem with a bamboo cane in windy places, otherwise just remove dead flower spikes. In hard winters the plant may lose its foliage or be cut to the ground by frost but it will quickly regrow come the following spring.
Other kinds to try *P. × rectus* 'Winchester Fanfare', similar but with dusky reddish pink flowers; *P. aequalis* 'Yellow Trumpet', primrose yellow flowers and green flower stems. Looks good with dark blue petunias.

PHYLLITIS SCOLOPENDRIUM HART'S TONGUE FERN

45cm (18in); evergreen hardy fern; **Zone 6**

Characteristics The thick roots or rhizomes give rise to long tongue-shaped leaves, which are slightly turned up at the edges, ribbed and sinuous. They are a bright shining green all year.
Position Reasonably wind tolerant, and given adequate water very light tolerant; from full sun to full shade.
Uses Invaluable for the darkest places where little else will grow. A terracotta pot or urn, or an old chimney pot with these "tongues" shooting up alongside a cloud of finer lighter green fronds of a maidenhair fern together with mind your own business (*Soleirolia*) to trail down, is a wonderful composition in green.
Compost Tolerant of all composts provided they can be kept reasonably moist, so an annual topdressing of organic matter is important.

Special maintenance Remove any dead leaves.
Other kinds to try 'Crispum', similar but the edges of the leaves are irregularly serrated and frilled.

PHYLLOSTACHYS NIGRA BLACK BAMBOO

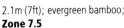

2.1m (7ft); evergreen bamboo; **Zone 7.5**

Characteristics Vertical canes are grooved and have little cupped swellings beneath each joint. They are greenish brown but when two years old or so they become a glistening black. The leaves are mid green, lance-shaped and they tend to hang down. The flowers are of no great significance.
Position Very wind and light tolerant; from full sun to full shade.
Uses A valuable background plant the dark stems are accentuated by lower-growing plants of finer texture and lighter colour such as *Chamaecyparis obtusa* 'Tetragona Aurea' or *Lonicera nitida* 'Baggesen's Gold'. *Hosta fortunei* 'Albopicta', which has broad yellow-centred leaves, and black bamboo look very oriental, a grouping that would suit a large glazed urn from the far east.
Compost Tolerates most composts given an annual topdressing of organic matter which will hold a reserve of moisture for the plant.
Special maintenance Remove any dead canes.
Other kinds to try *P. aureosulcata*, similar but sheaths on stems are striped and the browny green stems have yellow grooves.

 deciduous

 semi-evergreen

 evergreen

 flowering period

 full sun

 ¼ shade-¾ sun

 ½ shade-½ sun

 ¼ sun-¾ shade

 full shade

 needs winter protection

167

PIERIS FORMOSA FORRESTII
'WAKEHURST'

1.2m (4ft); evergreen shrub; **Zone 7.5**

Characteristics Bushy dense shrub with lance-shaped to oval pointed leaves slightly folded at the mid-rib. In late spring the new leaves are brilliant red, gradually becoming pink then creamy yellow and, by late summer, green. In spring clusters of flowers appear, composed of numerous tiny pendant urn-shaped white flowers.

Position Avoid strong winds but light tolerant provided the soil is kept moist; from full sun to full shade.
Uses A good background for other lime-hating plants such as *Rhododendron* 'Blue Diamond', whose flowers coincide with the red leaves of the pieris, and *Lithodora diffusa* 'Heavenly Blue' which will trail over the edge of the tub.
Compost An ericaceous (lime-free) compost is essential.
Special maintenance Remove dead flowerheads.
Other kinds to try P. 'Forest Flame', similar but taller and perhaps even redder in young leaf; *P. japonica* 'Variegata', slow growing, 50cm (20in), leaves narrower, edged creamy white at all times and only slightly flushed pink in spring. Valuable for its smaller stature and therefore appropriate for a windowbox.

PINUS MUGO
MOUNTAIN PINE

1m (3¼ft); spreading shrubby conifer; **Zone 3**

Characteristics The combination of low branches that tend to spread and upright branches make this a dense shrub. The dark green needle-like leaves are very thickly distributed on the shoots. This causes the foliage to look very dark which contrasts well with the young grey-white buds of winter.
Position Very wind tolerant, but prefers a light sunny position.
Uses This short slow-growing pine lends itself to container culture, and with a little pruning it can be used to create an oriental effect. Its dark background is a good foil for white flowers such as those of *Narcissus* 'Thalia', *Bergenia* 'Silberlicht' with broad leaves, and *Cyclamen neapolitanum album*.
Compost Tolerant of most composts given good drainage.
Special maintenance Train it to a particular shape or bonsai if required.

Other kinds to try 'Gnom', an even more compact and rounded bush, 45cm (18in) in five years; 'Mops', like a dark green mop head, 30cm (12in); *P. parviflora* 'Adcock's Dwarf', 1m (3¼ft), similar to the mountain pine but grey-green needles and less dense branching so that it looks more like a miniature pine tree; *P. sylvestris* 'Gold Coin', 45cm (18in), golden rounded bush.

PITTOSPORUM
'GARNETTII'

1.5m (5ft); evergreen upright to rounded shrub; **Zone 8**

Characteristics Upright branches with twiggy laterals have oval leaves about 2.5cm (1in) long. These are a greyish green, irregularly edged with white which becomes dotted with pinky purple in the winter – a most attractive effect. In late spring the small chocolate-coloured sweetly scented flowers open. These are not obvious from a distance but when observed closely they show up well against the white-edged leaves.

Position Wind and shade tolerant, although it also does well in sun.
Uses A plant for screening an unwanted view without creating any darkness and also as a light background for darker plants such as *Phormium tenax* 'Purpureum' or *P.* 'Dazzler'.
Compost Tolerant of most composts, so long as they do not dry out.
Special maintenance None, except to shape as required.
Other kinds to try 'Silver Queen', similar but with narrower leaves without the purple; 'Irene Paterson', leaves white with green spots, most distinctive; 'Abbotsbury Gold', smaller leaves green with a golden centre; 'Tom Thumb', 1m (3¼ft), slower growing, compact, leaves purple, Zone 7.5; *P. tobira* 'Variegata', 1m (3¼ft), rounded shrub with round to spoon-shaped leaves, greyish green with a white edge, many small deliciously scented cream flowers in late spring, Zone 7.5.

PLECTRANTHUS
COLEOIDES
'MARGINATUS'
(*P. coleoides* 'Variegatus')

60cm (24in); tender evergreen sub-shrub; **Zone 10**

Characteristics Sturdy stems square in section have pairs of oval to diamond-shaped leaves 5cm (2in) long. These are greyish green with a scalloped edge which is accentuated by a margin of white. The white flowers in summer are not a great attraction.
Position Avoid very windy places but plant thrives in sun or shade.
Uses This is a valuable foliage plant for containers including hanging baskets and urns. Its soft greyish colour associates well with many brightly coloured plants and provides a useful contrast in texture and form.
Compost Tolerant of all composts provided some extra organic matter is supplied to help retain moisture and thus keep the roots moist.
Special maintenance None, unless training to a particular shape is required.
Other kinds to try *P. hirtus* 'Variegatus', often confused with the above but it has a spreading and trailing habit which makes it much more suitable for a hanging basket or urn; *P. ciliatus*, another good trailer, grey-green leaves with silky hairs; *P. oertendahlii*, similar again but with oval to rounded leaves, bronzy dark green with a network of silvery veins. The stems and undersides of the leaves are purple and therefore are most attractive when viewed from below.

PLUMBAGO CAPENSIS
(*P. auriculata*)
CAPE LEADWORT

1.5m (5ft); evergreen shrub; **Zone 9**

Characteristics Green stems have oval to lance-shaped, mid to light green leaves well spread along the branches giving a light open effect. In summer clusters of five-petalled sky blue flowers shower the tops of the shoots.
Position A sheltered position is best away from very strong winds. Very light tolerant; from full sun to full shade.
Uses It can be trained to many shapes including a standard or a fan against a trellis. The outstanding flower colour and fairly upright growth make plumbago a fine plant for an urn or tub. Use *Lobelia erinus* 'Blue Cascade' for an edging around the base – its sky blue flowers match those of plumbago – and the daisies of *Argyranthemum* will provide a perfect contrast whether they be white, pink or primrose.

Compost Tolerant of most composts.
Special maintenance Train as required and remove dead flower-heads.
Other kinds to try 'Alba', white flowers; *P. rosea* (*P. indica*), deep pink to rose flowers, beautiful but not as hardy as the blue so place in a very sheltered position or take in for the winter.

POLYGONUM VACCINIIFOLIUM
(*Persicaria vacciniifolia*)
KNOTGRASS

10cm (4in); evergreen creeping perennial; **Zone 7**

Characteristics A mass of creeping stems produces numerous small oval pointed leaves. In late summer and autumn red shoots spring up from the foliage. These are clothed in small deep pink flowers that form dainty spikes.

Position Wind tolerant; from full sun to light shade.
Uses An attractive low carpet of green for most of the year that will pour over the edge of a windowbox or urn. It flowers at a time when there are few plants in bloom.
Compost Tolerant of most composts.
Special maintenance Remove dead flower spikes and trim back any long shoots as necessary.
Other kinds to try *P. affine*, 15cm (6in) similar but bigger leaves which go russet in winter and broader flower spikes; *P. capitatum*, 5cm (2in), half-hardy perennial, oval leaves are marked with darker green, pink flowerheads are ball-shaped and open in summer. Good for trailing from a hanging basket, Zone 9.

PORTULACA GRANDIFLORA
SUNDANCE

20cm (8in); slow-growing trailing annual; **Zone 10**

Characteristics Trailing stems bear fleshy green lance-shaped leaves. Cup-shaped semi-double flowers open in summer and early autumn and come in a range of colours including cerise, scarlet, rose, pink, apricot, yellow or white.
Position Flowers best in full sun but flowers will still open in half shade.
Uses Very good for containers that are difficult to water since the plants are drought tolerant. They will also trail over, softening the edge of the container.
Compost Well-drained compost is needed.
Other kinds to try 'Cloudbeater', fully double flowered.

POTENTILLA
'ELIZABETH'
SHRUBBY CINQUEFOIL

45cm (18in); deciduous spreading shrub; **Zone 3**

Characteristics Low spreading branches are covered with small leaves each divided into about five leaflets. Since they are slightly hairy they appear greyish green and form an uneven "rug". In autumn the leaves turn a russet colour. In late spring to mid autumn there is a succession of bright primrose yellow flowers, 2cm (¾in) across, not unlike single yellow roses.
Position Wind tolerant, but prefers a light sunny place.

Uses A good ground cover plant around the base of an evergreen with a strong outline, such as *Phormium tenax* 'Sundowner'. *Narcissus* 'Thalia' or *N.* 'Ice Follies' will give added colour in spring without a colour clash.
Compost Tolerant of all composts.
Special maintenance Trim if required.
Other kinds to try 'Red Ace', 60cm (24in), leaves mid green, flowers vermilion-red fading to soft orange in strong sun; 'Goldfinger', 75cm (30in), rounded bush with deep green leaves, flowers bright golden; 'Manchu' (*P. davurica mandschurica*), spreading bush with silvery grey-green leaves and white flowers; *P. arbuscula*, low rounded bush, silver grey leaves, yellow flowers.

deciduous

semi-evergreen

evergreen

flowering period

foliage/fruiting plant

full sun

¼ shade-¾ sun

½ shade-½ sun

¼ sun-¾ shade

full shade

needs winter protection

PRATIA PEDUNCULATA

12mm (½in); evergreen creeping perennial; **Zone 8**

Characteristics Tiny oval green leaves hug the ground. In summer star-shaped pale to mid blue flowers spangle the dark green carpet.
Position Wind tolerant, but prefers a shady place.

Uses A superb miniature carpet ideal for tiny bulbs such as crocus, snowdrops and tiny daffodils (for example *Narcissus bulbocodium*, *N.* 'Minnow' or *N.* 'Rip Van Winkle') to grow through. The bulbs will give colour in spring and pratia will provide the colour itself in summer. This combination is good in a windowbox, even a very narrow one, with a tiny bush of *Acer palmatum* 'Butterfly' to give a little height. This acer looks very pretty in late spring or autumn with its dainty white variegated and pink flushed leaves and casts the necessary shade.
Composts Most composts are suitable.
Special maintenance Make sure the compost is kept moist at all times.

PRIMULA × POLYANTHA 'CRESCENDO' POLYANTHUS

30cm (12in); herbaceous perennial grown as a biennial; **Zone 7**

Characteristics Bright light to mid green leaves, up to 10cm (4in) long and paddle-shaped, form an attractive rosette. From the centre of this rosette, from early spring to early summer, sturdy stems arise which divide at the top like the ribs of an umbrella. Each stem supports a rounded flower about 2.5cm (1in) in diameter. 'Crescendo' is available with red, rose, orange, yellow, lemon, white or blue flowers.
Position Will grow in most places, in sun or shade.
Uses Windowboxes, tubs and troughs look superb in late winter and spring carpeted with these cheerful plants.
Compost Tolerates most composts provided they are not allowed to dry out.

Special maintenance Remove dead flowerheads.
Other kinds to try 'Presto', similar to above but can start flowering in mid winter, 15cm (6in), in scarlet, rose, orange, yellow, white and blue. *P. vulgaris* (primrose), similar but only one flower to each stem; 'Carousel', 10cm (4in), compact, hardy and early, available in 14 colours; 'Charisma Fire', golden yellow flowers with a ring of flame; 'Charisma Rose', rose flowers patterned white and a gold eye. *P. vulgaris sibthorpii*, pink flowers with a cream eye. *P. auricula* 'Mark', grey indented leaves, flowers deep crimson with an ivory centre. *P. obconica*, clusters of lilac, purple or cerise flowers in winter and early spring, Zone 10.

PRUNUS ARMENIACA 'MOOR PARK' APRICOT

2.1m (7ft); deciduous fruit bush or tree; **Zone 8**

Characteristics A rounded bush or tree that can be trained to various forms. The flowers bloom in early spring on bare branches, the pale pink petals are a pleasant contrast to the purple-red sepals behind. The sweetly scented flowers are very prolific and after they fall the shiny oval to lance-shaped leaves open. These are a coppery red at first but turn to green later. By mid to late summer the fruits will be mature. They are orangy yellow with a red flush on the sunny side and about 4–5cm (1½–2in) diameter. In autumn the leaves turn a beautiful golden yellow.
Position A light sunny sheltered place will encourage bees to pollinate the early flowers.
Uses This plant is worth having for its many subtle attributes: its spring scented blossom, delicious fresh apricots, colourful young leaves and autumn foliage. An apricot in a tub against a south- or west-facing wall could be further enhanced by planting an eccremocarpus or thunbergia to trail over it in summer.
Compost Well-drained loam-based compost is best.
Special maintenance For most places it is best trained as a fan. If very windy during flowering, pollinate by hand. Spur prune in winter.
Other kinds to try *P. domestica* 'Early Transparent Gage', self-fertile gage, as above but hardier, almost white flowers, greenish yellow fruits, Zone 7; *P. persica* 'Peregrine', a peach, similar to apricot but larger fruit with a felted skin and mid pink flowers; *P. persica* 'Garden Lady', dwarf tree to 1.5m (5ft); *P.p. nectarina*, a nectarine, with smooth fruit. Treat the same as above, but as they are susceptible to leaf curl disease they will require spraying with Bordeaux Mixture.

PRUNUS 'CHEAL'S WEEPING' JAPANESE WEEPING CHERRY

2.1m (7ft); deciduous weeping tree; **Zone 5**

Characteristics This can be bought from the nursery trained as a tree with a 1.8m (6ft) trunk. Thereafter it produces shoots which are horizontal at first and then trail down to make a graceful umbrella-like tree. The flowers come in late spring, before the leaves open, and give an impressive display.
Position Reasonably wind tolerant; from full sun to half shade.
Uses Provided the main shoot is trained to the desired height, this tree makes a beautiful floral umbrella in spring in a tub, and an effective sunshade to sit under in summer. Daffodils can be planted around the base.
Compost Tolerant of most composts.
Special maintenance If the trunk is not sufficiently high then use a bamboo cane and ties to take the leader up as far as you need.
Other kinds to try *P.* 'Shogetsu' ('Shimidsu'), umbrella-shaped to round-topped tree, double white flowers on very long stalks which swing in the breeze; *P. sargentii*, upright to rounded tree, masses of light pink flowers, in autumn the leaves go a brilliant tangerine-orange; *P. subhirtella* 'Autumnalis', semi-double palest pink flowers in winter and spring; *P. subhirtella* 'Pendula Rubra', weeping branches bear deep pink flowers in spring; *P. avium*, fruiting cherry, can be grown in a tub if grafted on 'Colt' rootstock.

PYRACANTHA
'MOHAVE'
FIRETHORN

1.5m (5ft); evergreen shrub; **Zone 6**

Characteristics Bushy shrub easily trained to various shapes, evergreen leaves broadly oval and dark green. Clusters of tiny white flowers in early summer are quite pretty but it is the orange-red fruit of autumn that are the main attraction. The most disease-resistant pyracantha.

Position Thrives in most positions including full sun or full shade, although less flowers and fruit in shade.

Uses A valuable evergreen for covering an ugly wall or for training against a trellis as a living screen. The flowers and fruit give added interest and, when mature, it is an attractive plant for birds to nest in.

Compost Tolerant of most composts.

Special maintenance Train and prune to the required shape.

Other kinds to try P. angustifolia, similar but leaves grey-felted beneath and fruit an orange-yellow, normally left till late by the birds to give a long season of attraction; P. atalantioides, similar but leaves a glossy mid green and fruits brilliant red, again left till late by the birds.

PYRUS
'CONFERENCE'
DESSERT PEAR

1.5m (5ft); deciduous fruit tree or bush; **Zone 6**

Characteristics Upright bush with clusters of white blossom in early spring. Glossy oval to lance-shaped mid green leaves which in autumn turn an attractive golden yellow and, of course, the typical pear-shaped fruits. In 'Conference' these are normally quite long and slim and a russet colour.

Position Tolerates some wind but does best in a sheltered sunny place.

Uses The fruit is delicious when ripe. In spring a fan-trained or triple cordon bush in a half barrel can be very attractive when underplanted with *Tulipa greigii* 'Red Riding Hood', the scarlet globular flowers and broad green leaves contrast well with the white pear blossom.

Compost Most composts are suitable given good drainage.

Special maintenance This is a unique pear variety because, even without pollination, it still produces fruit. Therefore only training to shape is required.

Other kinds to try 'Williams' Bon Chrétien', well known as tinned or canned pears, golden with a slight pink flush, ripe in early autumn; 'Joséphine de Malines', stout greenish fruit that will store and is ready in winter. Both the above need cross-pollinating so two separate plants are required. They need a sheltered position out of the wind to encourage bees to visit.

RAOULIA AUSTRALIS

12mm (½in); evergreen carpeting perennial; **Zone 7**

Characteristics A gradually expanding mat of minute grey-green leaves. In summer tiny fluffy yellow flowerheads appear.

Position Sun or semi-shade needed for good healthy growth.

Uses Ideal as a carpet between other alpines and for the very slim-leaved tiny bulbs to grow through, such as the species crocus. Such a combination with a backing of a few dwarf conifers for height can create a beautiful scene in a trough or windowbox.

Compost Gritty peat or similar well-drained organic compost is required.

Special maintenance Do not allow compost to dry out in summer.

Other kinds to try R. haastii, as above but the leaves are apple green becoming chocolate brown in winter; R. hookeri albo-sericea, as above but silver leaves; R. lutescens, yellowish foliage.

RAPHANUS SATIVUS
'FRENCH BREAKFAST'
RADISH

15cm (6in); annual vegetable; **Zone 6**

Characteristics Fast-growing from seed, the mid to dark green spoon-shaped leaves soon shoot up and at their base the rapidly swelling root pushes its top out of the ground. The root is crimson shading to pink, and white at the base.

Position Wind tolerant, plant matures quicker in good light, so a sunny place is best.

Uses A common salad plant but in a raised bed the tops of the roots look attractive.

Compost Tolerant of most composts.

Special maintenance Keep well watered for crisp mild-tasting roots.

Other kinds to try 'Pink Beauty', round, rose pink, mild flavoured; 'Cherry Bell', similar to above, red roots; 'Long White Icicle', as its name suggests long white roots, crisp and tender if pulled when no more than 15cm (6in); 'Black Spanish Round', black-skinned round roots up to 455gm (1lb) can be produced. These can be left in the ground and pulled in winter as needed. Its foliage is a welcome source of green in the raised bed in winter.

deciduous

semi-evergreen

evergreen

flowering period

foliage/fruiting plant

full sun

¼ shade-¾ sun

½ shade-½ sun

¼ sun-¾ shade

full shade

needs winter protection

RHEUM × *CULTORUM* 'EARLY CHAMPAGNE' EDIBLE RHUBARB

75cm (30in); deciduous perennial vegetable; **Zone 6**

Characteristics A great thick root gives rise in early spring to the emerging leaves. These gradually expand and colour up to become the enormous triangular to heart-shaped glossy mid green leaves, familiar to most people. They may measure 30cm (12in) across with thick glistening crimson-rose leaf stems of about the same length.
Position Plant in a sheltered position as strong wind tatters the leaves. Very light tolerant; from full sun to full shade.
Uses The leaf stems are excellent when still young if stewed and used in pies and tarts. If grown in a half barrel it looks brilliant in full leaf with the red and green contrast. The advantage of growing rhubarb in a container is that it can be moved out of the way when it has died down or, better still, taken into a garage or shed in winter so the growth is forced and an early crop gained.
Compost Tolerant of most composts provided they have an adequate supply of fertilizer.

Special maintenance Remove any flowering shoots that appear.
Other kinds to try 'Timperly Early', early shoots, so good for forcing.

RHODODENDRON 'BLUE DIAMOND' RHODODENDRON

60cm (24in); evergreen shrub; **Zone 7**

Characteristics Small dark green leaves clothe this rounded compact bush. They provide a good background for the deep azure blue clusters of flowers that almost completely cover the bush in late spring.
Position Wind tolerant but requires good light; full sun to slight shade.
Uses As it is a slow-growing neat evergreen it looks well in a windowbox. It is a good background for dwarf bulbs of light colour such as *Narcissus* 'Thalia' which is white or *N.* 'Hawera', a 15cm (6in) primrose daffodil.

Compost An ericaceous (lime-free) compost is essential.
Special maintenance None.
Other kinds to try 'Winsome', similar to above but with rounder leaves and rose-vermilion flowers; 'Praecox', rosy mauve flowers in early to mid spring; 'Hinomayo', clear pink flowers in profusion in mid to late spring; *R. williamsianum*, pale pink flowers in mid to late spring, spreading habit and copper-coloured young leaves; 'Lady Alice Fitzwilliam', 1.5m (5ft), loose bunches of white funnel-shaped flowers flushed pink in mid to late spring, delicious heavy scent. In colder areas overwinter in a cold greenhouse or shed, Zone 8; *R. luteum*, 1.5m (5ft), deciduous azalea, leaves oblong to lance-shaped, clusters of yellow funnel-shaped flowers in late spring, extremely fragrant. Autumn foliage is orange-yellow, Zone 6.

RHUS TYPHINA 'LACINIATA' (*R. typhina* 'Dissecta') STAG'S HORN SUMACH

2.1m (7ft); open branched deciduous shrub or tree; **Zone 5**

Characteristics Sparsely branched with an upright habit, this plant has velvety brown shoots to which it owes its common name. The leaves are divided into numerous lance-shaped leaflets each toothed to give a light fern-like effect. In autumn they turn a brilliant orange-red. Clusters of tiny greenish flowers appear in summer, followed by autumn fruits.
Position Choose a sheltered spot or wind will quickly blow away the autumn leaves. Relatively shade tolerant.
Uses The great advantage of growing this plant in a large tub is that it can be brought to the fore for its glorious autumn colour and moved to the background when it is green. If it must be in a permanent position clothe its base with *Hedera helix* 'Glacier'. The white variegated greyish green leaves will not only trail over the edge of the tub they will also clothe the bare branches in winter.
Compost Tolerant of most composts.
Special maintenance Prune to achieve a tree form if required. As the roots tend to sucker the shoots may need thinning.

Other kinds to try *R. typhina*, the species, is almost as beautiful and it only lacks the dainty leaf serrations of the above; *R. copallina*, 1m (3¼ft), a dwarf kind with glossy dark green leaves that turn red-purple in autumn.

RIBES RUBRUM 'RED LAKE' REDCURRANT

1m (3¼ft); deciduous fruiting shrub; **Zone 7**

Characteristics An upright to rounded bush with three- to five-lobed broad green leaves. The tiny green flower clusters are not outstanding but in autumn the fruits swell and become a translucent red, like jewelled pendant earrings.
Position Choose a sheltered spot away from strong winds and in good light, preferably full sun.

Uses Delicious to eat or for making jelly. A plant in fruit is very attractive. It can easily be grown in a tub and trained as a fan to form a summer screen.
Compost Tolerant of most composts if enriched with organic matter, such as garden compost or leafmould, and drainage is good.
Special maintenance Spur prune in winter and train as required.
Other kinds to try 'Laxton's No.1', long bunches of fruit with small seeds; 'White Versailles', a whitecurrant. *R. grossularia* (gooseberry), spiny bush with plump, hairy green fruits.

ROBINIA PSEUDOACACIA 'FRISIA' GOLDEN FALSE ACACIA

2.4m (8ft); deciduous tree; **Zone 3**

Characteristics Round-headed tree of irregular form, the leaves are divided into many oval leaflets which are golden yellow in spring and autumn, and greenish yellow in summer. The flowers are white and hang in clusters in early summer, but the foliage is the main feature of 'Frisia'.

Position Choose a light sunny sheltered place out of strong wind.

Uses In a tub this tree will bring "sunshine" to a patio and, by virtue of its divided leaves, will not cast dense shade. The evergreen climber *Lonicera japonica* 'Aureoreticulata' can be planted to climb up and cover the bare branches with yellow-veined green leaves for a winter display.

Compost Tolerant of most composts.

Special maintenance None, except pruning to the required shape.

Other kinds to try *R. hispida*, 1.2m (4ft), deciduous shrub easily trained into a small standard plant or fan on a wall or trellis, it has bristly stems and soft green leaves. In early summer pendant racemes of deep rose pink attractive blossoms appear, Zone 6; *R. × ambigua* 'Bella-rosea', 2.4m (8ft), a tree with large pink flowers that hang down early in summer, Zone 5; *R. × margaretta* 'Casque Rouge' (*R. × margaretta* 'Pink Cascade'), is similar.

ROSA 'PINK PERPÉTUE' CLIMBING OR PILLAR ROSE

2.1m (7ft); deciduous climbing shrub; **Zone 7**

Characteristics Strong vertical stems are unbranched at first, but branch with height. Dark green leaves with three leaflets and double deep pink flowers smother the plant throughout the summer and autumn.

Position Relatively wind tolerant, most flowers are produced in a sunny place.

Uses A good example of a climbing rose with a continuous succession of flowers. In a half barrel this rose will grow up a trellis or over an arch, a source of delight all summer long. It can be further enhanced by a companion such as the sky blue flowers of *Clematis* 'Mrs Cholmondeley' in summer, or the winter flowers of *C. cirrhosa balearica*.

Compost Tolerant of most composts.

Special maintenance Remove dead flowers. Spur prune during the early spring and tie in extension growth.

Other kinds to try 'Danse du Feu' ('Spectacular'), a long succession of scarlet-crimson flowers; 'Climbing Iceberg', semi-double white flowers, disease tolerant; 'Zéphirine Drouhin', deep pink flowers, virtually thornless; 'Albéric Barbier', old-fashioned creamy white flowers with a gentle scent will tolerate a north-facing wall, evergreen; 'New Dawn', double pale pearl pink flowers all summer and autumn, shade-tolerant climber; 'Golden Showers', fragrant semi-double yellow flowers backed by glossy dark green leaves on crimson stems, moderate climber; 'Wedding Day', climber or weeping standard, single, open cream flowers turning white and finally pink flushed, prolific yellow fruit in autumn. 'Cécile Brunner', perfect miniature pointed light salmon pink flowers, ideal for buttonholes, available as bush or climber; *R. gallica* 'Versicolor' (*R. mundi*), a neat bush of old-fashioned pale pink flowers striped crimson; *R. damascena* 'Quatre Saisons', deliciously scented light pink old-fashioned flowers; 'Minijet', 30cm (12in), miniature pink-flowered rose, good for windowboxes; 'Baby Masquerade', miniature, red, yellow and pink flowers; other miniature and Garnette roses available in many colours.

ROSMARINUS OFFICINALIS 'SEVERN SEA' ROSEMARY

60cm (24in); evergreen spreading shrub; **Zone 7.5**

Characteristics At first branches grow fairly upright and then arch and spread. They are well covered with dark green very narrow needle-like leaves. The flowers are a deep sky blue, very prolifically borne in mid to late spring but spasmodic flowering usually ensures that there is no season without flower. Leaves can be used as a culinary herb.

Position Wind tolerant, but prefers a light sunny place.

Uses Valuable in a large windowbox, trough or tub for its long flowering period and attractive foliage. It looks good with *Coronilla glauca* which also produces colour throughout the year. The yellow flowers and grey foliage of coronilla contrast well with the blue flowers and dark green foliage of rosemary.

Compost Tolerates most composts given good drainage.

Special maintenance Prune to shape if necessary.

Other kinds to try 'Albus', 1m (3¼ft), upright growth, flowers white with a slight blue flush in late spring, Zone 7; 'Roseus', 1m (3¾ft), upright growth, flowers rosy mauve; 'Majorca Blue', 60cm (24in), spreading growth, needle-like dark green leaves, royal blue flowers, Zone 8; *R. lavandulaceus* (*R. officinalis* 'Prostratus'), 15cm (6in), prostrate growth, mid to dark green leaves, sky blue flowers in late spring. Excellent for trailing over the edge of containers, Zone 8.

deciduous

semi-evergreen

evergreen

flowering period

foliage/ fruiting plant

full sun

¼ shade-¾ sun

½ shade-½ sun

¼ sun-¾ shade

full shade

needs winter protection

173

S

RUBUS FRUTICOSUS
'MERTON THORNLESS'
THORNLESS BLACKBERRY

2.2m (7ft); semi-evergreen scrambling climbing fruit; **Zone 6**

Characteristics Upright to arching, purplish tinted stems bear leaves with three oval leaflets. In early summer clusters of white flowers appear on short side shoots and, if pollinated, these will form fruits which ripen from green to red and then purple-black.
Position Tolerant of full sun to full shade.
Uses Although grown primarily for the fruit the white flowers are very attractive to bees and butterflies and the fruit clusters are pretty at the multicoloured stage. In a container with a trellis attached this thornless kind makes a good visual screen which will not scratch skin or catch clothing.
Compost Tolerant of most kinds.
Special maintenance Train the stems as required, prune out some of the oldest stems in winter and ensure adequate water when the fruit is expanding.
Other kinds to try 'Himalayan Giant', larger plants with more deeply divided leaves and bigger fruits, but spiny.

RUTA GRAVEOLENS
'JACKMAN'S BLUE'
RUE

45cm (18in); evergreen bushy shrub; **Zone 6**

Characteristics Dense shrublet with strongly aromatic blue-green foliage. Each leaf is doubly divided into small oval to rounded lobes. The flowers are yellow and green held in clusters during summer, but these are not the main feature of the plant.

Position Wind tolerant, from full sun to partial shade.
Uses The blue-grey foliage looks well with purple leaves such as in a tub around the base of *Phormium tenax* 'Purpureum', 'Sundowner' or 'Dazzler' for year-round contrast. Alternatively with *Acer palmatum* 'Dissectum Atropurpureum' it also furnishes the container in winter.
Compost Tolerant of most composts given good drainage.
Special maintenance As the blue colour is more intense in young foliage, it is wise therefore to prune back or clip the foliage at least every other year. As a few people are allergic to the foliage it is advisable to wear gloves when handling this plant.
Other kinds to try 'Variegata', leaves blue-grey irregularly mottled cream which varies from season to season.

SALIX HASTATA
'WEHRHAHNII'
WILLOW

45cm (18in); deciduous upright shrub; **Zone 5**

Characteristics Deep purple upright branching stems are an outstanding contrast to the brilliant silver grey of the emerging catkins in early spring. A little later the stamens appear to surround the catkins with a golden halo. After flowering the oval bright green leaves open.
Position Wind tolerant, but prefers a sunny place.
Uses For a superb spring effect plant in a windowbox or tub with a carpet of golden crocuses, dainty pendant *Narcissus cyclamineus*, or its offspring 'February Gold'.
Compost Tolerant of most composts.
Special maintenance None.

Other kinds to try *S. caprea* 'Pendula' (*S. caprea* 'Kilmarnock'), similar catkins but a weeping standard form of a common native tree of Europe. Its height depends upon how high the main leader is trained so it can, if wished, become a sunshade of oval grey-green foliage for the summer. Autumn leaves yellow, Zone 5.

SALVIA BLEPHAROPHYLLA
EYELASH SAGE

30cm (12in); spreading rhizome-rooted perennial; **Zone 8**

Characteristics This spreading bush has oval bright mid green leaves, the edges of which have well-spaced long hairs like eyelashes. In summer and autumn slender spikes shoot up with brilliant scarlet crimson-lipped flowers.
Position Fairly wind tolerant, it prefers a light place.
Uses Plant this in an urn or trough.
Compost Tolerant of most composts provided drainage is good.
Special maintenance In Zones 7.5 or less it may not be hardy so take a few cuttings in autumn and over winter these inside for safety. Mulch over the top of the plant with 3–4cm (1–1½in) of straw or pulverized bark.
Other kinds to try *S. cacaliifolia*, 30cm (12in), brilliant blue flowers, broadly triangular leaves; *S. leptophylla*, 30cm (12in), brilliant blue flowers, narrow lance-shaped leaves; *S. buchananii*, 30cm (12in), velvet-textured cerise flowers, shiny dark green leaves; *S. officinalis* (common sage), 60cm (24in), hardy shrubby evergreen herb for cooking, oval rough-textured leaves, Zone 6; *S. officinalis* 'Purpurascens', as above, leaves purplish grey; *S. splendens* 'Phoenix Red', 25cm (10in), bushy sub-shrub grown as an annual, dark green oval leaves, scarlet flower spikes, Zone 10; *S. splendens* 'Fury', similar to above but starts to flower a little earlier; *S. farinacea* 'Victoria', 45cm (18in), deep blue flower spikes; *S. rutilans* (pineapple sage), 60cm (24in), red flowers.

SANTOLINA PINNATA NEAPOLITANA 'SULPHUREA'

60cm (24in); evergreen shrub; **Zone 7**

Characteristics Rounded and bushy this shrub has extremely fine cut, grey-green and aromatic foliage. In summer numerous small pin-cushion-like pale primrose flower-heads form. In this particular kind they look well in the haze of foliage.
Position Wind tolerant, but prefers a bright sunny place.

Uses It is frequently used as a contrast to dark shiny-leaved evergreens such as *Phormium tenax* 'Purpureum', 'Sundowner' or 'Dazzler'. It can be clipped easily to form a neat edging, even down to 15cm (6in), and therefore is suitable to surround a raised vegetable bed.
Compost Tolerates most composts given good drainage.
Special maintenance If required clip to shape, otherwise clip off the flowers with shears when they are past their best.
Other kinds to try *S. pinnata neapolitana*, this is similar but with harsh yellow flowers; *S. chamaecyparissus* (cotton lavender), similar but with even denser and greyish white foliage and harsh bright yellow flowers, good if clipped; *S. chamaecyparissus nana*, a dwarf form of the above, about 30cm (12in); *S. rosmarinifolia*, a green-leaved form.

SANVITALIA PROCUMBENS CREEPING ZINNIA

15cm (6in); annual; **Zone 10**

Characteristics This prostrate plant is covered in broadly oval pointed leaves which form a green carpet. Each of the daisy-like flower-heads has a large brown central disc and yellow rays, and is about 2.5cm (1in) across. The flowers are produced in abundance throughout the summer.
Position Choose a fairly sheltered place in the sun for this plant, although it will tolerate some wind.
Uses The outstanding flowers will enliven a windowbox or urn and they look well with the rusty red flowers and fine silver grey foliage of *Lotus berthelotii* planted to trail over the edge of the container.
Compost Tolerant of most composts.
Special maintenance Remove dead flowerheads.
Other kinds to try 'Mandarin Orange', similar in all respects except the flowers have brilliant tangerine-orange rays.

SAPONARIA OCYMOIDES TUMBLING TED

7.5cm (3in); evergreen perennial alpine; **Zone 7**

Characteristics Spreading mat of oval greyish hairy leaves. In summer flat, five-petalled, rose-pink flowers cover the plant.
Position Full sun encourages maximum flowering but half shade is tolerated.
Uses The greyish leaves and pink flowers have a softening effect visually, so that a windowbox of tumbling Ted planted together with a dwarf conifer, such as *Chamaecyparis obtusa*, for height and *Thymus serpyllum* 'Coccineus' to trail over the edge will be a pleasant change from gaudy bedding plants.
Compost Well-drained compost is essential.

Special maintenance After flowering the old flower stalks can be carefully clipped off with shears or scissors.
Other kinds to try *S. caespitosa*, similar but purplish pink flowers.

SAXIFRAGA STOLONIFERA 'TRICOLOR' MOTHER OF THOUSANDS

10cm (4in); evergreen perennial with runners; **Zone 8.5**

Characteristics The rounded leaves have frilly serrated edges. They are green in the centre with silvery veins and a wide but irregular margin of white, sometimes flushed with pink. The underside of the leaves and the stems are a purplish red as are the long runners that develop to produce little plantlets at their ends. Small white flowers open in summer.
Position Best in a sheltered place, but very light tolerant; from full sun to full shade.
Uses It looks charming in a hanging basket, urn or windowbox where it can trail down over the edge to display its decorative foliage. The umbrella-like leaves make a fine contrast with ivy and *Lotus berthelotii*, in both colour and texture.
Compost Adequate organic matter is important to hold moisture, otherwise most composts are suitable.
Special maintenance Ensure adequate watering during periods of drought.
Other kinds to try *S. stolonifera*, although the species lacks the white edge to the leaves it is also useful and hardier, Zone 7.5. *S. × urbium*, London pride, spreading evergreen mat, haze of tiny pale pink flowers in summer, Zone 7; *S. apiculata*, yellow spring flowers, Zone 7.5; *S. burseriana*, very low-growing, 5 cm (2in), with pure white early spring flowers.

---

deciduous

semi-evergreen

evergreen

flowering period

foliage/fruiting plant

full sun

¼ shade-¾ sun

½ shade-½ sun

¼ sun-¾ shade

full shade

needs winter protection

SCILLA SIBERICA
SIBERIAN SQUILL

10cm (4in); deciduous bulb; **Zone 6**

Characteristics Bright glossy green, broadly strap-shaped leaves spring from the bulb and dark blue shiny vertical stems bear several bright blue, bell-shaped, pendant flowers in early spring.
Position Happy in sun or shade.
Uses These dainty flowers associate well with the dark green bushy mounds and white flower clusters of *Iberis sempervirens* (evergreen candytuft) or the yellow of *Alyssum saxatile*. They all do well in a trough or windowbox.
Compost Tolerates most composts.
Special maintenance No special treatment required.

Other kinds to try
S. tubergeniana (*S. mischtschenkoana*), similar with pale blue flowers; *S. bifolia*, similar but stems produce a spike of up to 20 star-shaped flowers which can be mauve, blue, pink or white.

SEDUM LINEARE 'VARIEGATUM'
STONECROP

2.5cm (1in); succulent trailing perennial; **Zone 9**

Characteristics The round stems are very lax so they trail down when unsupported. The leaves emerge in threes and are very thin, lance-shaped, light greyish green and edged with creamy white. Yellow flowers open in summer, but are not the main feature of the plant.
Position Tolerant of windy places and full sun to partial shade.
Uses In a hanging basket long slender trails of foliage are formed. This sedum is ideal to grow beneath other succulents such as the upright pink *Echeveria gibbiflora* 'Rosea' or the blackish purple *Aeonium arboreum* 'Atropurpureum'.
Compost Happy in most composts given good drainage.
Special maintenance Remove any trails that eventually become brown. Do not overwater in winter.
Other kinds to try *S. morganianum*, similar habit to above but plumper blue-grey leaves; *S. spathulifolium* 'Cape Blanco', rosettes of spoon-shaped silver grey leaves form a carpet, Zone 8; *S. spathulifolium* 'Purpureum', similar but purple leaves; *S. album* 'Coral Carpet', round to egg-shaped leaves are green suffused with salmon-red. Leaves that are broken off often root to form a complete cover of plantlets. *S. acre* 'Aureum', forms a carpet of tiny pearl-like yellowish leaves. *S. spectabile*, 45cm (18in), attracts bees and butterflies.

SEMPERVIVUM TECTORUM
COMMON HOUSELEEK

2.5cm (1in); hardy succulent rosette; **Zone 7**

Characteristics Flower-like rosettes of oval leaves with little pointed tips all suffused a deep red. Offsets form more rosettes which will eventually spread to cover the compost. The reddish flowers in summer are not the main feature; they are on stems about 15cm (6in) high and some people like to remove them as they spoil the carpeting effect.
Position They will thrive in a windy place; full sun or deep shade.
Uses Of great value as a maintenance-free plant. Houseleeks will carpet the surface of a windowbox and creep over the edge. They look well with other sempervivums of different colour and around *Yucca flaccida* 'Bright Edge' with its upright dark green leaves edged white.
Compost Any compost will suit provided drainage is good.

Special maintenance None.
Other kinds to try *S.t.* 'Commander Hay', brighter red leaves than above. *S. arachnoideum* (cobweb houseleek), similar but leaves green with pinkish tips. The whole rosette is covered with cobweb-like silver threads; *S. montanum*, similar but mid green rosettes. All three look well together and there are hundreds more to choose from!

SENECIO 'SUNSHINE'

60cm (24in); evergreen bushy shrub; **Zone 7.5**

Characteristics This rounded to spreading shrub has grey-felted young shoots. The leaves are oval very grey at first becoming grey-green with grey-white undersides as they age. In summer clusters of golden daisy flowers are produced.
Position Very resistant to wind and salt, this plant also does well in full sun or full shade.
Uses The sturdy carpet of grey throughout the year looks well below the purple leaves of cordyline growing in a tub or half barrel.

Compost Tolerant of most composts.
Special maintenance Remove flowerheads before they open to encourage the production of young grey foliage.
Other kinds to try 'Moira Reid' ('Sunshine Variegated'), as the above but the grey-green leaves have a central blotch of creamy white; *S. compactus*, as 'Sunshine' but more compact growth; *S. bicolor cineraria* 'Silver Dust' (*S. maritima* 'Silver Dust'), 30cm (12in), evergreen bushy sub-shrub often grown as an annual. Silver grey leaves finely divided rather like carrot foliage. Yellow daisy-like flowerheads in summer are normally removed. A good plant for a light-coloured and textured effect in any display; *S. bicolor cineraria* 'Cirrus', similar to above but silver grey leaves oval and serrated. *S. hybridus* (*S. multiflorus*) (cineraria) 30cm (12in), bushy, large daisy flowers in blue, red, pink, white, Zone 10.

SKIMMIA JAPONICA REEVESIANA

45cm (18in); evergreen shrub;
Zone 7

Characteristics This fairly dense rounded shrub has smooth oval pointed mid green leaves which are aromatic. In late spring dense clusters of small scented white flowers appear. However, the main feature is the bright red fruits that develop in autumn and often remain well into winter. This plant is an hermaphrodite and therefore will produce fruit without a partner of the opposite sex.
Position Plant in a sheltered container out of the wind or else leaf tips will yellow; from full sun to full shade.
Uses A valuable plant for autumn and winter fruit, it looks well with variegated ivy trailing from beneath it in a tub or trough. Because of its small stature it is also worthy of windowbox planting.
Compost An ericaceous (lime-free) compost is needed for best growth.
Special maintenance None.

Other kinds to try S. japonica 'Rubella', 75cm (30in), similar to above but being a male plant it does not produce fruit. The flowers are very fragrant, pink in bud, and the flower stem is bronzy red, an attractive background to the 7.5cm (3in) clusters of white flowers.

SOLANUM JASMINOIDES 'ALBUM'
WHITE-FLOWERED POTATO VINE

2.4m (8ft); semi-evergreen climber;
Zone 8

Characteristics The scrambling branches are clothed with dark green oval to lance-shaped leaves, sometimes divided into lobes. In summer and autumn brilliant white star-shaped flowers with golden stamens show up well against the dark foliage.
Position Fairly wind and light tolerant; from full sun to full shade.
Uses Plant in a half barrel and this vine will quickly clamber over a trellis to make an attractive green arbour for a secluded seat. Grow *Salvia cacaliifolia* at the base to give cool blue spikes and trailing triangular foliage: most enjoyable on hot summer days.
Compost Tolerant of most composts.
Special maintenance Train as required.

Other kinds to try S. crispum 'Glasnevin', similar to above but more shrubby, lilac-purple flowers with yellow stamens.

SOLANUM MELONGENA 'RIMA'
AUBERGINE

30–60cm (12–24in); annual erect branching fruit; **Zone 10**

Characteristics The branches give rise to oval leaves about 10cm (4in) long, greyish green and often spiny on the main vein. The flowers are a dull violet colour and tend to be hidden by the leaves. The shiny fruits are an attractive dark purple-black, about 10cm (4in) long and 5cm (2in) in diameter.

Position A sheltered place out of the wind and in full sun is best.
Uses Although primarily for cooking and eating the fruits are also very attractive and the plant looks well in a tub.
Compost An enriched compost that retains moisture is important.
Special maintenance Plant out in late spring when frosts have finished.
Other kinds to try 'Little Fingers', fruit in clusters of three to six; 'Dusky', large fruit, disease resistant; *S. capsicastrum* (winter cherry), evergreen bushy sub-shrub grown as an annual, 30cm (12in), lance-shaped green leaves, small star-like white flowers in summer followed by numerous 12mm (½in) egg-shaped pointed fruits that turn yellow and finally bright red, at its best in autumn, Zone 9; *S. pseudocapsicum*, similar to above but with round fruits. *Solanum tuberosum* (potato), containers allow early spring planting, initially in a light shed or greenhouse using humus rich fertile compost. Place outside in late spring they will crop early if 'Vanessa' or 'Maris Bard' are used.

SOLEIROLIA SOLEIROLII
(*Helxine soleirolii*)
MIND YOUR OWN BUSINESS

2.5cm (1in); evergreen prostrate perennial; **Zone 8.5**

Characteristics Thread-like stems have minute, rounded but asymmetric, bright green leaves. The stems spread to form a green moss-like mat of foliage. The insignificant flowers are only occasionally produced.
Position Does best in a sheltered position out of the wind and shaded from the sun.
Uses In a dark moist corner planted in a terracotta pot with ferns it will cover the compost and trail down the sides in a most attractive manner.
Compost Tolerates most composts provided they do not dry out.
Special maintenance Keep it within bounds and ensure it is kept moist.
Other kinds to try 'Aurea', golden yellow leaves, less invasive; 'Variegata', leaves edged white, very pretty, less invasive but tends to revert to green unless the green shoots are removed regularly.

 deciduous

 semi-evergreen

 evergreen

 flowering period

 foliage/ fruiting plant

 full sun

 ¼ shade-¾ sun

 ½ shade-½ sun

 ¼ sun-¾ shade

 full shade

 needs winter protection

SORBUS VILMORINII
VILMORIN'S MOUNTAIN ASH

2.4m (8ft); deciduous tree; **Zone 6**

Characteristics Slow-growing tree with spreading branches as it matures. Extremely elegant fern-like leaves composed of 19 to 29 elliptical leaflets of a dark sea green. These become orangy bronze in autumn. In late spring clusters of small white flowers appear. The delightful deep pink fruits, each about 5mm (¼in) diameter, persist on the bare branches as birds leave the berries until very late in the year.
Position Avoid very windy places or the autumn leaves will fast be blown away. Light tolerant; from full sun to partial shade.
Uses This is an excellent tree for a large urn or half barrel.

Compost Tolerant of most composts.
Special maintenance Stake the trunk and then any minor shaping as required.
Other kinds to try *S. cashmiriana*, similar but with about 15 leaflets, attractive pink-flushed white flowers in early summer and 12mm (½in) diameter long-lasting white fruits in 5–7.5cm (2–3in) clusters; *S.* 'Joseph Rock', similar but bright green leaves turn orange-red and purple in autumn, long-lasting yellow fruits; *S. aria* 'Lutescens', 7.5cm (3in) oval leaves, silver when young becoming grey-green, soft orange fruits, Zone 5; *S. reducta*, 30cm (12in), white flowers followed by pink berries.

SPHAERALCEA MUNROANA

20cm (8in); trailing woody-based perennial; **Zone 8**

Characteristics Vigorous trailing stems spill down the sides of a container. The grey-green oval round-toothed leaves are hairy and well spaced along the stems. The coral pink saucer-shaped flowers, 2cm (¾in) across, arise from the leaf axils. They bloom for a very long period, from late spring to late autumn.
Position Reasonably wind and light tolerant; from full sun to partial shade.
Uses The trailing stems will soften the outline of an urn on a pedestal, a windowbox or a hanging basket. Its soft pink flowers and greyish foliage associate well with almost any plant including the dainty white daisies of *Argyranthemum*, blue plumbago and also the strong fiery colours of *Salvia splendens* and brilliant oranges of *Tagetes* (French and African marigolds).
Compost Tolerant of most composts.

Special maintenance Reduce unwanted trails should they get too long.
Other kinds to try *S. ambigua*, similar to above but bushier, more branching growth.

SYRINGA MICROPHYLLA
'SUPERBA'
DWARF LILAC

60cm (24in) deciduous shrub; **Zone 7**

Characteristics Rounded bushy shrub with broadly oval, mid green leaves produces rounded spikes of numerous highly scented lilac-pink flowers in late spring to late summer.
Position Fairly light tolerant.

Uses Few background shrublets give better scent than this, therefore ideal for a windowbox where the perfume can drift indoors on summer days and nights.
Compost Tolerates most composts.
Special maintenance Dead flowers can be removed.
Other kinds to try *S. meyeri* 'Palibin', similar but 1m (3¼ft), slightly more open growth; *S. × persica*, similar but 1.5m (5ft), narrowly oval leaves, less rigid growth and masses of light mauve-lilac flowers in late spring.

TAGETES ERECTA
'PERFECTION YELLOW'
AFRICAN MARIGOLD

30–45cm (12–18in); upright annual; **Zone 10**

Characteristics Sturdy upright growth bears mid to dark green shiny leaves divided into five to fifteen lance-shaped toothed leaflets. This strong smelling foliage forms a dense but pleasantly textured background for the large blooms. Each flower is a great ball composed of numerous clear yellow petals, about 10cm (4in) across, and very weather resistant in this kind. The flowering period goes all through summer and into autumn.
Position Fairly wind and light tolerant; from full sun to partial shade.
Uses A brilliant filler for any large urn, trough or windowbox. They look well with the broad red leaves of canna spearing in between and *Lotus berthelotii* trailing over the edge.
Compost Tolerant of most composts.
Special maintenance Remove dead flowerheads.
Others kinds to try This series is available in gold, orange and mixed; Inca Series, similar but 25–30cm (10–12in), also in yellow, gold, orange and mixed; 'Golden Age', 30cm (12in), golden flowers, odourless foliage; Jubilee Series, 60cm (24in), in gold, orange and yellow, for a tall background; *T. erecta* × *T. patula* (Afro-French marigolds), this hybrid group contains triploids (they have an odd number of chromosomes so they do not set seed) so the plant is not weakened even if deadheading is overlooked – useful for an inaccessible container. Fireworks Series are an example, 30–35cm (12–14in), yellow, gold, orange and red flowers up to 7.5cm (3in) across.

TAGETES PATULA
'AURORA FIRE'
FRENCH MARIGOLD

20–25cm (8–10in); bushy erect annual; **Zone 10**

Characteristics The sturdy green stems have mid to dark green shiny leaves divided into about nine leaflets giving a dense but pleasantly textured background for the flowers. Each bloom is double but with fewer petals than an African marigold. Each petal is deep bronzy red edged with gold, which in total gives beautifully patterned flowers for summer to autumn.
Position Wind and light tolerant; from full sun to partial shade.
Uses Excellent carpeting plant for windowboxes. Such is the variation within *Tagetes* that this can be used with taller yellow African marigolds and an edging of *T. tenuifolia*.
Compost Tolerant of most composts.
Special maintenance Remove dead flowerheads.
Other kinds to try Aurora Series includes 'Yellow Fire', yellow marked red, and 'Gold'; Boy-o-boy Series, 15–20cm (6–8in), double – 'Yellow'; 'Gold'; Orange'; 'Harmony', red and gold; Disco Series, 15cm (6in), single – 'Viva', yellow, 'Orange', 'Red'; 'Naughty Marietta', yellow marked mahogany red; Mischief Series, 30cm (12in), single – 'Yellow'; 'Gold; 'Red and Gold'; 'Mahogany'; *T. tenuifolia* (*T. signata pumila*), compact, produces a multitude of tiny single flowers, a very even colour effect, ideal for a neat edging for windowboxes; Gem Series, 20cm (8in), includes – 'Lemon'; 'Gold' and 'Tangerine'. Starfire Mixed, similar to Gem but brighter.

TANACETUM PTARMACIFLORUM
(Pyrethrum argenteum)
SILVER FEATHER

30cm (12in); sub-shrub grown as an annual; **Zone 8.5**

Characteristics This small shrub with branching upright growth is one of the daintiest foliage plants. It has very finely divided leaves of silvery white. The flowers are silver grey and merge in with the foliage in summer.
Position Wind tolerant, this plant thrives in full sun.
Uses The light-coloured lacy foliage contrasts superbly with the glossy round succulent crimson leaves of *Begonia semperflorens* 'Ambra Red' or *Beta vulgaris* Hortensis in say a tub. Alternatively they can be used in any container as a feathery plume to lighten heavy colour or texture.

Compost Tolerant of most composts if drainage is good.
Special maintenance Remove flowerheads to help maintain vigour.
Other kinds to try *T. densum amani*, 20cm (8in), evergreen sub-shrub with divided silver grey leaves gradually forming a ground cover. Yellow flowerheads are best removed. Good in a windowbox with other alpines, Zone 7; *T. vulgare* (common tansy), a herb once used as an insect repellant (it was rubbed into meat to keep flies away), 60cm (24in), upright spreading herbaceous plant. The green leaves are finely cut and a good background for the clusters of yellow disc-like flowers. A pretty herb for a pot.

TAXUS BACCATA
'AUREA'
GOLDEN YEW

1m (3¼ft); slow-growing coniferous tree; **Zone 4**

Characteristics Sturdy dark brown branches clothed with very narrow golden leathery leaves and at first forms a dense bush. Female plants, if left unpruned, will bear bright red fruits, the inner seed of which is very poisonous.
Position Wind and light tolerant; from full sun to partial shade.
Uses Yews tolerate clipping very well so they can be trained to many shapes. (Clipping, of course, also deters fruiting.) Formal shapes like cones, balls or pyramids look well in fine terracotta pots, urns or wooden Versailles tubs. Placed on either side of a doorway they create an imposing effect.
Compost Tolerant of most composts given good drainage.
Special maintenance Clip and train to the shape required.

Other kinds to try 'Fastigiata' (Irish yew), dark green foliage, upright habit; 'Fastigiata Aurea', as above, golden; 'Dovastoniana', spreading, with weeping branchlets, dark green; 'Dovastonii Aurea', similar to above but golden.

THUJA PLICATA
'STONEHAM GOLD'
ARBOR-VITAE

75cm (30in); slow-growing conifer; **Zone 3**

Characteristics This conifer develops an irregular cone-shaped outline. The very dense foliage is composed of huge numbers of fan-shaped shoots covered with minute flattened scale-like leaves of a coppery gold colour.

Position Wind and light tolerant; from full sun to partial shade.
Uses Since it grows slowly it is useful planted each end of a windowbox to give a little height. *Hedera helix* 'Goldheart' with its yellow-centred deep green leaves looks good carpeting the compost and around the base of the conifers, and trailing over the edge of the container.
Compost Tolerant of most composts.
Special maintenance None.
Other kinds to try 'Zebrina', faster growing, with foliage banded yellow, useful in a half barrel; *T. occidentalis* 'Rheingold', slow-growing, foliage coppery bronze in winter and coppery yellow in summer.

deciduous

semi-evergreen

evergreen

flowering period

foliage/fruiting plant

full sun

¼ shade-¾ sun

½ shade-½ sun

¼ sun-¾ shade

full shade

needs winter protection

179

THUNBERGIA ALATA
BLACK-EYED SUSAN

2.4m (8ft); annual climber; **Zone 9**

Characteristics Twining stems have triangular leaves with a heart-shaped base and a coarsely toothed margin. The rounded orange-yellow flowers are composed of five broad overlapping petals in distinct contrast to the dark brown to black centre. It blooms all summer and into autumn.
Position It flowers best in a warm sheltered place out of the wind and in full sun.

Uses It is quite happy in a tub or trough and its fast growth makes it valuable for cladding a trellis, wall or even an unattractive tree.
Compost Tolerant of most composts.
Special maintenance It needs a support to twine around.
Other kinds to try This plant is sometimes available in white, tangerine and mixed colours; *T. grandiflora*, evergreen twining climber, woody but half-hardy, oval leaves about 12.5cm (5in) long, glossy green and somewhat succulent, trumpet-shaped pale to mid violet-blue flowers in summer. Plant in a tub, prune back to a main rod and house over winter.

THYMUS SERPYLLUM
'COCCINEUS'
WILD RED THYME

5cm (2in); evergreen prostrate sub-shrub; **Zone 5**

Characteristics Tiny creeping stems have minute oval leaves about 2mm ($\frac{1}{10}$in) long. The overall effect is a dense mat of dark green that hugs the soil level and trails down over the edge of the container. In summer little flower stems spring up to about 5cm (2in) terminating in a cluster of tiny lipped flowers of reddish purple.
Position Withstands salt gales and thrives in bright light and full sun.
Uses A low carpet suitable for the smallest bulbs to grow through. Light-coloured crocus such as 'Blue Pearl' (pale blue), 'Ladykiller' (white and purple) or 'Cream Beauty' look superb against this dark background in spring. By summer they will die down and the thyme will flower; a good succession for a windowbox or herb pot.

Compost Tolerates any compost provided drainage is good.
Special maintenance None.
Other kinds to try *T.s. albus*, white-flowered form; *T. pseudolanuginosus*, grey-green leaves, pink flowers; *T. × citriodorus* 'Silver Queen', 10cm (4in), spreading shrub with wiry upright branches, tiny leaves have a lemony fragrance when crushed and are dark green edged white, flowers lilac; *T. × citriodorus* 'Aureus', as above, but leaves golden yellow; *T. vulgaris* (garden thyme), common herb, 20cm (8in), branches become gnarled with age, leaves elliptic, dark green with greyish tinge, lilac flowers in early summer to late autumn.

TOLMIEA MENZIESII
'TAFF'S GOLD'
(*T. menziesii* 'Variegata')
PICK-A-BACK PLANT

20cm (8in); evergreen to semi-evergreen perennial; **Zone 8**

Characteristics The tufted plant has heart- to ivy-shaped leaves, 5cm (2in) across, held on stems about 5cm (2in) long. The edges have rounded teeth and where the leaf stem joins the blade a young plantlet develops. The leaves are a bright mid green mottled with yellow in varying degrees from leaf to leaf. The spikes of small tubular to bell-shaped green and brown flowers appear in spring. Although quite dainty they are not the main feature of the plant.
Position A shaded spot is best although these plants are fairly wind tolerant.

Uses A plant to brighten up dull shady spots, it forms a colourful ground cover around the larger ferns like *Matteuccia struthiopteris* with its ostrich feather-like green plumes. Since it is virtually evergreen tolmiea can be used with the deciduous hostas to give some winter interest.
Compost Tolerant of most composts.
Special maintenance Remove dead leaves and flowers occasionally.
Other kinds to try *T. menziesii*, the ordinary green form, is a good foil for brightly variegated, shade-loving plants such as *Iris foetidissima* 'Variegata'. It will also tolerate full sun.

TRACHELOSPERMUM JASMINOIDES
'VARIEGATUM'
STAR JASMINE

1.5m (5ft); evergreen twining climber; **Zone 8**

Characteristics The twining stems are green suffused with purplish brown and clothed with leathery shining elliptic leaves about 5cm (2in) long arranged in pairs. The leaves have dark green patches towards the centre, surrounded by irregular grey-green areas and white towards the margins. In winter the foliage often becomes flushed with rose. In summer very fragrant white flowers open in clusters. Each blossom is about 12mm ($\frac{1}{2}$in) across and has five curiously twisted and wavy edged petals.
Position Does best in a shady place sheltered from the wind.
Uses A lovely foliage plant for a trellis and quite content in a half barrel against a shady wall on the patio. For spring effect plant tulip 'Captain Fryatt' at its base for a good ruby-purple contrast to the decorative foliage.
Compost Grows best in a compost with plenty of organic matter.
Special maintenance Train as required.
Other kinds to try *T. jasminoides*, the species, has longer green leaves, is more vigorous and stands full sun better; *T. asiaticum*, is similar but with smaller leaves 2.5cm (1in) long, creamy yellow flowers with less scent, hardier, Zone 7.5.

TRACHYCARPUS FORTUNEI
(*Chamaerops excelsa*)
CHUSAN PALM

1.5m (5ft); evergreen unbranched hardy palm; **Zone 7.5**

Characteristics This slow-growing palm gradually forms a thick vertical hairy trunk at the top of which sprout large fan-shaped leaves. These "fans" are about 45–90cm (18–36in) wide and have stems of about the same length. Eventually the plant will flower when numerous small yellow flowers will appear near the top of the stem early in summer. The Chusan palm can reach 7.5m (25ft).
Position Tolerant of different light conditions; from full sun to full shade.
Uses For a tropical or an oriental effect what could be better? It is easily accommodated in a large planter or tub on the patio and being hardy it can remain there in winter. Should a little more colour be required, *Eccremocarpus scaber aurantiacus* will climb up the trunk and produce yellow flowers, and *Lysimachia nummularia* 'Aurea' will clothe the base of the palm and trail over the edge of the container.
Compost Tolerant of most composts.
Special maintenance Remove old brown leaves: cut them off with secateurs (do not pull them off).

TRADESCANTIA FLUMINENSIS 'VARIEGATA'
WANDERING JEW

15cm (6in); evergreen trailing perennial; **Zone 10**

Characteristics Succulent stems at first grow upright but soon tend to become horizontal or hanging and spread by rooting at the nodes. Oval to elliptic pointed leaves which clasp the stem at the base are bright green striped with creamy primrose. It has small white flowers from time to time but the leaves are the main decorative feature.
Position Avoid windy places or the trailing stems will be blown away, but very light tolerant; from full sun to full shade.
Uses Commonly used as a trailing plant, it is useful in hanging baskets and for the edges of windowboxes and troughs.
Compost Tolerates most composts provided they do not dry out in a very sunny place.
Special maintenance In early autumn take a few cuttings to overwinter on a windowsill for next year. They will root easily in compost or water.
Other kinds to try 'Albovittata', similar but with green and white stripes; *T. albiflora* 'Variegata', similar to above but rounder leaves, green striped white and a strong purple beneath, very pretty; *T. zebrina* (*Zebrina pendula*), leaves dark green with two metallic silvery bands and purple beneath, mauve-purple flowers; *T. zebrina* 'Quadricolor', as above but white and mauve stripes too; *T. zebrina* 'Purpusii', leaves completely mauve-purple; *T. sillamontana*, leaves covered in grey-white hair.

TRIFOLIUM REPENS 'PURPURASCENS'
PURPLE-LEAVED CLOVER

7.5cm (3in); semi-evergreen mat-forming perennial; **Zone 7**

Characteristics The stems spread and root to form a carpet which is covered with clover leaves. Each leaf has three or four rounded leaflets but is unusual in being purple edged with green. Round flowerheads of white pea-like flowers emerge in summer to dot the purple background.
Position Happy in sunlight or shade.
Uses A good carpet for filling in between dwarf shrubs or for bulbs to grow through. The scented white flowers attract bees and the foliage attracts the common blue butterfly to lay its eggs on the leaves.
Compost Tolerates all composts.
Special maintenance None, save cutting it back if it spreads too far.

TROPAEOLUM MAJUS 'ALASKA'
NASTURTIUM

30cm (12in); spreading bushy annual; **Zone 10**

Characteristics Succulent spreading stems have long-stalked leaves with almost circular blades. In this kind they are green irregularly marbled white. In addition it produces trumpet-shaped flowers with spurs and rounded petals in shades of red or yellow in summer and autumn.
Position Fairly tolerant of wind and different light conditions; from full sun to partial shade.
Uses Plant in a windowbox with spiky green-leaved plants, such as *Cordyline australis*, to give contrasting flower colour and foliage. Nasturtium will trail down the sides of the container too.
Compost Tolerant of most composts.
Special maintenance None unless it grows too fast, then trim as required.

Other kinds to try 'Empress of India', deep crimson flowers and coppery green leaves; Gleam Series, semi-double flowers of yellow, orange and red, trailing habit, useful for high windowboxes, hanging baskets and urns on pedestals; Whirlybird Series, single flowers including yellow, orange, rose, scarlet and mahogany which sit upright and open-faced above the foliage; *T. peregrinum* (*T. canariense*), vigorous climber to about 2.1m (7ft), the mid green glossy leaves are attractive and five-lobed. The plant is covered by a succession of small fringed yellow flowers. A valuable temporary screen.

deciduous

semi-evergreen

evergreen

flowering period

foliage/fruiting plant

full sun

¼ shade-¾ sun

½ shade-½ sun

¼ sun-¾ shade

full shade

needs winter protection

V

TULIPA GREIGII
'RED RIDING HOOD'
BOTANICAL TULIP

20cm (8in); bulb; **Zone 5**

Characteristics In very early spring the oval pointed stalkless leaves emerge. In the Greigii group the foliage is very beautiful being bluish green with stripes and mottles of purple. In early spring the brilliant red cupped flowers open.
Position The short-stalked flowers are reasonably wind resistant; from full sun to full shade.
Uses Valuable for windowboxes.
Compost Very tolerant of most composts given good drainage.
Special maintenance Remove seedheads if desired.
Other kinds to try Greigii group – 'Cape Cod', yellowish apricot; 'Oriental Spendour', scarlet and yellow; *T. turkestanica*, flowers up to eight per stem, white, yellow centre, 20cm (8in), early spring; *T. praestans* 'Unicum', four flowers per stem, orange-scarlet, 25cm (10in), mid spring; **Fosteriana group** huge chunky flowers, 50cm (15in), mid spring – 'Mme Lefeber', scarlet; 'Candela', yellow; 'Purissima', white; **Double Early group**, open flower bulging with petals, 25cm (10in), mid spring – 'Peach Blossom', pink; 'Mr Van der Hoef', yellow; 'Oranje Nassau', orange-red; **Single Early group** single flowers, 35cm (14in), mid spring – 'Pink Beauty', rose; 'Couleur Cardinal', red and yellow; 'Princess Irene', salmon-buff; **Triumph group** single flowers 40cm (15in), mid to late spring – 'Garden Party', white and carmine; 'Apricot Beauty', apricot-rose; 'Attila', violet; 'Kansas', white; **Lily-flowered group** elegant tapered reflexed petals, 50cm (20in), mid to late spring – 'China Pink', satin pink; 'West Point', yellow; 'Marilyn', white, red tip and base; 'Queen of Sheba', dark red, edged yellow.

VACCINIUM CORYMBOSUM
'BLUECROP'
HIGHBUSH BLUEBERRY

1m (3¼ft); deciduous upright fruiting shrub; **Zone 6**

Characteristics The upright to slightly arching branches are clothed with oval, mid green leaves. In spring and early summer the tips of side shoots give rise to clusters of small pendant urn-shaped flowers. These are followed by edible berries which are most decorative, being mid to slate blue. The leaves normally turn to shades of red before they fall. 'Bluecrop' bears heavy crops of fruit in late summer.
Position Fruits better with sunshine but shade tolerant too.
Uses Tasty fruit in addition to decorative flowers plus fruit and foliage with seasonal variations make this a very worthwhile container plant.
Compost Acid compost essential.

Special maintenance After a few years prune out old branches with poor growth in the spring.
Other kinds to try 'Goldtraube 71', large crops and faster growth than above.

VERBENA
'SISSINGHURST'

15cm (6in); semi-evergreen perennial, often grown as an annual; **Zone 9–10**

Characteristics Spreading stems are daintily clothed with mid grey to green leaves made up of several divided leaflets. Rounded clusters of tiny flowers appear in continuous succession in summer and autumn. In this particular kind they are a strong rose pink.
Position Fairly wind and light tolerant.
Uses With its dainty foliage and spreading habit this plant is ideal for hanging baskets, raised urns and windowboxes. It looks superb with the white daisies of *Argyranthemum*.
Compost Tolerant of most composts.
Special maintenance Only train if required.
Other kinds to try Trailing kinds for baskets, raised urns, etc., as above – 'White Knight' ('Cascade'), white, cream eye; 'Blue Knight' ('Cascade'), blue; 'Carousel' ('Aphrodite'), purple and white striped; 'Showtime Belle', carmine; 'Red Cascade', scarlet; 'Royal Purple', purple; 'Silver Anne', pink, scented; **Compact bush kinds** to form a dense carpet in a trough or raised bed – 'Novalis Rose Pink Eye', rose with white eye; 'Novalis White', white; 'Novalis Scarlet Eye', scarlet with white eye; 'Novalis Deep Blue Eye', deep blue with white eye; 'Aubletia Perfecta', deep purplish rose; **Upright kinds** mix well with stocky plants, e.g. pelargoniums, as their thin stems and tiny flowerheads give a light textured effect – *V. venosa* (*V. rigida*), 30cm (12in), violet-mauve; *V. venosa* 'Polaris', 30cm (12in), soft lavender blue.

VINCA MINOR
'ATROPURPUREA'
PURPLE LESSER PERIWINKLE

15cm (6in); prostrate evergreen sub-shrub; **Zone 5**

Characteristics Wiry spreading stems have oval to lance-shaped dark green glossy leaves about 3cm (1⅛in) long. When the plant matures it can form a complete carpet. From early spring to early summer, and sometimes in between, rosy purple flowers open. The petals are offset, reminiscent of a propeller blade.
Position Wind tolerant, this periwinkle grows well in full sun to full shade.
Uses It forms an excellent permanent carpet beneath bushy shrubs and one through which medium to large bulbs can easily grow. *Narcissus* 'Ice Follies' and *N.* 'Thalia' look very good.
Compost Tolerant of most composts.

Special maintenance None.
Other kinds to try *V. minor* (lesser periwinkle), sky blue flowers; *V. minor* 'La Grave', larger lavender blue flowers; *V. minor* 'Bowles' Variety', larger white flowers; *V. minor* 'Multiplex', double purple flowers; *V. minor* 'Alba Variegata', flowers white, leaves edged creamy yellow; *V. minor* 'Argenteovariegata', flowers blue, leaves edged white; *V. major* (greater periwinkle), 45cm (18in), broadly oval leaves 6.5cm (2½in) long and sky blue flowers; *V. major* 'Variegata', as above but leaves have a wide creamy white margin; *Vinca rosea* (*Catharanthus rosus*), evergreen tender shrub often grown as an annual to about 45cm (18in), fairly succulent erect branching stems, oval glossy leaves, flowers white with a crimson eye or rose pink with a crimson eye, from late spring to early autumn.

VIOLA
'UNIVERSAL RED WING'
PANSY

15cm (6in); bushy perennial usually grown as a biennial; **Zone 7.5**

Characteristics Compact when young somewhat spreading later, this plant has shiny oval leaves with rounded teeth, of a fresh green colour. The flowers in this kind are rounded yellow with a black "face". The top two petals are a contrasting deep red. Flowers open during mild spells in winter and throughout the spring into summer.

Position Fairly wind tolerant, pansies thrive in full sun to full shade.
Uses An excellent plant for carpeting windowboxes and troughs.
Compost Tolerant of most composts.
Special maintenance Dead flowers can be removed.
Other kinds to try Universal Series has 18 different colours through virtually the whole spectrum; Ultima Series is similar with 24 different colours and patterns; Summer-flowering kinds, these start in late spring and continue throughout the summer; Turbo Series, available in 14 different colours; Joker Series, these have a lighter centre and a dark face, light blue and white, mahogany and gold, violet and gold, purple and orange; Cornuta Series, very neat plants with smaller but more prolifically borne flowers, more like the old cottage heartsease; 'Johnny Jump Up', violet-lavender and yellow with a fascinating "face"; 'Cuty', white "face", yellow eye, blue-purple "whiskers" and back petals; 'Prince Henry', deep purple-violet with yellow "whiskers"; 'Prince John', yellow; 'Blue Princess', violet-blue, yellow eye, blackish purple "whiskers".

VITIS VINIFERA
'PURPUREA'
PURPLE-LEAVED GRAPEVINE

3m (10ft); deciduous climber; **Zone 7**

Characteristics Vigorous woody stems give rise to large attractive three- to five-lobed leaves and tendrils which anchor the plant as it climbs. The leaves are greyish with short hairs when young becoming purple as they mature. In summer clusters of tiny pale green flowers occur, mostly hidden by the leaves. These develop into small grapes.
Position Happy in sun or shade.
Uses An excellent cover for an ugly wall or a trellis to screen an unwanted view. The purple leaves look well behind the grey rounded foliage of *Eucalyptus perriniana* and the white daisy blooms of *Argyranthemum*.

Compost Tolerant of most kinds provided drainage is good.
Special maintenance When the vine has filled its allocated space prune back side shoots in winter to one or two buds.
Other kinds to try *V.* 'Brant', as above but green leaves turning scarlet in autumn and larger sweet black fruit; *V.v.* 'Seyval Blanc', green leaves and light green grapes for dessert or wine making; *V.v.* 'Madelaine Sylvaner', greeny white fruits ripening earlier than above (late summer), heavy cropping, makes good wine.

YUCCA FLACCIDA
'IVORY'

1m (3¼ft); evergreen very short-stemmed shrub; **Zone 5**

Characteristics From a short thick stem grow tufts of dark green narrow lance-shaped leaves. These are about 5cm (2in) wide and 45cm (18in) long on a mature plant and have fine fibres along the edges. Strong stems spring up vertically in mid summer to mid autumn and these are covered with hanging bell-like flowers each about 5cm (2in) long. The flowerheads make a superb contrast to the foliage.
Position Wind tolerant, but choose a sunny position as it encourages more flowers to form than in shade.
Uses This is an impressive and regal plant even in winter. It looks good in a tub with the cream-edged leaves and white spring flowers of *Vinca minor* 'Alba Variegata'.
Compost Tolerant of most composts provided it has adequate drainage.
Special maintenance Remove dead flower spikes and old leaves, to allow birds to catch any hidden snails which can damage the leaves.

Other kinds to try *Y.f.* 'Bright Edge', as above but leaves have a white edge; *Y.f.* 'Golden Sword', leaves green with bright yellow centre; *Y. filamentosa* 'Variegata', slightly wider leaves than any of the above, broadly edged white which becomes pink flushed in winter; *Y. aloifolia*, 2m (7ft) tree with stiff sharp, green leaves.

ZINNIA
PETER PAN
'FLAME'

20cm (8in); annual; **Zone 10**

Characteristics Sturdy upright shoots branch later to produce broad oval stalkless 5–10cm (2–4in) long leaves. These are a bright green and provide a good background to the orange-scarlet flowers which open throughout the summer. These are very big compared with the size of the plant and measure 10cm (4in) in diameter. The petals are interestingly quilled and there is a central tuft of yellow stamens.
Position Fairly wind tolerant, they enjoy a place in full sun.

Uses This short-growing zinnia is very good for brightening up a sunny windowbox. It looks good with an edging of *Lotus berthelotii* with fine silvery hanging foliage and rusty red flowers.
Compost Tolerant of most composts given good drainage.
Special maintenance Remove dead flowers.
Other kinds to try Peter Pan Series includes 'Gold', 'Orange', 'Scarlet', 'Plum'; Fairyland Series, 29cm (11in), with double 7.5cm (3in) diameter flowers in mixed colours; Thumbelina Series, 12cm (5in) high, with double 4cm (1½in) flowers in mixed colours; 'Lilliput' ('Minipompom'), 23cm (9in) high, in mixed colours.

 deciduous

 semi-evergreen

 evergreen

 flowering period

 foliage/fruiting plant

 full sun

 ¼ shade-¾ sun

 ½ shade-½ sun

 ¼ sun-¾ shade

 full shade

 needs winter protection

USING THE ZONE MAPS

These zone maps are an aid for those inspired readers who may wish to introduce the plants featured in this book into their own gardens.

If you can determine that the desired plant overwinters outside in the garden where you have seen it, you should be able to identify both the zone where it is growing and the zone where you live. Bearing in mind that in the smallest garden the same plant can succeed in one corner yet die in another, use of the zone maps should at least allow you to determine whether a trial with the desired plant is worthwhile.

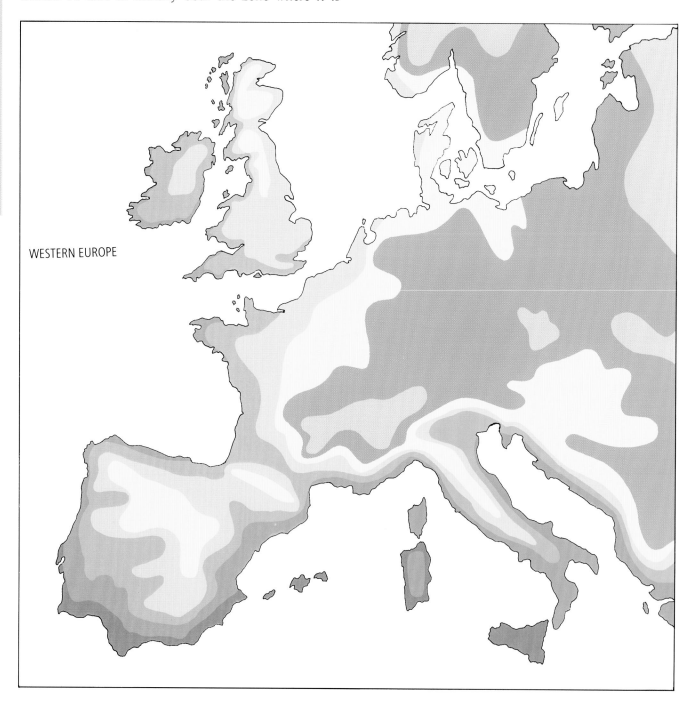

WESTERN EUROPE

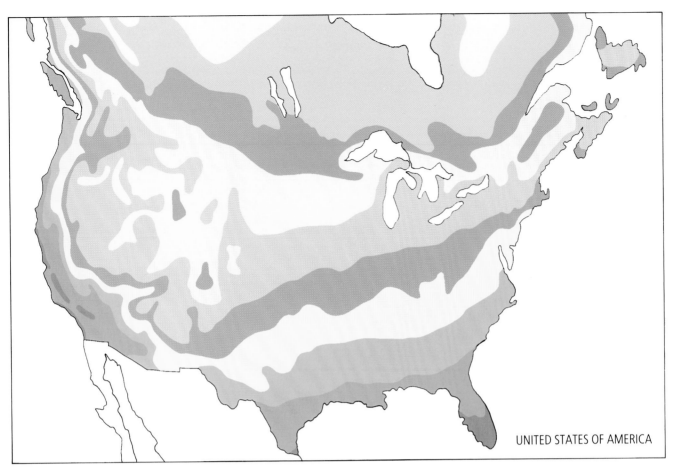

UNITED STATES OF AMERICA

ZONE KEY

Zones designate the lowest range of temperatures that a plant will normally survive. Thus a plant in zone 9 will normally survive between −6°C and −1°C (20°F and 30°F). If a plant has been given a zone rating not shown in this key, for example 9·5, it suggests that it will survive only at the higher end of range 9 i.e. −3°C and −1°C (25°F and 30°F).

Zone 1	below −45°C	below −50°F
Zone 2	−45°C to −40°C	−50°F to −40°F
Zone 3	−40°C to −34°C	−40°F to −30°F
Zone 4	−34°C to −29°C	−30°F to −20°F
Zone 5	−29°C to −23°C	−20°F to −10°F
Zone 6	−23°C to −18°C	−10°F to 0°F
Zone 7	−18°C to −15°C	0°F to 5°F
Zone 7·5	−15°C to −12°C	5°F to 10°F
Zone 8	−12°C to −6°C	10°F to 20°F
Zone 9	−6°C to −1°C	20°F to 30°F
Zone 10	−1°C to 5°C	30°F to 40°F

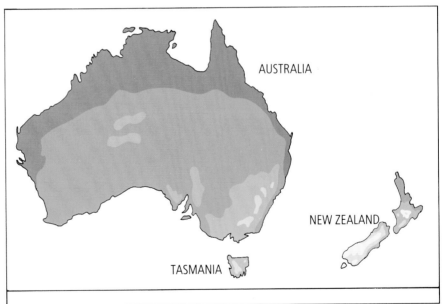

AUSTRALIA

NEW ZEALAND

TASMANIA

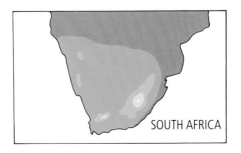

SOUTH AFRICA

INDEX

CREDITS

Quarto would like to thank the following for their help with this publication and for permission to reproduce copyright material.

Front cover; Liz Eddison, Photo/Nats, Derek Fell; p. 8-9 Harry Smith Collection; p. 12 Peter McHoy, p. 13 Peter McHoy; p. 14 ar Peter McHoy, br Harry Smith, p. 15 Liz Eddison; p. 18 al Peter McHoy, p. 19 ar Photo/Nats; p. 20 ar Harry Smith Collection, p. 21 cl Peter McHoy br Quarto; p. 22 Liz Eddison, p. 23 Peter McHoy; p. 24 bl Derek Fell, p. 25 ar R Cheek, bl R Cheek; p. 26 ar R Cheek, bl Liz Eddison, p. 27 Peter McHoy; p. 28 br Derek Fell, c Peter McHoy, p. 29 bl Liz Eddison, a & br Peter McHoy; p. 30 ar Liz Eddison, p. 31 a & b Derek Fell; p. 32 bl Peter McHoy, ar Derek Fell; p. 33 al Derek Fell, ar Photo/Nats; p. 34 bl Liz Eddison ar Photo/Nats, p. 35 a Peter McHoy, bl Peter McHoy; p. 37 al Peter McHoy, bl Peter McHoy; p. 41 ar Peter McHoy; p. 42 br Peter McHoy, p. 43 a Peter McHoy; p. 46 Peter McHoy; p. 47 Liz Eddison; p. 49 a Roy Cheek; p. 50 Peter McHoy, p. 51 Liz Eddison; p. 53 Photo/Nats; p. 54 bl Peter McHoy, p. 55 ar Peter McHoy, bl Liz Eddison; p. 58 ar Liz Eddison, al Harry Smith Collection; p. 61 ar Peter McHoy; p. 66-67 Liz Eddison; p. 71 br Peter McHoy; p. 75 Liz Eddison; p. 84 & 85 ac, bc Harry Smith Collection; p. 86 al Tim Miles; p. 87 cr Liz Eddison; p. 88 & 89 c Tim Miles; p. 90 ar Liz Eddison; p. 93 al Harry Smith Collection, p. 96 bl Harry Smith Collection; p. 99 bl Harry Smith Collection; p. 100 cr Liz Eddison, p. 101 a Liz Eddison; p. 103 al Tim Miles; p. 104 al Harry Baker; p. 106 ar Harry Smith Collection; p. 108 br Stephen Crisp; p. 109 ar Harry Smith Collection; p. 111 Derek Fell; p. 113 Liz Eddison; p. 114-5 Harry Smith Collection.

Key: a = above, r = right, b = below, l = left, c = centre.